K.V

A PRACTICAL GUIDE TO GROWING
VEGETABLES
FRUIT & HERBS

A PRACTICAL GUIDE TO GROWING
VEGETABLES
FRUIT & HERBS

a complete how-to handbook for gardening for the table,
from planning and preparation to harvesting and storing,
with every technique shown in over 800 clear illustrations

RICHARD BIRD

with photographs by Jonathan Buckley

southwater

This edition is published by Southwater, an imprint of Anness Publishing Ltd, Hermes House, 88–89 Blackfriars Road, London SE1 8HA; tel. 020 7401 2077; fax 020 7633 9499

www.southwaterbooks.com;
www.annesspublishing.com

If you like the images in this book and would like to investigate using them for publishing, promotions or advertising, please visit our website www.practicalpictures.com for more information.

UK agent: The Manning Partnership Ltd; tel. 01225 478444; fax 01225 478440; sales@manning-partnership.co.uk
UK distributor: Grantham Book Services Ltd; tel. 01476 541080; fax 01476 541061; orders@gbs.tbs-ltd.co.uk
North American agent/distributor: National Book Network; tel. 301 459 3366; fax 301 429 5746; www.nbnbooks.com
Australian agent/distributor: Pan Macmillan Australia; tel. 1300 135 113; fax 1300 135 103; customer.service@macmillan.com.au
New Zealand agent/distributor: David Bateman Ltd; tel. (09) 415 7664; fax (09) 415 8892

Publisher: Joanna Lorenz
Executive Editor: Caroline Davison
Designer: Ruth Hope
Production Controller: Ann Childers
Illustrator: Liz Pepperell

ETHICAL TRADING POLICY
Because of our ongoing ecological investment programme, you, as our customer, can have the pleasure and reassurance of knowing that a tree is being cultivated on your behalf to naturally replace the materials used to make the book you are holding. For further information about this scheme, go to www.annesspublishing.com/trees

A CIP catalogue record for this book is available from the British Library.

Previously published as *The Fruit and Vegetable Gardener*

PUBLISHERS' NOTE
In the United States, the burning of plants or bulbs (if they are diseased, for example) is prohibited.

Page One A bay tree clipped into a spiral.
Page Two Vegetable plots can be decorative as well as productive.
Page Four Brick paths divide up this large informal vegetable garden.

contents

introduction

ABOVE **Retaining a kitchen garden with dwarf box hedging is the ideal way to keep the area neat and tidy. Here, sunflowers add the perfect decorative touch to the garden.**

BELOW **These terracotta forcers are used to hurry vegetables such as rhubarb into growth. They also serve an ornamental purpose, dressing up what can be a dull vegetable plot.**

At the beginning of the 21st century it may seem something of an anachronism that people in the so-called civilized world should be growing their own vegetables. Not only are they readily available from supermarkets, but there is also so much else to do with our time. But take a look at people who do grow their own produce and you will usually find healthy, happy souls who enjoy good food – there's more to it than saving a little money.

In the days when spending a few pennies on seed saved much more at the greengrocers, growing vegetables used to be the cheap option, but this is no longer necessarily true, particularly if you include your own time in the equation.

People's reasons for growing vegetables and fruit vary widely, but nearly all vegetable gardeners would say that the crops you grow yourself are far superior to those you buy. There is, of course, an element of one-upmanship about this, but this is far from the whole story.

Above all, vegetables from your own garden are fresh. They can be in the ground one minute and in the pot the next. Once you have tasted fresh vegetables you realize the vast difference between them and the glossy, but days-old ones in the supermarkets. Mass-produced vegetables have been bred to different criteria from those that we grow in the garden. Greengrocers and supermarkets want fruit that will arrive at the shops looking fresh and undamaged, and so the produce has tough skins, which also give them a long shelf life. Fruit and vegetables from the garden do not have to travel.

Farmers want to harvest a crop all at once, so it is important that all the peas, for example, are ready for picking on the same day. Gardeners, on the other hand, want the reverse – they want as long a season as possible. Supermarkets want all the vegetables they stock to be the same size and to look the same, but gardeners, provided they are not interested in exhibiting, are not so fussy.

At the bottom of the list of qualities that are demanded by shops and supermarkets, and frequently not on the list at all, is taste. Customers go back to buy carrots every week without any thought to what the last batch tasted like. Gardeners, however, have a wide choice of carrot seeds, many selected for flavour, and they can choose the variety with the taste they like best.

Another advantage, allied to taste, is that gardeners know what has been put on the food. Today, gardeners choose to use few chemical sprays and powders, but crops bought from supermarkets have been doused in an ever-increasing number of compounds to make sure that, among other things, they come to the shops in a totally unblemished state. Gardeners can know that their food is completely untainted by chemicals.

Garden vegetables are the ultimate in convenience food. Admittedly, you have to wash them, but they sit there just waiting to be harvested when you want them. You may need only one stalk of celery, so why go and buy a whole bunch, when you can quickly cut one stalk from the garden? This is much more economical and saves on time spent shopping. Excess produce can be frozen or stored, and used when you need it.

Kitchen gardens can be decorative, too. Even a simple garden with everything grown in rows or blocks is likely to be attractive, but when they are planted as part of a potager, vegetables can be arranged in even more decorative ways.

Lastly, as well as having healthy food, the gardener gets plenty of exercise and fresh air. There is also a sense of closeness to nature. A cliché perhaps, but there is still something fundamental about getting your hands dirty and listening to the birds as you work.

That is the end of the philosophy of the kitchen garden. From this point the book becomes a practical one. It concentrates on describing the techniques required to produce an attractive and productive kitchen garden. With this book as a guide you will soon not only be growing your own produce but acquiring a whole set of skills, many of them traditional ones, handed down over the centuries, and others that are the result of modern experience.

ABOVE **Here, pink-flowered chives, red lettuce and purple cabbage as well as fennel and parsley create an informal vegetable garden.**

designing
a kitchen garden

Before you even contemplate putting a spade in the soil, it is a very useful exercise to sit down and think about what you are trying to achieve in your kitchen garden. Firstly, you need to consider whether you have the time, space and conditions to achieve what you want.

The design of a kitchen garden can then be approached in two ways. It can be either purely functional, in which case you simply have to ensure that the layout and planting of the garden will produce the largest possible volume of produce. Alternatively, you might like to adopt a more decorative approach, orchestrating the design so that the garden is pleasing to look at as well as productive.

There is also a variety of more technical considerations to take into account. For example, how you are going to get the best out of your plot? Will there be any limitations to your plans caused by lack of space, problem soils and difficult weather conditions, and how can the overall layout help to prevent the influx of pests and diseases? Once you have thought through questions such as these, you can start having fun and planning your garden in greater detail.

RIGHT **This is a traditional kitchen garden, with vegetables neatly lined up in rows. Although it is autumn, there will be plenty of vegetables in season over the next few months.**

There are several factors to consider when planning the overall design of a kitchen garden. Many of these relate to more specific issues and are dealt with later in more detail but are mentioned here in a general context.

What do you want?

The first priority is to work out what you want. Do you want a productive garden that will provide food for a large family or for selling or giving away? If so, you will probably be planting varieties of vegetables in bulk, which reduces the possibility of using intricate patterns. If, however, you are thinking in terms of a decorative feature, with the vegetable crops as a secondary consideration, you are going to need a different approach to laying out the kitchen garden. What do you want to include? Are you hoping to grow fruit and herbs as well as vegetables? This kind of decision will influence how much space you need and how you use it.

Do you want a greenhouse? If so, is it going to be within your kitchen garden or will it be tucked away, out of sight in a corner of the garden? What are you going to do with items such as sheds, cold frames and compost bins? Someone with a working kitchen garden is likely to position these where they are convenient. If you want a decorative kitchen garden, you may well consider that these structures are eyesores and better located in a separate area, perhaps screened by a hedge.

How much time?

If you are going to do it properly, a kitchen garden takes up a tremendous amount of time. If you have help in the garden this may not be a problem, but if you do it all yourself, at weekends for example, you may find that time runs short during a critical period if there are two

LEFT **This is a highly decorative kitchen garden, in which a selection of flowering plants grows among the vegetables.**

wet weekends followed by one when you are away from home. In other words, design the garden to suit the amount of time available. A large kitchen garden that has been neglected is a sad sight.

How much space?

It may not be a question of deciding how much space you want to devote to vegetables; this may already be decided by the amount of space actually available. Do not try and squeeze too much into a small space. Remember that there may be a call on the space for other purposes – children playing, for example.

Suitability of the space?

An important point to consider is whether the space you want to use is suitable for vegetables or whether you will have to modify the design to allow for problem areas. For example, there is no point in trying to grow vegetables under trees. Nor can they be grown on swamp-like ground. Removing the trees or, at least, reducing the shade they cast is possible, but it may be undesirable or too expensive. Wet ground can be drained, of course, but this, again, may be too expensive, and it may be better to turn that part of the garden into a pond.

What's the weather like?

Although it is not a serious problem for the design of the garden, the weather does play a part in your plans. A vegetable garden should have plenty of sunshine, so if you want to reserve the sunny part of the garden for relaxation and sunbathing, there may well be nowhere to grow vegetables. If the bottom of the garden is a frost hollow, growth will be delayed there, and this may upset the overall decorative balance of your garden even if it does not affect its productivity. Prevailing dry, wet, cold or warm climates may affect what you can grow and therefore limit the productive or decorative qualities of your intended garden.

ABOVE **A well-ordered garden is attractive in its own way. Many gardeners take great pride in keeping everything neat and tidy, which not only looks good, but also increases productivity.**

The Vegetable Plot

In the working vegetable garden, the overall visual design may not be important. Vegetables are, of course, decorative in their own right, and even the most regimented plot, where everything is grown in rows, usually has some visual appeal. With this type of garden, however, the design is subordinate to convenience and output, with rectangular blocks composed of rows or blocks of crops.

ABOVE **Lack of space is not a problem if you want to grow your own vegetables. Even this small border functions as a working vegetable garden.**

Permanent structures

The first consideration is the position of more permanent items, such as greenhouses, cold frames, sheds and compost bins. The green-house needs plenty of light and should be away from cold winds. It should also be near the house because it often needs attention in the winter and at night. This also applies to cold frames. The shed and the compost bins can be more or less anywhere, although not too far away. If the compost bin is a long way away, you may be tempted to leave rotting ve-getation lying around rather than clearing up.

All these structures need access paths, which again will dictate their position. A compost bin on the far side of a bed may fill a space, but it will be of little use if you have to walk over the bed to get to it. Putting in a path to it, however, will take up valuable growing space.

Bed design

The positioning of the beds should have prime consideration. Practice varies consid-erably on the shape and method employed. Most gardeners prefer to have large rectangu-lar plots, 3.6m/12ft wide and as long as the garden allows. Typically, there are two such plots, one each side of a central path. Within these plots rows of vegetables are set out across the beds, with temporary narrow paths between each row.

Recent years have seen the reintroduc-tion of a different method, which had fallen out of favour. This is the use of deep beds,

only 1.2m/4ft wide. Such beds, can, in fact, be easily superimposed on the old system by dividing up the long plot into any number of 1.2 x 3.6m/4 x 12ft beds. The significance of the 1.2m/4ft width is that the whole bed can be reached from either side. These smaller beds have permanent paths on each side, which can be paved or left as bare earth.

Permanent planting

Most planting in the kitchen garden is done on an annual basis and changes every year, but there are some plants that stay in the same position for several, if not many, years. Vegetables such as rhubarb, globe artichokes and asparagus need a permanent base. Most fruit is permanent or is moved only every few years. Tree fruit, in particular, must be con-sidered as a long-term addition to the garden.

These types of plants are usually kept together, partly for convenience and partly because they can all be protected against birds by being included in one fruit cage.

Paths

Paths in a productive kitchen garden tend to be for access purposes and not seen as part of a decorative pattern.

RIGHT **This large traditional vegetable garden contains a great variety of foliage, which can be highly decorative.**

A Walled Vegetable Garden

*A vegetable garden is basically a utilitarian space for growing vegetables,
but it frequently becomes much more than that. Vegetables are decorative in
their own right and a well-planned vegetable plot can usually become
a very attractive part of the garden.*

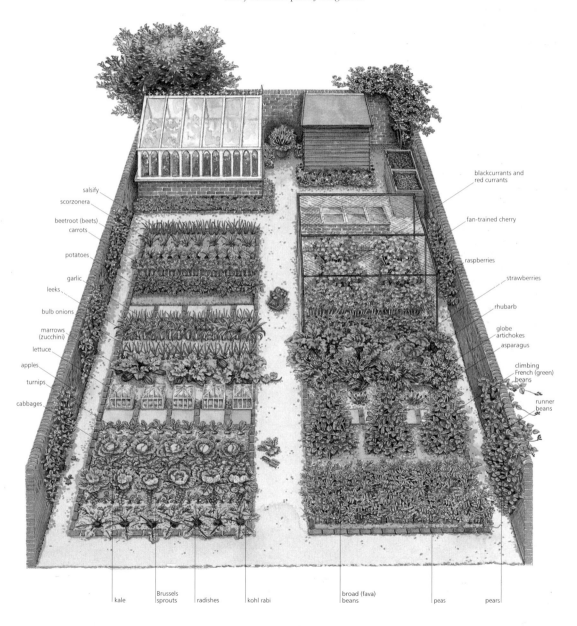

salsify

scorzonera

beetroot (beets)

carrots

potatoes

garlic

leeks

bulb onions

marrows
(zucchini)

lettuce

apples

turnips

cabbages

blackcurrants and
red currants

fan-trained cherry

raspberries

strawberries

rhubarb

globe
artichokes

asparagus

climbing
French (green)
beans

runner
beans

kale

Brussels
sprouts

radishes

kohl rabi

broad (fava)
beans

peas

pears

Decorative Fruit and Vegetables

One tends to think of vegetables and fruit as being grown either in special gardens or in beds within gardens that are devoted solely to them. There is, however, no reason why they should not be mixed with plants that are grown for decorative purposes. Most gardens have flowering and foliage plants, so why not mix a few vegetables in with them?

ABOVE **Many vegetables are decorative in their own right. Both the flowers and foliage of these climbing beans are purple.**

Decorative vegetables

Some vegetables seem to have been created for inclusion in decorative schemes. Ruby chard, also known as red-stemmed Swiss chard or rhubarb chard, is a perfect example. Although it is good to eat, its vivid red stems and deep purple foliage make it an ideal border plant, particularly in a position where a touch of bright colour is required. Beetroot (beets), while perhaps not quite as colourful, can be used in the same way.

Colour is not all. The foliage of carrots may not be particularly unusual in colour, but it has a wonderful filigree shape and soft texture. These qualities can be used to soften or link two neighbouring colours, or to break up an area of rather solid foliage.

Climbing plants, such as beans, peas, marrows (zucchini) and squashes, can be used to cover arbours and pergolas. Colourful squashes and marrows hanging down in a walkway can be an attractive, if unexpected, sight.

Decorative fruit

Fruit is even more adaptable than vegetables. Apple or plum trees create a dappled shade that is perfect for sitting under or for creating beds in which to grow shade-loving plants. They can be grown against walls as cordons, espaliers or fans, where they create beautiful two-dimensional patterns that can be even more attractive than conventional climbers. In addition to the shape, there are the blossom and the fruit to enjoy, and the leaves of some varieties of pears have wonderful autumn colours.

Walls are not the only way to display trained fruit trees. They can be used to decorate arbours, pergolas and arches. Grapes can also be used in this type of position, rather than training them in a regimented way against wirework in a fruit garden.

Some bush fruit, red currants and gooseberries in particular, can be grown as tree-form standards – that is, they have a thin, unbranched trunk with the "bush" sitting on top. These can look extremely attractive in borders and beds, especially

LEFT **Many vegetables, such as these purple-leaved Brussels sprouts, have dramatic leaves that make a vegetable plot look very striking.**

An Ornamental Fruit Garden

Fruit gardens should be laid out in the most productive way possible, ensuring that each plant has sufficient space to grow and develop as well as plenty of air and light. However, this does not prevent a fruit garden from being designed in an attractive way that makes the most of the natural beauty of the fruit trees and bushes.

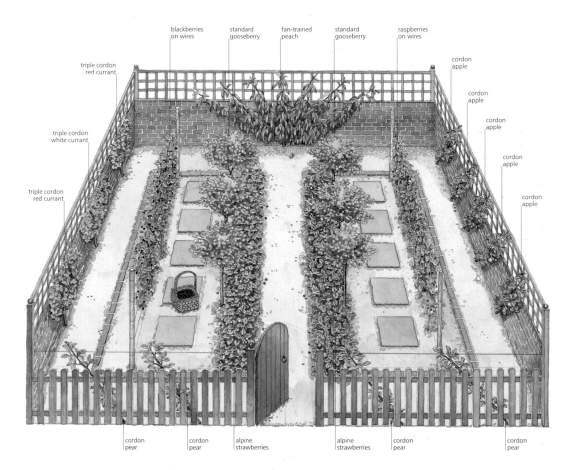

blackberries on wires

standard gooseberry

fan-trained peach

standard gooseberry

raspberries on wires

cordon apple

triple cordon red currant

cordon apple

cordon apple

triple cordon white currant

cordon apple

triple cordon red currant

cordon apple

cordon pear

cordon pear

alpine strawberries

alpine strawberries

cordon pear

cordon pear

if they are the centrepiece. Naturally, they look best when they are in full fruit.

Even strawberries can be used in a decorative manner. Alpine strawberries make good edging plants for borders. A single line between the border and a path, for example, can be extremely effective, especially as they have a long flowering season. They work really well around the edge of herb gardens but can be used in any type of border.

Decorative herbs

Although herbs can be kept together in a separate garden, they do lend themselves particularly well to being spread around the garden in the decorative borders. Shrubby plants, such as rosemary, sage and thyme, have an obvious decorative function, but so do many of the herbaceous varieties. The thin, grass-like leaves of chives, for example, contrast well with the bolder shapes of

hostas, and they are also particularly good for edging paths. The frothy leaves of parsley can be used in much the same way.

Many herbs can be grown in decorative borders for their flowers rather than their leaves. The leaves of bergamot (*Monarda*), for example, are used as a herb, but the flowers, which are a bright bold red, are exceptionally decorative, making this a superb border plant.

Potagers

Strictly speaking, a potager is simply a kitchen garden, but it has taken on romantic overtones and is now taken to mean those kitchen gardens that have a decorative as well as productive function.

ABOVE **Flowers are often mixed in with the vegetables in a potager. Sweet peas are one of the most popular choices among gardeners.**

Overall design

The simplest design for a potager is a square or circle, and in many ways these take a lot of beating. Many gardeners, however, enjoy having much more complicated patterns than this, going on to divide the basic shape like the spokes of a wheel or creating four squares, perhaps. Much more intricate patterns can be created, with circles within squares or squares within circles. And so the list of design ideas expands.

The patterns do not have to be geometric. Some gardeners prefer more free-flowing plots, divided with swirls and curved lines. Although these can be extremely attractive, they can be difficult to plant effectively.

Sources of inspiration for such gardens may be visits to actual gardens or pictures in magazines or books. Other useful sources which are often overlooked are arts and crafts that use similar patterns. A book on patchwork, for example, can highlight all kinds of design ideas that can be mixed and matched with further ideas from other gardens.

Structural elements

The shapes of the beds are usually delineated by paths, which are both decorative in their own right and also useful in that they provide access to the beds. These can be paved with brick or stone, or covered with gravel. Although properly laid paths are ultimately best, it is possible to lay them in a temporary fashion until you are certain that you like the layout, or if you want to change the overall plan every few years. Simply lay paving stones, for example, directly onto the levelled soil.

A further way to delineate the beds is to surround them with low box hedging. This creates a permanent structure but it increases its attraction. The box plants will take a few years to become established but the effort and wait are worth it.

Other structural elements are more three-dimensional. Arches, for example, can be used, particularly in the centre of the garden, perhaps covered with fruit. Small trees and standard fruit bushes can be used as centrepieces for individual beds. All add to the shape and texture of the garden.

Designing with plants

The vegetables are the least permanent part of the garden. Just planting them out in lines or blocks will produce an attractive effect, but more interest can be generated by consciously

LEFT **Here, the flowers are situated close enough to the fruit and vegetables to become an integrated part of the potager.**

A Potager Garden

*A potager is simply a kitchen garden, but it is used, increasingly,
to mean a kitchen garden that has been laid out in a decorative manner. Instead
of plants filling more or less random rows, a more complex and involved
plan is drawn up, and the garden takes on a new dimension.*

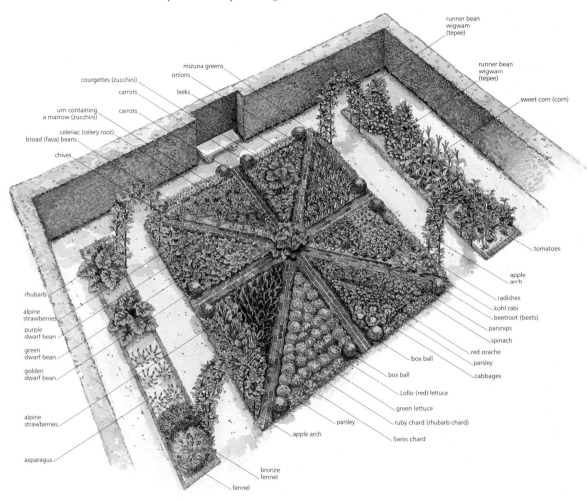

runner bean wigwam (tepee)

mizuna greens
onions
courgettes (zucchini)
carrots
leeks
urn containing a marrow (zucchini)
carrots
celeriac (celery root)
broad (fava) beans
chives

runner bean wigwam (tepee)

sweet corn (corn)

tomatoes

apple arch

rhubarb
alpine strawberries
purple dwarf bean
green dwarf bean
golden dwarf bean

alpine strawberries

asparagus

radishes
kohl rabi
beetroot (beets)
parsnips
spinach
red orache
box ball
parsley
box ball
cabbages
Lollo (red) lettuce
green lettuce
parsley
ruby chard (rhubarb chard)
apple arch
Swiss chard

bronze fennel
fennel

planning each bed, thinking about the plants' colours and textures. Red-leaved lettuces, for example, can be used as winding threads through green vegetables. Parsley can be used as edging, or as a boundary between groups of vegetables. Rows of beans growing up canes can divide beds into sections or they can be grown over archways. Plants need not be planted in blocks, they can be laid out in circles with other plants growing in the middle or around the outside.

However, there is a serious problem with such designs and that is whether to eat the vegetables or not! A meticulous design with every plant in its place is utterly ruined if one is taken off for use in the kitchen. This is something that you must plan for and a less formal style may be the answer.

Another factor to be borne in mind is that it is bad gardening practice to grow the same plants on the same ground each year. Because crops should be rotated, it is not possible to use the same pattern each year unless you create it using different plants.

Herb Gardens

Herb gardens tend to fulfil two functions. The first, and obvious one, is to provide herbs. The second arises from the fact that herbs can be highly decorative, making an attractive garden on their own.

Herbs as herbs

Although we grow almost as many herbs as our ancestors, they are primarily included in our gardens for romantic reasons. The number of herbs that most gardeners use in the kitchen is relatively small. But small as this number is, those we do use regularly are important. When you are designing a herb garden, make certain that these herbs are readily accessible from the path, and put those that are never or rarely used in the more inaccessible parts of the border.

The most frequently used herbs should be placed as near to the kitchen door as possible so that the cook can grab a handful when necessary. This means that either the herb garden should be located here or the important herbs should be mixed in with other plants in a decorative border. Another solution is to grow these particular herbs in a container or containers, which can then be placed near the kitchen door for easy access.

Herbs for atmosphere

Although many people regularly use a large number of herbs, most of the gardeners who maintain herb gardens do so because of their romantic associations. And there is no doubt that herbs are romantic. This is partly their history and partly the atmosphere they create in the garden. Herbs tend to be gentle plants, and only occasionally do we come across brash ones. The colours are muted and soft, the atmosphere they create is hazy. On sunny days the garden is perfumed by their scents and is drowsy with the sound of

ABOVE **Coriander (cilantro) is a popular herb with a pungent taste. Its delicate flowers and leaves are also decorative.**

bees. This is the perfect garden in which to sit and relax, so you should remember to include a seat in your design.

Herbs by design

The layout of a herb garden depends largely on the space available, of course, but also on the time you can spend in it. Remember that a large one will take a lot of looking after.

It is possible to create quite small herb gardens, and the herb wheel is one of the most popular plans. An old cartwheel is laid out on prepared ground and the spaces between the spokes are filled with different herbs. When real wheels are not available, the same design can be created from

Important culinary herbs	
Basil	Marjoram
Bay	Mint
Chives	Parsley
Dill	Rosemary
French tarragon	Sage
Lovage	Thyme

LEFT **Box hedges associate well with herb gardens. They add order to what, at times, can be an untidy collection of herbs.**

A Formal Herb Garden

Herb gardens need to be carefully planned if they are to be attractive. Primarily a herb garden is a place for growing herbs for the kitchen, but it should also be a peaceful haven where the scents and colours of the plants can be enjoyed. However, it is worth remembering that a well maintained herb garden needs more attention than a vegetable plot.

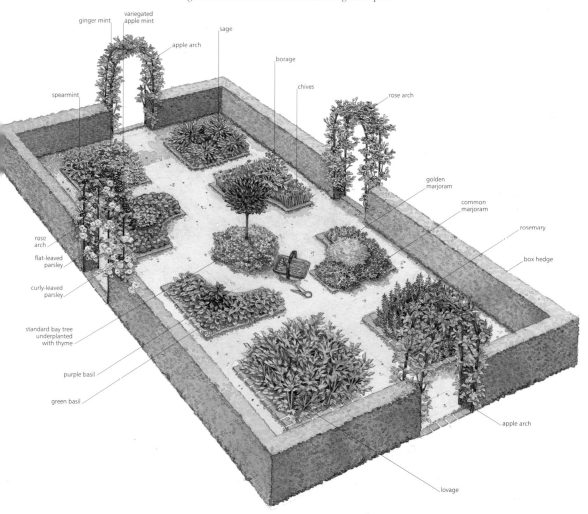

ginger mint
variegated apple mint
sage
apple arch
borage
chives
rose arch
spearmint
golden marjoram
common marjoram
rosemary
rose arch
box hedge
flat-leaved parsley
curly-leaved parsley
standard bay tree underplanted with thyme
purple basil
green basil
apple arch
lovage

bricks. Remember not to use herbs that are too rampant – a sage bush, for example, will soon become big enough to cover the whole area of the wheel. If you want to use the more vigorous plants in a small area, regularly dig them out and replace them.

If you are working on a larger scale, almost any of the patterns mentioned as suitable for potagers can be used. It is worth mentioning that the only time of year when the internal divisions of the garden will be clearly seen is in the winter when the vegetation has died back. During the growing seasons, the lush growth will be such that the outlines of the beds are not easily seen. If you want to see the demarcations, edge the beds with low box hedges, which will also give good definition to the overall design.

Containers

Increasing interest is being shown in containers as a method of growing a few vegetables in a small space, perhaps on the patio or possibly even on a balcony or roof garden. This interest is fuelled by the range of beautiful containers that is now available from garden centres and nurseries.

ABOVE **A surprising amount can be grown in a relatively small space, as can be seen from this collection of herbs and vegetables in pots.**

The containers

Virtually any container can be used to grow vegetables, but success is more likely if it is reasonably large – the bigger the better, in fact. Most vegetables do not like to dry out and the greater the volume of compost (soil mix) that is available, the less chance there is of this occurring. A larger amount of space also allows you to grow several different plants in the same container, which is much more decorative than using just one type.

Terracotta pots are extremely attractive, but the porous nature of the material allows water to evaporate more quickly through the sides of the pot than through, say, a glazed one. Most pots are heavy even without compost (soil mix), so make sure you position them before you fill them. Large, black plastic buckets are practical and can be used successfully, although they are not as attractive as ceramic pots.

Growing bags

If you do not mind their utilitarian appearance, growing bags – plastic sacks filled with a formulated growing medium – are an inexpensive way of growing vegetables. They are particularly useful for tomatoes, but they can be used for many other vegetables as well. They were originally developed for use in the greenhouse (where their appearance does not matter), but they can be used outside just as well. A warm corner, against a wall, is the ideal location.

ABOVE LEFT **More than just a taste of peas can be grown in a container. However, it is important not to let the tub dry out.**

LEFT **Cabbage may not be the first planting idea that springs to mind when thinking of containers, but here four good specimens are growing happily in a plastic tub.**

Hanging baskets

Hanging baskets are not ideal for growing vegetables, mainly because they are too small, but a basket of decorative lettuces, perhaps a mixture of green and bronze varieties, can be eye-catching. Some varieties of tomato are trailing, producing tiny, bite-sized fruit, and these are ideal for baskets. A little imagination should allow you to create something productive as well as attractive.

The position

Containers of vegetables can be placed together with purely decorative containers, although they should not be grown in shade. Although plants such as aubergines (eggplants) and peppers are better grown in a warm situation, most other vegetables prefer not to get too hot, and you should bear in mind that plants grown in pots do not have the solid mass of earth around their roots to keep them cool during the day and it is possible that the roots can become too hot.

A Courtyard Kitchen Garden

You do not need a garden in order to grow vegetables. A patio, courtyard or even a balcony is sufficient to produce a few crops. With care, an attractive arrangement can be made which makes an original alternative to most container plantings. There is less weeding involved than in a conventional plot, but a container garden requires a great deal of watering.

leeks

tomatoes

carrots

half-barrel planted with runner beans climbing up a wigwam (tepee)

half-barrel planted with a pole apple

strawberry pot

thyme

parsley

chilli peppers

chives

lettuce

mint

courgettes (zucchini)

water butt

marjoram

gravel

paving slabs

tarragon

compost bin

Another problem with siting the containers in a warm place is that they will need watering several times a day.

You should, therefore, choose a warm but not hot place, preferably one where there is plenty of air circulating, but not causing a draught (draft).

From a decorative point of view, vegetables can be grown wherever they will fit in. A group of containers can make an attractive feature. You could include a tripod of beans and a tub of golden courgettes (zucchini) and tomatoes, with yellow as well as red ones to vary the scheme. Other pots might contain

sweet or bell peppers or aubergines (eggplants), both of which are decorative. It is a question of using your imagination as well as checking growing times and choosing your favourite tastes that should determine what you do. If you do not like the results, you can always try something different next year.

planning
the crops

For most vegetable growers, the ultimate goal is their produce: they want to grow the best possible vegetables. In order to achieve this, the gardener needs to plan his or her crops very carefully, especially if lack of time and the size of garden are possible limitations. There is little point in taking on a large kitchen garden if you cannot maintain it and, similarly, it is inadvisable to expect large harvests from a small plot of ground.

However, with planning and a careful use of space and time, a surprising amount can be grown. Some parts of the planning stage are largely aesthetic, but others will influence the quantity and quality of your crops. Techniques such as crop rotation, successional cropping and intercropping are particularly important in this context.

One of the first decisions to be made is whether to grow the vegetables in rows or in blocks. There are advantages and disadvantages to both systems, and in the end it is really a question of personal choice.

The consideration of all these factors will eventually become second nature to you. The experienced gardener does not have to think twice about them, but if you are approaching kitchen gardening for the first time, it is important to think about them carefully.

RIGHT **This kitchen garden has been packed with vegetables. No rows are left unfilled and the spaces between them have been mulched with grass clippings to keep the weeds at bay and to prevent the evaporation of water.**

While it is important to get pleasure out of a vegetable garden by arranging it in a pleasing and attractive style, it is equally important to remember that there is a range of practical considerations to be borne in mind when you are planning how to group your crops.

What do you want to grow?

The first factor is, of course, deciding what crops you want to grow. If no one in the family likes beetroot (beets), do you really want to grow them, even if they do look attractive? If space is short should you be growing something else that will be eaten? Potatoes are comparatively inexpensive from greengrocers and farm shops, and, since they take up a lot of space, is it worth your while growing them? If you really want to grow potatoes, perhaps you could compromise and grow a few earlies for that wonderful flavour that only potatoes cooked straight from the soil have, but buy in your maincrop, which will probably not taste all that different from those you would grow yourself.

It is also worth thinking carefully about how much of each crop you need to grow. Go by what you need and not by the quantity of seed in the packet. It is easy, for example, to plant out all the runner bean seeds you have bought only to find that the plants that result will produce far more beans than you could ever eat. Balance the space available against what you want to grow and the quantities that you will require of each. This leads on to the fact that you

BELOW **Rows of spring onions (scallions) have been alternated here with rows of carrots. This is a traditional way of deterring carrot root fly and is effective because the strong smell of the onions masks that of the carrots.**

should sow only to meet your immediate requirements. There really is no point in sowing a whole row of lettuce if you get round to eating only a few of them before they have bolted (run to seed). It is better to sow a third of a row now and another third in a couple of week's time and so on, in order to get a succession of vegetables rather than a glut which you probably won't be able to consume.

ABOVE **This small raised bed is not only decorative but very productive, and demonstrates just how much can be grown in a small garden.**

Designing the beds

Once you have decided what to grow, there is the layout to consider. Most gardeners use the traditional way of growing their plants in rows, but blocks are becoming more popular. One of the advantages of this method is that more plants can be grown in a single area, and it is thus ideal for a garden where space is limited.

Crop rotation is another important consideration. Gardeners have long known that it is not a good idea to grow the same crop on the same ground in successive years, and so the crops are "rotated". This is not difficult to achieve, but it does mean that if you are designing a decorative garden you cannot use the same design for two consecutive years unless you use different plants.

Allowing for more permanent plants

A point to consider when planning the layout is that some crops will remain in the ground over winter. It is rare to start off with a completely bare plot each spring. Sprouting broccoli, for example, will still be growing until late spring, while plants such as garlic and broad (fava) beans, planted in late autumn or early winter, will be there until summer. Remember to allow for these crops when you draw up your plan. Fruit trees and bushes also need a permanent position, as do some vegetables such as rhubarb that are not moved for years.

Crop Rotation

Crop rotation has been practised by farmers and gardeners for generations as a simple and effective precaution against pests and diseases. The basic idea is that if you grow the same type of plant on the same patch of ground every year, the soil will harbour pests and diseases from one season to the next. If you move the crop to another piece of ground, the pests and diseases will lose their host and will die out.

ABOVE **In a four-year rotation, courgettes (zucchini) would be grown in plot three. Alternatively, they can be grown on a compost heap.**

The practical side of this philosophy is the division of the vegetable garden into four or five areas. The different types of crops – brassicas, beans and so on – are moved from one plot to another so that they return to the same piece of ground only every fourth year.

For four-year crop rotation, the crops are divided into four groups – the fifth bed is used for the permanent plants, which obviously do not move. Look at the list of vegetables that you wish to grow for the coming year and divide them into their various groups. Allocate planting areas to each. Do the same for the following year, but move all the crops to another plot. If space is limited, a three-year rotation is better than nothing.

BELOW **Globe artichokes stay in the ground for several years, so they are grown in a permanent plot and do not form part of the rotation plan.**

Four-Year Crop Rotation

Plot 1
Peas
Broad (fava) beans
French (green) beans
Runner beans

Plot 2
Cabbages
Brussels sprouts
Calabrese (Italian sprouting broccoli)
Broccoli
Kale
Radishes
Swedes (rutabaga or yellow turnips)
Turnips
Kohl rabi

Plot 3
Bulb onions
Spring onions (scallions)
Shallots
Leeks
Garlic
Sweet corn (corn)
Marrows (zucchini), squashes and pumpkins
Lettuce

Plot 4
Potatoes
Parsnips
Beetroot (beets)
Carrots
Salsify
Scorzonera
Celery
Celeriac (celery root)
Tomatoes

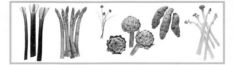

Plot 5 (permanent)
Rhubarb
Asparagus
Perennial herbs
Globe artichokes
Jerusalem artichokes
Seakale

Four-Year Crop Rotation

In many gardens, the differentiation between the plots is hardly discernible,
but it makes life easier to split the garden into individual plots.

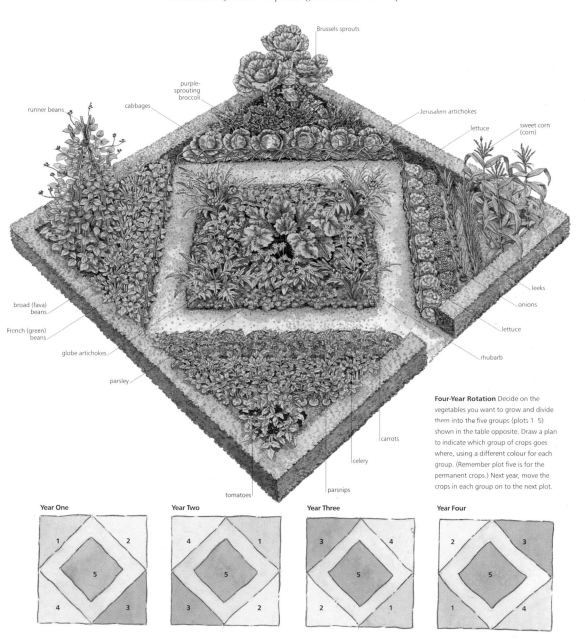

Brussels sprouts

purple-
sprouting
broccoli

runner beans

cabbages

Jerusalem artichokes

lettuce

sweet corn
(corn)

broad (fava)
beans

French (green)
beans

globe artichokes

parsley

leeks

onions

lettuce

rhubarb

carrots

celery

parsnips

tomatoes

Four-Year Rotation Decide on the
vegetables you want to grow and divide
them into the five groups (plots 1–5)
shown in the table opposite. Draw a plan
to indicate which group of crops goes
where, using a different colour for each
group. (Remember plot five is for the
permanent crops.) Next year, move the
crops in each group on to the next plot.

Year One

1   2

5

4   3

Year Two

4   1

5

3   2

Year Three

3   4

5

2   1

Year Four

2   3

5

1   4

Three-Year Crop Rotation

This is a more conventional method of dividing up the garden into separate plots, keeping each group of plants together for rotating.

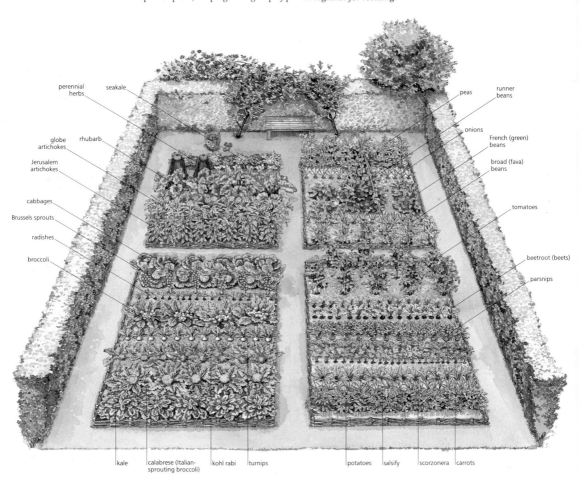

perennial herbs · seakale · peas · runner beans

globe artichokes · rhubarb · onions · French (green) beans

Jerusalem artichokes · broad (fava) beans

cabbages · tomatoes

Brussels sprouts

radishes

broccoli · beetroot (beets)

parsnips

kale · calabrese (Italian-sprouting broccoli) · kohl rabi · turnips · potatoes · salsify · scorzonera · carrots

Three-Year Rotation
Decide on the vegetables you want to grow and divide into the four groups (plots 1–4) shown in the table opposite. Draw a plan to indicate which group of crops goes where, using a different colour for each group. (Remember plot four is for permanent crops.) Move the crops in each group to the next plot the following year.

Year One

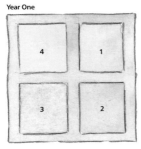

4 | 1
3 | 2

Year Two

4 | 3
2 | 1

Year Three

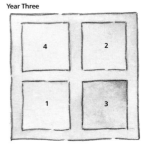

4 | 2
1 | 3

Three-Year Crop Rotation

Plot 1
Peas
Broad (fava) beans
French (green) beans
Runner beans
Bulb onions
Leeks
Sweet corn (corn)
Marrows (zucchini), squashes and pumpkins
Lettuce

Plot 2
Potatoes
Parsnips
Beetroot (beets)
Carrots
Salsify
Scorzonera
Tomatoes

Plot 3
Cabbages
Brussels sprouts
Calabrese (Italian sprouting broccoli)
Broccoli
Kale
Swede (rutabaga or yellow turnips)
Turnips
Kohl rabi
Radishes

Plot 4 (permanent)
Rhubarb
Asparagus
Perennial herbs
Globe artichokes
Jerusalem artichokes
Seakale

ABOVE **In a three-year crop rotation, tomatoes are grown in plot two, along with root crops such as parsnips and carrots.**

ABOVE **Rhubarb is planted in the permanent bed when crops are rotated, and can stay in the same position for up to 25 years.**

As well as having advantages in terms of pests and diseases, there are other reasons for moving crops around. Some crops will tolerate newly manured ground while others cannot. Thus, one plot can be heavily manured when it is dug in the autumn during the first year and cabbages and related plants can be planted in it in spring. In the following year the plot is simply dug, and the root crops, which do not like the soil too rich, are planted there.

Strict crop rotation is not the easiest of things to maintain. Many gardeners start off with good intentions and manage it for a few years, but gradually things begin to slip. Some brassicas that have been left in

the ground over winter may block the space that is required for some other plants, or perhaps a few plants have been slipped in to fill a gap. Leaving plants in the ground until the following year so that you can collect your own seeds also plays havoc with rotation if you have only a small amount of space. If you find this happening, there is no need to worry.

In a small kitchen garden, crop rotation, although it is admirable in theory, is not that important in practice. One of the main difficulties is the amount of space required to put strict rotation into effect. In agricultural situations the crops are fields apart; even in a large garden, the distances involved can be

quite large. In a small garden, however, it is often impossible to get the plots far enough apart for the pests or diseases not to be able to find their host plant. The other problem is that, in practice, four years is not always long enough to kill off all the diseases anyway.

This does not mean that crop rotation is unimportant, however, because it still has some effect. Yet it does mean that you should not lose any sleep if you are not able to follow the sequence to the exact letter. Most gardeners do not grow the same crop on the same ground for two years running in any case – with the exception of plants such as runner beans – but they do not follow strict crop rotation.

Rows

Vegetables have traditionally been grown in rows. Although some gardeners challenge the claims made for this method, suggesting that blocks and deep beds are better, rows are probably still the most widely used system.

The basic idea is simple: the vegetables are grown in a single line, with some crops, such as beans and peas, being grown in a double line. The lines or rows are separated by a distance somewhat wider than the breadth of the plants, so that there is bare earth between the rows. This bare earth acts as a path, allowing access for maintenance, such as weeding and watering, as well as for harvesting.

Growing vegetables in rows is an attractive way of producing them. The varying heights, shapes, textures and colours all show up well, with the rows looking like decorative ribbons stretched across the garden. Their appearance is not, however, the principal reason for growing vegetables in this way. There are practical considerations, too.

Access is one of the important benefits provided by individual rows. The paths between the rows allow the gardener to move freely among the plants without having to stretch. Each plant can be examined for condition as well as for pests and diseases. Pests have less chance of being overlooked if the plant can be clearly seen from at least two sides, and individual plants can be tended to if necessary. The bases of the plants can be easily seen for inspection, weeding and watering.

Another advantage is that there is plenty of air circulating among the plants, which helps considerably to reduce mildew-type diseases. The plants generally have plenty of space in which to develop, and the leaves are able to open out to receive the maximum amount of light. Finally, rows are easy to cover with the majority of cloches available.

Needless to say there are also disadvantages. The use of so many "paths" means that a lot of space is unproductive when you look at the plot as a whole, an important factor in a small garden, where space is limited. Another disadvantage is that the paths allow

light to reach the soil, so increasing the number of weeds that germinate, although this is offset to some extent by the ease with which it is possible to hoe. With constant use, the paths become compacted, which does not help the soil structure. Although the whole bed will be dug each year, because it is so large it is necessary to walk over it

LEFT **Traditional rows of vegetables, filling all the available space, can be very decorative.**

while the ground is being prepared, again adding a certain degree of compaction. Constant hoeing will help overcome this by breaking up the soil and keeping it aerated. However, in dry weather, hoeing should be avoided as it encourages water loss. An alternative is to lay planks of wood between the rows. This not only helps to prevent soil compaction but also acts as a mulch which will help retain the moisture in the soil as well as keep weeds down.

ABOVE **The decorative quality of vegetables can be clearly seen in these rows. All the leaves are green and yet the variety of greens and the shapes of the leaves form a very attractive picture over a long season.**

LEFT **It is important to leave plenty of space for young plants to fill out. Rows with plenty of space between them also allow for access and easy weeding.**

Blocks and Deep Beds

Growing vegetables in blocks as opposed to rows is an old method that more or less dropped out of use in many countries but that has been reintroduced in recent years. The basic idea is to grow the plants in a square or rectangle, say five plants wide by five plants deep, rather than in a single row.

ABOUT **These blocks of contrasting lettuces have been planted in deep beds that are almost flush with the ground. The beds have been dug deeply rather than built up.**

RIGHT **Each of these blocks of vegetables and herbs is about 1.2m/4ft wide, which allows access from the paths running across the plot.**

The vegetable plot is divided into smaller plots, each about 1.2m/4ft across and spanning the width of the main plot. These smaller beds are permanent, unlike rows, and between each is a path, either trodden earth or more substantial paving slabs or bricks. The width of the smaller beds is determined by the gardener's reach – 1.2m/4ft should allow access of about 60cm/24in from each side so that the entire bed can be reached without compacting the soil. Keeping off the beds means that the soil structure is always kept in top condition.

Some gardeners simply dig the soil in the existing plot, adding organic material to it as they go. Others prefer to create a deep bed system, either by digging deeper, using a double digging method, or by raising the height of the bed with boards or a low wall and then adding a mixture of good loam and organic material. The bed is worked from the path so that the soil is never compacted.

The advantage of a rich soil in good condition is that it will support more plants, and so most gardeners plant much more closely than in the conventional rows. This means that productivity is improved considerably, and many more plants can be raised from the same area of ground. As well as being productive, close planting also means that weed seeds have little chance of germinating.

A solid block of plants, however, makes it more difficult to get at any weeds, as well as making it harder to see if there are any pests and diseases lurking below the leaves. Because the plants are close together, there is likely to be less air circulating than around vegetables grown in rows, and this increases the possibility of diseases that like damp conditions with stagnant air. It is also not as

easy to water the base of individual plants. Watering can, in fact, become erratic, with some areas ending up drier than others as water runs off the leaves. Another disadvantage is that it is not as easy to cover the vegetables with cloches, and although it is, of course, possible to construct a cover, this will not be as mobile as individual cloches.

You can take advantage of both methods by using deep beds, with their rich soil conditions, and planting short rows across the beds instead of blocks. This method works well for those gardeners who feel that digging destroys the structure of the soil. They dig the soil initially, adding plenty of organic material, but thereafter only top-dress the surface with more organic material, perhaps hoeing it in or allowing the worms to move it below the surface. Although this benefits the soil, most gardeners prefer the more traditional method of digging at least once a year because this has other advantages.

LEFT **Boards create a greater depth of fertile soil, so vegetables can be planted much closer together.**

Intercropping

There can be few gardeners who have enough space to grow everything they wish, and this is particularly true of those with small gardens. One way partly to overcome the problem is to make sure that every available piece of land is in use and to avoid letting ground lie idle.

There are two main ways to ensure that the land is used efficiently. The first is to plant quick-growing crops among slower ones so that the former have been harvested before the latter have grown sufficiently to fill the space. Brussels sprouts, for example, are planted at anything up to 75cm/30in apart, depending on the size of the variety. For several weeks after they have been planted there is a lot of empty space around each plant. This can be filled with a crop such as lettuce or radishes that takes only a short while to come to maturity.

Some plants, however, cannot be planted out in the early part of the season, and rather than leave the ground empty, it can be filled

BELOW **Intercropping carrots with lettuces – here a tinted variety known as 'Nelson' – makes for a very decorative effect.**

with a temporary crop. For example, a bed of lettuces can be planted and the first ones to be harvested can be replaced by young sweet corn (corn), the rest of the lettuces being harvested as the corn develops.

A similar idea can be used with station-sown seeds. For example, parsnip seeds can be sown in groups of three at, say, 23cm/9in intervals. In between each group a few radishes can be sown. This method has advantages in that not only will the quick-growing radishes make use of the ground before the parsnips need it, but, because parsnips are slow to germinate, the radishes will actually mark the row, making it easier to hoe off any weeds without disturbing the parsnips, which are still below ground.

Another aspect of intercropping is purely decorative. A simple example is to intercrop red-leaved lettuces with green ones.

To create these effects, it is best to raise the plants in trays or modules and plant them out in a pattern when they are large enough.

When you are intercropping for visual effects, take care in the choice of neighbours. There is little point in planting decorative lettuces next to potatoes, which will eventually flop over and smother them. However, from the productive point of view it is a good idea to plant lettuces between rows of potatoes before the latter have emerged or have reached any height, because the lettuces will be cropped before the ground is smothered by the potato leaves.

ABOVE **Here, a short row of radishes is being sown between individual cabbages. They will crop long before the cabbages have grown large enough to cover them.**

ABOVE **As an alternative to sowing, individual lettuces can be planted between slow-growing plants such as cabbages.**

Successional Crops

Closely related to the question of intercropping is that of successional sowing and planting. The idea behind this is to phase the crops so that your plot provides a continuous stream of produce and not a series of sudden gluts. In other words, this is another method of ensuring that you get the most out of your ground.

Many gardeners have a tendency to sow a complete row right across their plot, whether they need that amount of produce or not, simply because a whole row looks better than a short one. This can be wasteful, because two-thirds of the row may bolt before you have consumed it and then you are left with nothing. It is far better to sow a third of a row of, say, spinach, wait two or three weeks and then sow another third and finally the last section two or three weeks later still. This means that the crops will reach maturity at two- to three-week intervals, spreading out so that you have spinach for two months or more rather than for the two to three weeks that would have been the case if you had sown the whole row at once.

Another way of securing a succession of crops is to choose varieties that mature at different times. Peas, for example, are classified into first earlies and maincrop types, and within these groups some varieties produce peas sooner than others. Choosing several different varieties rather than just one will provide a much longer harvesting season.

The same principle is true of fruit. Choosing different varieties of raspberries, for example, will enable you to harvest fruit from early summer right through to late autumn. This also applies to strawberries, apples and many other types of fruit.

There may, of course, be times when you do not want to spread the harvesting. For example, if you like to freeze vegetables for

winter use it is easier if, for example, all your peas mature at once so that you can quickly freeze them and replant the ground with another crop of something else – late turnips perhaps. Vegetables that all crop at once are usually marked in the seed catalogues as being suitable for freezing.

If you are creating a vegetable garden as a decorative feature as well as a productive one, successional sowing and planting becomes

doubly important. Any crop removed, whether it is a single lettuce or a row or a wigwam (tepee) of peas will leave a gap and the sooner it is filled the better the garden will look.

Both from the productive and the visual point of view it is always worthwhile having a few plants coming along in pots ready to plant out. Lettuce, Swiss chard and parsley, for example, can be sown at two-week intervals in modules to provide a good supply of plants to fill the gaps.

Another aspect of successional cropping is replacing one crop with another as soon as it is finished. Thus, replant the ground occupied by broad (fava) beans with a late crop of leeks as the beans are finished or plant out spring cabbage in the space that becomes available when the onions are harvested. Keep the ground producing for you even if you only sow green manure, which is dug back into the soil later in the year.

RIGHT **Some crops are better planted at intervals so that they do not all mature at the same time. To facilitate this, it is often easier to fill long rows with several different types of vegetables rather than leave gaps to be sown later.**

greenhouses

sheds and equipment

Considering the large number of tools and equipment that is now
available from the average garden centre, the gardener can actually get
by with buying surprisingly few of them, as long as they are chosen
carefully and with a view to what is actually needed. Starting a
vegetable garden need not be a costly business. You do not, for example,
have to invest in a large greenhouse or in cold frames, although a shed
will prove useful if you do not want to perform unhygienic gardening
tasks in the kitchen. A wheelbarrow is the only mechanical device that
most gardeners will require although many may use a rotavator
(rototiller) for digging larger plots. There are also many excellent
second-hand tools to be had, very often at a fraction of the price of new
ones that may be of an inferior quality, so it is worth spending a little
time on finding the best tools.

ABOVE **Greenhouses are available in a variety of shapes and sizes, which means that you should be able to find one to suit your garden.**

In many ways gardening is a very personal hobby and no more so than in the choice of tools and other equipment. Everybody has their favourite selection of tools and feels lost if, for example, they are working in someone else's garden without these items.

What do you really need?

Life is much easier in the garden if you have items such as a wheelbarrow, but bear in mind that, in a small garden, you can grow an extra couple of plants in the space needed to store it. Indeed, most things, such as weeds and compost, can be carried in a bucket in small-scale gardening.

One of the problems with owning a lot of tools and equipment is that you need somewhere to keep them, and that means there is even less garden for growing once you have erected the requisite shed. The advantage of having just a few hand tools is that they will usually fit into the back of the garage or even under the stairs in the house. Once you own a large rotavator (rototiller), no one will be pleased when it is trundled across the carpet to put it away or its sharp tines scratch the side of the car as you try to manoeuvre it into and out of a tightly packed garage.

Once you start to use a rotavator (rototiller) your gardening will be on a scale that usually means having a shed devoted to tools, and you may want to consider having a combined tool and potting shed – it should be a simple matter to put a bench down one side of a tool shed. Having a potting shed may seem to be rather an old-fashioned idea, but once you have had one you will find it difficult to manage without. However, it is not essential, and many successful gardeners manage quite well without one.

Do you need a greenhouse or cold frame?

Just as a handful of tools are all that you need to get started, it is also not essential to have a greenhouse and cold frames. There is no doubt that such structures are useful and will make your life much easier in many ways, but they are expensive in terms of both cost and space – and also in terms of the

time you will spend in them if you have only a limited number of hours available for gardening. In any case, most of the things that you will do in a greenhouse can be carried out elsewhere. Any propagation, for example, that is necessary can be done on the kitchen windowsill (as long as the cook is sympathetic), while tomatoes and cucumbers, which are the most common greenhouse crops, can be grown in the open, even if it means they crop later.

If, however, you intend to garden on a large scale and do wish to invest in a greenhouse, then bear in mind that the design is very much a matter of personal preference. Often your choice of greenhouse will be dictated by what you can comfortably fit into the available space in your garden as much as by its aesthetic appeal. In spite of the wide variety of greenhouses now on the market, there is still ample scope for the keen amateur to design and build a greenhouse suited to his or her own specifications and requirements. If you are not that practically minded, however, and do not want to go to the expense of buying a greenhouse, you might like to consider using polythene (plastic) tunnels instead. Although not very attractive, these tunnels are a cheap and practical alternative to the traditional greenhouse.

ABOVE **A small vegetable and herb garden such as this does not require a large battery of tools.**

BELOW **Terracotta pots, which are used for blanching seakale and other vegetables, such as endives, make striking ornaments in the garden.**

Greenhouses

The ultimate goal of most gardeners is to have a greenhouse, for it extends the possibilities of the garden tremendously. Such a structure can be used for propagation, for growing tender or winter crops and for overwintering plants that cannot be safely left outside. There is a fourth, often unspoken, use and that is to keep the gardener dry and warm in winter.

Most of the horticultural operations that are done in a greenhouse can be achieved perfectly satisfactorily in cold frames. Most gardeners, however, prefer to carry them out in the warmth and comfort of the greenhouse, rather than bending over a cold frame in a cold or wet wind.

Choosing a greenhouse

As with any equipment, the first thing to consider are your reasons for making the purchase. Why do you want a greenhouse? What are you going to do with it? This is an important stage, because answering these questions will help to determine the size.

BELOW **This standard straight-sided greenhouse is made of aluminium, but it has been painted green, rather than being left silver, so that it blends in better with the colours of the garden.**

Cost and the available space will also obviously influence the size, but if possible, make use the prime consideration. Most gardeners, slightly tongue in cheek, will tell you to work out the size and then double it. There is some truth in this old saw, and many, if not most, gardeners wish that they had bought a larger greenhouse than the one they did. So buy larger rather than smaller if you possibly can.

Material

These days the choice is mainly between wood and aluminium, although it is still possible to find old iron-frame greenhouses, and some more expensive ones are a combination of materials, such as brick and wood. For most gardeners the choice is simply an aluminium frame, because it is the cheapest style available, but there are other factors to be taken into consideration. For example,

ABOVE **The marigolds planted with a row of tomatoes in this greenhouse will ward off potential pests, a technique known as companion planting.**

wooden greenhouses are far more attractive than aluminium ones. However, although they usually fit more sympathetically into the garden, they are more expensive and the upkeep is more time-consuming. Wooden greenhouses are slightly warmer in winter. It is possible to make your own, working to your own design and dimensions.

Aluminium greenhouses are cheap and easy to maintain. The cheaper ones may, however, be rather flimsy, and in exposed positions the sides may flex and the glass fall out! They normally come in standard sizes, but because they are modular, there is a choice of the number of windows and their position. Some companies will build to your specifications, but this is obviously a more expensive option. It is now possible to buy aluminium greenhouses where the frame is painted, which partially disguises the aluminium.

Glass can now be replaced with plastic. Most gardeners prefer the traditional material, but if there are children around it is often more sensible to go for plastic on safety grounds.

RIGHT **An unusually shaped greenhouse with a steeply pitched roof that not only looks different from conventional greenhouses, but has the added advantage that the steep sides absorb the low winter sun more easily.**

LEFT **It is vital not to let greenhouses over-heat. Opening the windows at the right time is not always possible if you are not at home during the hottest part of the day, but automatic window-openers will do the job for you.**

Octagonal greenhouses are suitable for small sites, and many people find them more decorative than the traditional shapes. Because they are almost round, the "aisle" is just a central standing area, thus saving a lot of wasted space. However, the amount of useful space is still quite small.

Lean-to greenhouses can be built against walls, which not only saves space but also makes use of the warmth that is usually found in the wall, especially house walls. These are obviously much cheaper than a full greenhouse, but the amount of useful space within them is limited because the light does not come from all directions and plants can get drawn. Painting the wall white helps because more light is reflected back onto the plants.

Digging in

The old-fashioned idea of sinking the greenhouse into the ground is a good one as long as you can overcome any drainage problems. Steps lead down to the door, and on to a central aisle, dug out of the soil. The side benches are laid on the natural soil level and the roof springs from a low wall on the ground. The advantage of this system, apart from the fact that it is relatively cheap, is that the soil acts as a vast storage heater. Gardeners using such a greenhouse find that as long as they provide some form of insulation, no heat is required to overwinter tender plants. Traditionally, a wooden framework would have been used for the roof, but aluminium would do just as well.

Shape

The shape of the greenhouse is a matter of personal preference. Traditional styles have vertical sides, but some new ones have sloping sides, which allow in more light – especially useful during winter when the sun is low or if you have trays of seedlings on the floor.

Ventilation

When you buy a greenhouse, make sure that it has as many opening windows as you can afford because the free passage of air through the structure is of the utmost

ABOVE **Insulating the greenhouse is important during the cold winter months, helping to keep heating costs down as well as preventing any violent fluctuations in temperature. Polythene (plastic) bubble insulation is cheap and efficient.**

LEFT **Some plants, such as peppers, grow better in a greenhouse than they do outside in the open air. In a greenhouse, they are assured of a constant temperature and humidity.**

importance. Stagnant air in a greenhouse is a killer, as all kinds of fungal diseases are likely to develop very quickly. Openings can either be covered with conventional windows or with louvres. If you are away during daylight hours in summer, the time when windows need to be opened on hot days, automatic openers can be used. The mechanism opens the windows as soon as a specified pre-set temperature is reached. Having a door at each end helps on larger houses. In winter, windows should be left open as much as possible, and, when it is necessary to close them, use a fan to keep the air circulating.

Heating

There are various methods of heating a greenhouse, but one of the most versatile is with electricity. Although the cost per unit of heat may be greater, the control of its output through the use of thermostats is such that no heat (or money) is wasted, because the appliance comes on only when the temperature drops below a certain point. Thermostatically controlled gas heaters are also now becoming available. Paraffin heaters are cheap, but they need to be regularly filled and maintained and they produce large amounts of water vapour, which encourages disease unless the greenhouse is ventilated.

Heating bills can be reduced by insulating the greenhouse. Double glazing is the ultimate but is expensive. A cheaper alternative is to line the house with sheets of clear polythene (plastic), preferably containing air bubbles. If you have only a few plants that need protecting, it is cheaper to close off one end of the greenhouse with polythene and heat just this area. If the number of plants is small enough, a heated propagator or a cloche over a heated bench may be sufficient.

Shading

Greenhouses need to be as light as possible, especially during the winter, but at the same time bright sunshine should be kept out as this will raise the temperature too much. It is possible to buy shade netting, which can be draped over the outside or clipped to the inside of the glass. This is easy to remove in overcast periods. An opaque wash applied to the glass reduces the effect of

the sun considerably, but it is time-consuming to keep removing it during dull weather, so it is usually left in place from early summer to mid-autumn. There is one form of wash that becomes transparent when it rains, thus letting in more light.

Fittings

The full height of the greenhouse is needed for tomatoes and cucumbers, which can be grown in growing bags on the floor. Benching or staging is a useful addition, at least down one side, and can be made of wood or longer-lasting aluminium.

If the staging has raised sides it can be filled with sand. This is useful for sinking pots in to help keep them warm and moist. Heating cables can also be used to keep the bench warm, and building a polythene (plastic) or glass cabinet or lid on top will turn it into an effective propagating bench.

Polytunnels

Polythene (plastic) tunnels are a cheap alternative to greenhouses. They are ideal for growing winter and early spring vegetables and for housing and propagating plants until they are ready to plant out. They are, however, rather ugly and can get very cold, and the polythene will need replacing every three years or so.

Tools and Equipment

To look in the average garden centre you would imagine that you need a tremendous battery of tools and equipment before you could ever consider gardening, but in fact you can start (and continue) gardening with relatively few tools and no equipment at all.

Tools are personal things, so one gardener may always use a spade for digging, no matter how soft the ground, whereas another would always use a fork as long as the ground was not too heavy. The type of hoe for certain jobs is another subject on which gardeners hold widely different opinions.

Buying tools

It is not necessary to buy a vast armoury of tools when you first start gardening. Most of the jobs can be done with a small basic kit.

When you are buying, always choose the best you can afford. Many of the cheaper tools are made of pressed steel, which soon becomes blunt, will often bend and may even break. Stainless steel is undoubtedly the best, but tools made of this tend to be expensive. Ordinary steel implements can be almost as good, especially if you keep them clean. Avoid tools that are made of aluminium. Trowels and hand forks especially are often made of aluminium, but they wear down and blunt quickly and are not good value for money.

Soil Testers

The chemical composition of the soil can be tested by the gardener by using one of a range of soil testers. The most commonly used checks the acidity/alkalinity of the soil. It is chemical based and involves mixing soil samples with water and checking the colour against a chart. More complicated tests indicate whether there is a shortage of minerals or trace elements. The balance can then be adjusted by adding lime or fertilizers to the soil.

Second-hand

A good way to acquire a collection of tools is to buy them second-hand. There are advantages to this. One is that they are usually much cheaper than new ones. Frequently, too, they are made of much better steel than cheap, modern ones and still retain a keen edge, even after many years' use. In the past gardening tools were made with a much greater variation in design and size. If you go to buy a modern spade, for example, you will probably find that the sizes in the shop are all the same – designed for the "average" gardener. Old tools come in all shapes and

spade

fork

trowel

hand fork

dibber

pruning saw

Labelling and Tying
When working in the garden, it is useful to have a tray of odds and ends, such as string, raffia, plant ties and labels. You never know when you might need them. For example, it is always difficult to remember what has been planted or sown where – it may be weeks before seed you have sown is visible above ground.

raffia

plant ties

string

plant labels

sizes, and if you find modern tools uncomfortable to use you are more likely to find an old one that is made just for you.

Not all old tools are good by any means, of course, but by keeping an eye out and buying only good quality ones you will end up with tools that will more than see you through your gardening career and at a relatively modest price. Car boot fairs (garage sales) and rural junk shops (second-hand stores) are the places to look out for them. Avoid antique shops where such tools are sold at inflated prices to be hung as decorations on the wall rather than to be used.

Care and maintenance

Look after your tools. If you do this they will not only always be in tip-top working condition but will last a lifetime. Scrape all the mud and any vegetation off the tools as soon as you have used them. Once they are clean, run an oily rag lightly over the metal parts. The thin film of oil will stop the metal from corroding. This not only makes the tools last longer but also makes them easier to use because less effort is needed to use a clean spade than one with a rough surface of rust.

In addition, keep the wooden parts clean, wiping them over with linseed oil if the wood becomes too dry.

Keep all blades sharp. Hang tools up if possible. Standing spades and hoes on the ground, especially if it is concrete, will blunt them over time. Keep them away from children.

Equipment

It is possible to run a vegetable and fruit garden with no mechanical aids at all. However, if you have grass paths, a lawn mower will, obviously, be more than useful – it will be essential. Hedge cutters, too, are useful, although hedges can be cut by hand much more easily than grass paths.

In the vegetable garden itself the only mechanical device that you may require is a rotavator (rototiller), which can be used for digging and breaking up the soil. Unless you have a large garden, however, this is not absolutely necessary, although it does make life easier if you want to break down a heavy soil into a fine tilth.

Keep all your equipment maintained. There is nothing worse than wanting a piece of machinery to use in a hurry only to find that it will not start. After the weather, machinery is the most stressful part of gardening.

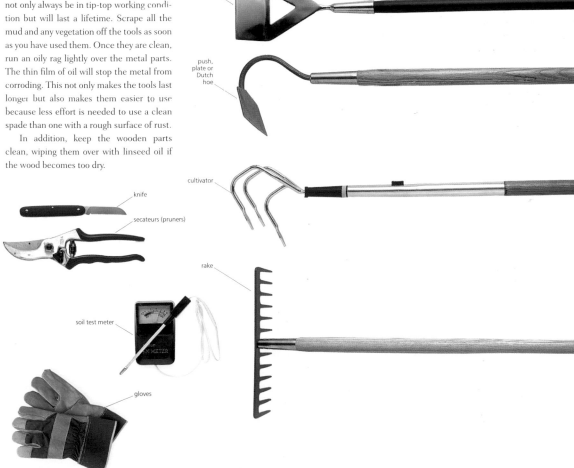

draw hoe

push, plate or Dutch hoe

cultivator

knife

secateurs (pruners)

rake

soil test meter

gloves

Tool Sheds

The larger the garden and the more tools you have, the bigger the problem you will have in storing them. It is possible to keep a handful of items in a cupboard in the house or hanging on the garage wall. Gradually, however, more and more space is required.

When gardening, you will accumulate bags of compost (soil mix) to be stored as well as a multitude of pots, and, depending on where you live, the wheelbarrow might be best stored under cover. The ultimate solution to these problems is to get a tool shed.

Buying

As with a greenhouse, whenever you buy a shed it always seems to be too small soon after you get it, so think carefully before you buy. What do you need it for? If it is just to store tools, then it is possible to buy a small shed that is no more than a cupboard. This might have just enough space to hang tools and stand a couple of sacks of compost (soil mix) and some pots on the floor, but there will not be enough room to walk into it.

If you want to keep non-gardening things in there as well – a couple of bicycles, perhaps, as well as the garden furniture – you are obviously going to need far more space.

BELOW **Although it is not absolutely essential, a potting shed is a useful place to work, especially on a wet day.**

It is worth considering whether you want to use it as a combined tool and potting shed, and this would obviously require yet more space. Ultimately, the decision is likely to depend on how much money you want to spend and the amount of room available.

Materials

Most tool sheds are made out of wood, and they are usually purchased in prefabricated sections that are bolted together on site. The cheaper softwoods will last for years if they are treated with preservatives at regular intervals. The more expensive cedar sheds will last much longer, although they, too, benefit from treatment with preservatives. Cheap plastic and sheet metal sheds are also available, but they generally look cheap and do not last long. If that is all you can afford, tuck it out of sight – behind a hedge or screen, for example.

There is no reason why you should not make your own shed. This would not necessarily work out cheaper than buying one, but at least it can be tailor-made to the site and to your requirements. Wooden structures can be dismantled and moved elsewhere, but for a more robust and warmer building, it could be made from brick. Remember to check local planning laws before you begin work on it.

Cheaper sheds are supplied without floors and are simply set on the ground – but it is preferable to have a concrete base. Concrete is cold and unyielding to feet if you have to stand on it for any length of time – while

ABOVE **As well as being the ideal place to store your tools, equipment and other gardening materials, a tool shed can be attractive in its own dusty way.**

potting, for example. A wooden floor, set above the earth or concrete, is warmer, but unless it is well supported from below, it flexes as you walk on it and in some cases the whole shed may rock. Windows take up valuable wall space, but if your shed is a reasonable size or if you are using it for potting, they are essential to let in light.

Organization

Most hand tools can be hung on the walls using ready-made racks or by using wooden dowel pegs set into a strip of wood. If there is space it is a good idea to build a potting bench along one wall, preferably under a window. Equipment or bags of compost (soil mix) can be stored below the bench, while shelves above it can carry pots or smaller tools. An old bathroom cabinet or a similar small cupboard with a child-proof lock is useful for keeping chemicals in if you use them. Open bags of compost tend to get spilt, so it is a good idea to store them in plastic dustbins (containers) that fit under the bench.

RIGHT **This selection of tools is still in working order, even after many years' work. Clean and well oiled, they should give many more years' good service.**

Cold Frames

Cold frames are rather underrated by many gardeners. They are not only useful in their own right but they can also be used for most of the jobs that are undertaken in the greenhouse. They are less expensive than greenhouses, take up less space and are cheaper to keep warm. Their main disadvantage is that the gardener works outside and not inside in the warm and dry as with a greenhouse.

Uses

In the vegetable garden, cold frames are frequently used for producing winter or early crops of such vegetables as carrots. The frame can be in a permanent position in the garden or moved, rather like a large cloche, onto the vegetable bed itself. The vegetables can be grown either directly in the soil or in growing bags. Later in the year, the cold frame can be used for growing cucumbers or melons.

Another basic use is to afford protection and warmth to trays of seeds or seedlings. Once the plants are ready to go out, the lights can be opened over a period of a week or two to harden off the plants before they are planted out.

Materials

As with greenhouses, the cheaper cold frames are made from aluminium. Their advantage is that they are light enough to move around, but they are not good at retaining heat. Wooden ones are better at this, and cold frames with solid walls made from brick, concrete or even old railway sleepers (ties) provide much better protection during the winter.

Aluminium-framed cold frames can be designed to include glass in the sides, which allows in more light. Solid-sided ones are much warmer but light can enter only through the glass above. It is a good idea to paint the inside of the walls white to reflect some of the light.

Lights (lids) that are glazed with glass are generally preferable, but plastic can be used where there is danger of accidents – if children or elderly people are in the garden, for example.

Heating

Most cold frames, as their name suggests, are not heated. However, it is easier and cheaper to provide some warmth than in a greenhouse, and if you want to propagate or overwinter tender plants it may be possible to supply some form of heat. Electric heating cables installed in the sand below the pots and around the walls of the frame is the easiest method. It is also the most efficient if the cables are connected to a thermostat that switches the electricity on only when heat is required.

Hotbeds

A traditional way to heat cold frames is to set them on a pile of farmyard manure, usually horse dung. As the dung breaks down it releases more than enough heat to keep the frames warm. Soil can be laid on top of the manure and a wide range of vegetables grown in it during the winter. The manure should be fresh, and once it has rotted down and no longer generates heat, it can be spread on the garden and dug in.

Insulation

It is easy to insulate cold frames because they are small. The simplest way is to throw an old carpet over the frame on cold nights.

LEFT **When the seedlings are fully acclimatized and ready to be planted out, the lights (lids) can be left off altogether.**

This may be sufficient to hold in the residual heat, so no extra heating is required to keep the frame above freezing. More efficient methods would be to cover the frames with bubble polythene (plastic) or even to line the inside of the lights with it.

Ventilation

When it is not necessary to keep the frames tightly shut to avoid heat loss, it is sensible to open them slightly, even if it is just a crack, to let air circulate among the plants. This helps prevent various fungal diseases, especially botrytis, which cause seedlings to die through rotting.

RIGHT **A cold frame with a partially opened light (lid) so that the greenhouse-grown seedlings gradually become acclimatized to the outside conditions.**

BELOW **A brick cold frame with a soil bed for growing winter and early spring vegetables.**

Cloches

Cloches are portable forms of protection, rather like miniature cold frames. They are mainly employed during the winter and early spring, but they can be used at any time of year to bring on a crop or to protect it.

ABOVE **A rigid plastic cloche is easy to use. The sections butt up against each other and can be pegged into the soil. Endpieces are also available.**

Uses

There are frequently times when you want to cosset a few plants. They may need protection from the cold or it may be that they are not particularly worried by the cold but need a little warmth to make them grow faster. One row of strawberries, for example, can be covered with cloches to make them fruit one or even two weeks earlier than they would if uncovered. During the winter, broad (fava) beans will come on better if they are protected not only from the cold but also the extremes of rain and wind. Cloches can also be used to protect plants from predators.

In wet and cold areas cloches can be used to cover the ground so that it both dries out and warms up ready for sowing. This will often enable the gardener to sow several weeks earlier than the weather would otherwise allow in the unprotected garden.

In autumn, cloches can be used to cover ripening or harvested vegetables. For example, cordon tomatoes can be lowered to the ground onto straw and allowed to ripen under cloches, while onions that have been harvested in a wet summer can be placed under cloches to "harden off" before storing.

Materials

Some of the earliest cloches were glass bell jars – like upside-down glass vases – which were placed over individual plants. Other traditional cloches were made from sheets of glass, and the earliest types were held in iron frameworks, and resembled miniature greenhouses. Later, cloches became simpler, and the glass was held together by metal or, more recently, plastic or rubber clips. These were known as barn or tent cloches because of their shapes, and could cover a single plant or a whole row when arranged in a line.

Glass is still used, but most cloches are made of polythene (sheet vinyl or plastic) or rigid plastic. There are two main types. One is made up of individual units, which link up in some way, and the other is like a miniature polytunnel, with a single sheet of polythene stretched along the length of the row.

All cloches will do the job they are designed to do. Glass should last the longest, unless you are careless. Although plastics and polythene (sheet vinyl) have a more limited lifespan, they are generally cheaper to replace and are usually lighter and easier to store.

Making your own

Bought cloches may not fit the length or width of the rows in your garden, especially if you are growing in deep beds or blocks. It is relatively simple to make your own. For smaller rows, several hoops of galvanized wire are pushed into the earth at intervals of 60cm/24in and a sheet of polythene (plastic) is laid over them. Place more wire hoops over the first, so that the polythene is trapped between them and held securely. For real security the sides and the two ends of the polythene can be buried in the earth.

For larger beds hoops can be made from lengths of plastic water pipe. Place a stick or iron stake in the ground on each side of the block or row and place the end of the pipe over the stake, forming a hoop. Proceed as before, using more hoops to hold the polythene (plastic) in place, or use strings stretched over the polythene next to the hoops and attached to wire hooks sunk into the ground.

LEFT **Glass bell jars are simple cloches for covering one plant. They are expensive, but plastic sweet jars make a good, if not as attractive, alternative.**

RIGHT **Old-fashioned cloches are particularly good for decorative vegetable gardens. However, they are also very expensive.**

soil

The soil in your garden is your most valuable asset, and it should be cared for accordingly. Some gardeners are lucky and inherit soil in good condition, others find that their soil was once good but is now a little tired and in need of attention. Unlucky gardeners start with virgin soil, often a heavy clay and filled with builder's rubble. Even good soil needs care, while the other two types of soil, especially the heavy soil, need plenty of attention. However, given time and energy even a heavy soil will become fertile and workable, and produce good vegetables.

The main tool in the gardener's armoury is organic material: farmyard manure, garden compost and many other well-rotted forms of humus. It is never possible to have too much of this if you want good soil. Gravel and sharp sand can also be used in the battle against heavy soil. When added to clay, these fine crushed stones separate the particles of clay and allow water to drain through.

Once you have improved your soil, you will find that there is nothing more satisfying than turning a barren soil into a fertile one.

RIGHT **A soil that is well worked is ideal for growing vegetables as long as its structure and fertility are maintained by the addition of well-rotted organic material.**

Know your soil

All soils are different, and even in a single garden the soil may vary from place to place. Look at your soil: notice how it absorbs water, how well plants grow, what does well and what does not. Check several sites around the garden with a soil test kit – small kits are available from garden centres. The more you study and get to know your soil, the better gardener you will become and the better crops you will grow. The two main aspects to consider are its structure and its fertility. If you can get these right, the rest of your gardening should be easy.

Working the soil

Some people are lucky: they take over a garden that has been well worked. Others are not so fortunate: they inherit a new site that is little more than pure clay. However, although the people who have a well-worked garden may think they can relax, it is important that they keep on treating the ground with respect. If they neglect to feed the soil, it will become tired and infertile; if they stomp around on it after heavy rain, the soil will become compacted and the beautiful structure that has been built up over the years will be lost.

BELOW **Using raised beds is one method of creating a controlled medium, away from the influence of the native soil. For example, a fertile loam can be imported and used in a bed on top of a heavy clay, thus providing an "instant" garden.**

Those with a new garden will have to work hard, especially if it is heavy clay, but gradually, season by season, the soil will improve until eventually it will be unrecognizable. I remember my father moving to a garden in which the soil was nothing but solid yellow clay; by the time he hung up his boots for the last time, it was possible to dig the ground with a fork in midwinter, such was the extent to which its condition had been improved. It does not take a lifetime to improve the soil, however, and even a few seasons will make a real difference.

There are few soils that the average householder will encounter in which it is impossible to grow vegetables. Simply digging and sowing will produce results – not necessarily good results, especially if you do just that every year, but nonetheless, it will produce results. However, if it is fed with organic material the soil will soon not only be easier to work but will also produce better crops.

Better crops

By better crops we mean bigger and tastier vegetables. Vegetables that
are half-starved or that grow in dry soils are often tough and bitter tasting.
Compost and similar materials help to retain moisture in the soil, releasing
it to the plants over a long period, thus reducing the risk of drought and dry
soil. Quantity is also improved, because a richer soil will support more plants.
It is worth remembering, too, that undernourished, struggling plants are more
susceptible to pests and diseases, and providing good soil is, therefore, a way
of protecting your plants and reducing the need for chemicals.

There's nothing like muck

The greatest soil improver of them all is well-rotted organic material of some
sort. This is relatively cheap, especially if bought in quantity, and in some areas
stables give horse manure away free to anyone prepared to collect it – a bargain
that should never be overlooked. There is also a great deal of garden and
kitchen waste that can be recycled.

BELOW **Working from wooden planks is a useful way of avoiding walking directly on the soil, which can cause it to compact. This precaution is especially important when the soil is wet.**

Types of Soil

*Vegetables can, within reason, be grown on most soils, but, as one
would expect, there is an optimum soil in which the best vegetables can
be grown. Most soils can be persuaded, with varying degrees of effort,
to move towards that optimum, but the starting point is often different.*

ABOVE **The better the soil, the better the crops will
be. Keeping the soil in good condition is the key
to successful kitchen gardening.**

Clay

When they work well clay soils can be fertile, but their structure is the despair of most gardeners. Clay is heavy and the particles cling together, making the soil sticky. Clay soil compacts easily, forming a solid lump that roots find hard to penetrate and that is difficult to dig. Try not to walk on clay soils when they are wet. This tendency to become compacted and sticky means that clay soils are slow to drain, but, once drained, they "set" like concrete, becoming a hard mass. They also tend to be cold and slow to warm up, making them unsuitable for early crops.

Clay soil is not, one would think, a good basis for growing vegetables, yet many of the best gardens are on clay. Clay soils are usually rich, and all the hard effort needed in the initial stages to improve the soil will pay off in the long term.

Sandy soils

Soils that are made up of sand and silts are quite different. They have few of the sticky clay particles but are made up of individual grains that allow the water to pass through quickly. This quick passage of water through the soil tends to leach (wash) out nutrients, so the soils are often poor. But they also tend to be much warmer in winter and are quicker to warm in spring, thus making it easier to get early crops. Silts contain particles that are a bit more clay-like in texture than those found in sandy soils, and they hold more moisture and nutrients.

Both types of soil are easy to improve and are not difficult to work. Sand does not compact like clay does (although it is still not good practice to walk on beds), but silty soils are more susceptible to the impact of feet and wheelbarrows. Adding organic material can temper their insatiable thirst.

Loams

The soil of most gardeners' dreams is loam. This is a combination of clay and sandy soils, with the best elements of both. They tend to be free draining, but at the same time

BELOW **Soil that has been well worked, as the
soil in this garden clearly has, is essential to the
production of good crops of vegetables.**

COMMON TYPES OF SOIL

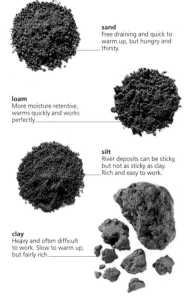

sand
Free draining and quick to
warm up, but hungry and
thirsty.

loam
More moisture retentive,
warms quickly and works
perfectly.

silt
River deposits can be sticky,
but not as sticky as clay.
Rich and easy to work.

clay
Heavy and often difficult
to work. Slow to warm up,
but fairly rich.

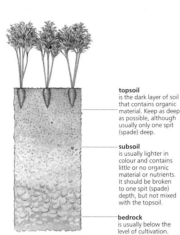

topsoil
is the dark layer of soil that contains organic material. Keep as deep as possible, although usually only one spit (spade) deep.

subsoil
is usually lighter in colour and contains little or no organic material or nutrients. It should be broken to one spit (spade) depth, but not mixed with the topsoil.

bedrock
is usually below the level of cultivation.

Soil profile A typical soil profile usually consists of three main elements: an upper layer of dark, fertile topsoil; a middle layer of lighter, infertile subsoil; and a lower layer of bedrock, which ranges from a few to hundreds of metres (yards) deep.

moisture retentive. This description – free draining and moisture retentive – is often used of soils and potting mixes and it may seem a contradiction. It means that the soil is sufficiently free draining to allow excess moisture to drain away, but enough moisture is retained for the plant without it standing in stagnant water. Such soils are easy to work at any time of the year, and they warm up well in spring and are thus good for early crops.

Acid and alkaline soils

Another way of classifying soils is by their acidity or alkalinity. Those that are based on peat (peat moss) are acid; those that include chalk or limestone are alkaline. Gardeners use a scale of pH levels to indicate the degree of acidity or alkalinity. Very acid is 1, neutral is 7 and very alkaline is 14, although soils rarely have values at the extremes of the

pH values	
1.0	extremely acid
4.0	maximum acidity tolerated by most plants
5.5	maximum acidity for reasonable vegetables
6.0	maximum acidity for good vegetables
6.5	optimum for the best vegetables
7.0	neutral, maximum alkalinity for good vegetables
7.5	maximum alkalinity for reasonable vegetables
8.0	maximum tolerated by most plants
14.0	extremely alkaline

scale. Although they can be grown on a wider range of soils, vegetables are usually grown in soils with a pH of 5.5–7.5, with the optimum conditions being around 6.5. So, the best pH for growing vegetables is slightly on the acid side of neutral. A test with a soil kit will show the rating in your own garden. You can adjust the acid soils of a garden, but it is more difficult to alter alkaline ones.

TESTING THE SOIL FOR NUTRIENTS

1 Collect the soil sample 5–8cm/2–3in below the surface. Take a number of samples, but test each one separately.

2 With this kit, mix one part of soil with five parts of water. Shake well in a jar, then allow the water to settle.

3 Draw off some of the settled liquid from the top few centimetres (about an inch) for your test.

4 Carefully transfer the solution to the test chamber in the plastic container, using the pipette.

5 Select a colour-coded capsule (one for each nutrient). Put the powder in the chamber, replace the cap and shake well.

6 After a few minutes, compare the colour of the liquid with the shade panel of the container.

Improving Drainage

Few garden plants, and certainly no vegetables, like to sit in stagnant water – watercress, of course, likes water, but it must be running. A free-draining soil is of the utmost importance if you want to grow decent crops. In the majority of gardens this simply means improving the soil, but in a few gardens, where the problem is serious, it will mean installing a drainage system first.

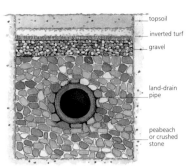

topsoil
inverted turf
gravel

land-drain
pipe

peabeach
or crushed
stone

Working the soil

In many gardens wet soil can be improved simply by improving the soil itself so that the water drains away. One way to achieve this is to add organic material to improve the soil's fertility. The fibrous material contained in the organic matter helps to break up the clay particles, allowing water to pass through. This material eventually breaks down and so it should be added every time the soil is dug.

The other method is to add gravel or grit to the soil. The best material for this is what used to be known as horticultural grit – that is, grit up to about 5mm/¼in in diameter. Flint grit that has been crushed is best because the angular faces allow water to

drain away better than the rounded surfaces of the uncrushed grits, such as peabeach. It may seem sacrilege to add stones to soil, but these fine gravels will make all the difference.

Drainage systems

Of course, it is no good improving the soil if the water still does not have anywhere to go. In fact, the situation could become worse because the well-drained soil in the bed could become a sump, with water running off adjacent paths and lawns into it. If water lies in the garden, then there is nothing for it but to install proper drainage. This can be a big undertaking, and many gardeners may prefer to get professional help.

Section through a land drain This cross-section of a typical land drain shows the various layers of materials from which it is constructed, including the topsoil, an inverted turf or perforated plastic membrane, gravel, peabeach or crushed stone, and the land-drain pipe.

The basic idea is to channel the water away from the garden. It may be possible to send it into a ditch, but under no circumstances should you connect it to the main drainage system from the house because this is bound to be breaking all kinds of local laws and regulations. If you do not have a ditch, there are two possible solutions. The first is to dig a soakaway. This is a deep hole, usually at least 2m/6ft deep, filled with clean rubble. Water runs out of the drainage pipes into the hole from which it slowly soaks away into the surrounding soil, well below the level of the beds. Alternatively, if the lay of the land allows it, excess water can be piped into a decorative pond, along with other surface water – such as that from the roof of the house, for example.

The drainage system that removes the water from the land is constructed by digging a series of trenches about 60cm/24in deep. There is one main trench, and the others join it at an angle. The trenches should slope towards the soakaway if the

LEFT **Good drainage ensures that this garden is able to support a diverse array of flowers and vegetables, including cabbages and sunflowers.**

inverted turf

topsoil

gravel

land-drain pipe

large pebbles

drainage ditch

Land drain on a flat site This is a section through a land drain on a flat site, showing the fall of the pipe – in this case the angle is exaggerated – which slopes down into a drainage ditch. The water percolates through the soil and pebbles and into the pipe, which then delivers it to the drainage ditch.

inverted turf

gravel

large pebbles

side branch

Land drain on a sloping site An aerial view of the drainage system, showing the side branches, which are constructed in the same way as the main pipe. When the ground slopes, the pipes are laid parallel to the ground, so that the water can drain away.

side branch

large pebbles

outflow to drainage ditch

topsoil

inverted turf

subsoil

bricks

drainage pipe

infill of stones

Laying a soakaway If there is no ditch or drain available, then the water must be directed into a soakaway. This is a large hole filled with clean rubble or large stones. In lighter soils, it should be lined with bricks to prevent it filling with soil.

ground is flat, but should run parallel to the surface if the ground slopes. Perforated plastic tubing that comes in a continuous reel is the cheapest form of piping. This is laid on gravel with more gravel laid on top. Upturned turves are then laid on the top of the gravel (to prevent soil from washing into the gravel and blocking the drainage) and the topsoil is replaced. If turf is not available, a pervious plastic membrane can be used.

As an alternative to plastic piping, traditional tile drains can be used. These are short lengths of ceramic pipe laid with a small gap between each. A less efficient, but traditional, method is to use French drains – fill a trench with rubble and top it off with upturned turves and topsoil.

WORKING IN ORGANIC MATTER

1 Soil that has been dug in the autumn can have more organic matter worked into the top layer in the spring. Spread the organic matter over the surface.

2 Lightly work the organic material into the top layer of soil with a fork. There is no need for full-scale digging.

Soil Structure

Perhaps the most important task in any garden is to improve and maintain the quality of the soil. Good-quality soil should be the aim of any gardener who wants to grow vegetables or fruit. To ignore the soil is to ignore one of the garden's most important assets.

ABOVE **Green manure helps to improve both the structure and fertility of the soil. Sow it when the ground is not being used for anything else and then dig it in before it flowers and seeds**.

Organic material

The key to improving the soil in your garden is organic material. This is an all-embracing term that covers any vegetable matter that has been broken down into an odourless, fibrous compost. It includes such things as rotted garden waste, kitchen vegetable waste, farmyard manures (which are plant materials that have passed through animals) and other plant waste material.

It is important that any such material should be well-rotted. If it is still in the process of breaking down, it will need nitrogen to complete the process and will extract it from the soil. This, of course, is the reverse of what the gardener wants – the gardener's aim is, in fact, to add nitrogen to the soil. If you are unsure, a good indicator that the material has broken down sufficiently is that it becomes odourless. Even horse manure is free from odour once it has rotted down, and manuring a garden should not be the smelly occupation it is often depicted as being.

Some substances contain undesirable chemicals, but these will be removed if the material is stacked and allowed to weather. Bark and other shredded woody materials may contain resins, for example, while animal and bird manures may contain ammonia from urea. These chemicals will evaporate or be converted by weathering.

Digging in

The best way to apply organic material to the vegetable garden is to dig it in. In this way it becomes incorporated into the soil. If possible, double dig the bed, adding material all the way to the bottom of both spits. This will help to retain moisture and supply nutrients where they are needed, which is down by the roots. It will also encourage roots to delve deeply rather than remaining on the surface where easy water can be obtained from the odd rain shower or watering can. The deeper the roots go the more stable will be the plant's water supply and the plant will grow at a regular pace rather than in unproductive fits and starts. This will produce much better plants.

Top-dressing

Once the ground has been planted, especially with permanent vegetables and fruit, it is impossible to dig in organic material to anything more than a couple of inches. The damage done by disturbing roots makes it pointless to attempt to go any deeper. The answer here is to top-dress with well-rotted matter. A 10cm/4in layer of, say farmyard manure, will be slowly worked into the soil by the earthworms. As well as being taken into the soil, such a dressing will also act as a mulch, protecting the ground from drying out as well as preventing any weed seeds from germinating.

The top-dressing should also be free from any weed seeds or you will be creating problems rather than solving them. Properly made compost and the other types of material that can be used should always be weed free and suitable for use in this way.

Fruit and permanent plantings

For any type of plant that will be in position for several if not many years, it is important that the soil is in the best possible condition before planting begins. Once planted it will be impossible to dig in more material, and

IMPROVING SOIL FERTILITY......................

The fertility of the soil is much improved by the addition of organic material, but a quick boost can also be achieved by adding an organic fertilizer, spreading it over the surface and then raking it in.

REDUCING SOIL ACIDITY.................................

The acidity of the soil can be reduced by adding lime some weeks before planting and working it in with a rake. Check the soil with a soil testing kit to see how much lime is required.

you will have to depend on top-dressing. Although this is a good supplement, it is not an alternative to proper preparation in the first place. The ground should be double dug if possible, and you should add as much organic matter as you can get, especially in the lower layers of soil.

Improving the soil's pH

The other aspect of improving soil is to improve the pH level. For vegetables, as we have noted, the level to aim at is pH6.5, but anything between 6 and 7 is still good, while 5.5–7.5 is acceptable.

If the soil is too acid, the pH can be adjusted somewhat by adding lime to the soil. Three types of lime can be used for reducing soil acidity. Ordinary lime (calcium carbonate) is the safest to use. Quicklime (calcium oxide) is the strongest and most caustic, but it may cause damage. Slaked lime (calcium hydroxide) is quicklime with water added; it is not as strong as quicklime and is therefore less dangerous. Always take safety precautions when you are applying lime and follow the quantities recommended by the manufacturer on the packet. Do not add lime at the same time as manure, because this will release ammonia, which can damage the plants. Spread the lime over the soil at the rate prescribed on the packet and rake it in. Do not sow or plant in the ground for at least a month. Do not over-lime.

It is not as easy to reduce the alkalinity of soil. Peat (peat moss) used to be recommended for this purpose, but not only is collecting peat environmentally unsound, it breaks down quickly and needs to be constantly replaced. Most organic manures are on the acid side and help to bring down the levels. Leafmould, especially that from pine trees, is also acid.

Spent mushroom compost contains lime and is useful for reducing acidity, but it should not be used on chalky (alkaline) soils.

When not to add manure

Not all crops like to be grown in soil that has been freshly manured. Root crops, such as parsnips, for example, tend to "fork" when the soil is too rich. This means that, instead of the single, long, tapering roots, they have short stubby roots with several branches. The parsnip may taste the same, but it is not so convenient to clean and peel.

The way to prevent this happening is to avoid manuring before planting. Either use soil that has been manured from a previous crop – follow the brassicas, for example – or add the organic material during the previous autumn so that it has had a chance to break down before the root crops germinate and start to grow.

IMPROVING SOIL STRUCTURE

1 One of the best ways to improve the structure of the soil is to add as much organic material as you can, preferably when the soil is dug. For heavy soils, this is best done in the autumn.

2 If the soil has already been dug, then well-rotted organic material can be worked into the surface of the soil with a fork. The worms will complete the task of working it into the soil.

WORKING ON WET SOIL

It is best to avoid working on wet soil, but sometimes it is necessary. To ensure that the soil is not compacted and its structure destroyed, it is advisable to work from a plank of wood.

Soil Conditioners

Quite a range of organic conditioners is available to the gardener. Some are free – if you do not count the time taken in working and carting them. Others are relatively cheap, and some, usually those bought by the bag, can be quite expensive. However, not everyone has a stable nearby or enough space to store large quantities of material, and these gardeners will therefore need to buy it as required.

Farmyard manure

A traditional material and still much used by many country gardeners, farmyard manure has the advantage of adding bulk to the soil as well as supplying valuable nutrients. The manure can come from any form of livestock, although the most commonly available is horse manure. It can be obtained from most stables, and many are so glad to get rid of it that they will supply it free if you fetch it yourself. There are often stables situated around the edge of towns, so manure is usually available to town gardeners as well as to those in the country.

Some gardeners do not like the manure when it is mixed with wood shavings rather than with straw, but it is worth bearing in mind that the former is often less likely to contain weed seeds, and as long as it is stacked and allowed to rot down it is excellent for adding to the soil as well as for use as a top-dressing.

All manures should be stacked for a period of at least six months before they are used. When it is ready, it will have lost its dungy smell.

Garden compost

All gardeners should try to recycle as much of their garden and kitchen vegetable waste as possible. In essence, this is simply following nature's pattern, where leaves and stems are formed in the spring and die back in the autumn, falling to the ground and eventually rotting and returning to the plants as nutrients. In the garden some things are removed from the cycle, notably vegetables and fruit, but as much as possible should be recirculated.

ABOVE **Farmyard manure should be left stacked in a heap until it has lost its smell and has finished rotting down.**

Compost is not difficult to make, and, of course, it is absolutely free. If you have the space, use several bins so there is always some available for use.

Unless weeds that are in seed or diseased plants have been used, compost should be safe to use as a soil conditioner and as a mulch.

Leafmould

Leafmould is a natural soil conditioner. It is easy to make and should not cost anything. Only use leafmould made by yourself; never go down to the local woods and help yourself because this will disturb the wood's own cycle and will impoverish the soil there.

SOME ORGANIC MATERIALS

well-rotted
farmyard manure

well-rotted garden
compost

Four stakes knocked into the ground with a piece of wire-netting stretched around them will make the perfect compound for making leafmould. Simply add the leaves as they fall from the trees. It will take a couple of years for them to break down and what was a huge heap will shrink to a small layer by the time the process is complete.

Add leafmould to the soil or use it as a top-dressing. It is usually acid and can be used to reduce the pH of alkaline soil. Leafmould from pine needles is particularly acid.

Peat (peat moss)

This is expensive and does little for the soil because it breaks down too quickly and has little nutritive content. It is also ecologically unsound to use it.

Spent mushroom compost

Often available locally from mushroom farms, the spent compost is relatively cheap, especially if purchased in bulk. It is mainly used in the ornamental part of the garden, but it is still useful in the vegetable garden if it is allowed to rot down. It is particularly useful if the soil is on the acid side because it contains chalk.

Vegetable industrial waste

Several industries produce organic waste material that can be useful in the garden. Spent hop waste from the brewing industry has always been a favourite among those who can obtain it. Coco shells are now imported, although these are better used as a mulch than as a soil conditioner. Several other products are locally available. Allow them to rot well before using.

Green manure

Some crops can be grown simply to be dug back into the ground to improve the soil condition and to add nutrients. They are particularly useful on light soils that are left vacant for any length of time, such as over winter.

Green manures	
Broad (fava) beans	nitrogen fixing
Italian ryegrass	quick growing
Lupins	nitrogen fixing
Mustard	quick growing
Phacelia	quick growing
Red clover	nitrogen fixing
Winter tare	nitrogen fixing

Green manures can be sown in early autumn and dug in during spring. Alternatively, if you plant fast-growing varieties, you can use them whenever land becomes available during the growing season.

Avoid letting the green manure flower and seed, otherwise it will self-seed. Most of the foliage and stems can be used in the compost bin.

BELOW **Green manure can be grown as a separate crop or it can be grown between existing crops. Here, clover is grown amongst cabbages, where it not only fixes nitrogen in the soil, but also provides a ground cover, keeping the weeds down.**

Making Compost

Compost is a valuable material for any garden, but it is especially useful in the vegetable garden. It is free, apart from any capital required in installing compost bins, but these should last a lifetime and the overall cost should be negligible. A little bit of effort is required, but this is a small price to pay for the resulting gold-dust.

ABOVE **A range of organic materials can be used, but avoid cooked kitchen waste or any weeds that have seed in them.** *Clockwise from top left:* **kitchen waste, weeds, shreddings and grass clippings.**

The principle

The idea behind compost-making is to emulate the process in which a plant takes nutrients from the soil, dies and then rots, putting the nutrients back into the ground. In the garden, waste plant material is collected, piled in a heap and allowed to rot down before being returned to the soil as crumbly, sweet-smelling, fibrous material.

Because it is in a heap the rotting material generates heat, which encourages it to break down even more quickly. The heat also helps to kill pests and diseases as well as any weed seed in the compost. If the rotting material is to break down properly, a certain amount of moisture is needed, as well as air. If there is too much water, however, the process is slowed down; if there is insufficient air, the heap will go slimy and smell bad.

The process should take up to about three months, but many old-fashioned gardeners like to retain the heap for much longer than that, growing marrows and courgettes (zucchini) on it before they break it up for use in the garden.

The compost bin

Gardeners always seem to generate more garden waste than they ever thought possible and never to have enough compost space, so when planning your

bins, make sure you have enough. The overall aim is to have three: one to hold new waste, one that is in the process of breaking down, and the third that is ready for use.

The bins are traditionally made from wood (often scrap wood), and because these can be hand-made to fit your space and the amount of material available, this is still the best option. Sheet materials, such as corrugated iron, can also be used. Most ready-made bins are made of plastic, and although these work perfectly well, they may be a bit on the small side in a busy garden.

A bin should contain at least a cubic metre/3.5 cubic feet of compost for it to heat up adequately. If you have a large garden, a

bin double this size would be even more efficient. The simplest bin can be made by nailing together four wooden pallets to form a box. If the front is made so that the slats are

RIGHT **Only a small proportion of the vegetables and flowers for cutting in this plot will be used. This means that most of the foliage and stems can be put in the compost bin.**

slotted in to form the wall, they can be removed as the bin is emptied, making the job of removing the compost easier. This is a refinement, however, and not essential.

Materials

Any plant garden waste can be used for composting as long as it does not contain weed seeds. (In fact, it is useful to have a separate bin for anything that contains seeds, because the compost can be used for permanent plantings such as trees. Compost used for this purpose will never come to the surface, and any seeds will be prevented from germinating.) You should also avoid including perennial weeds. Woody material, such as hedge clippings, can be used, but shred it first.

Kitchen vegetable waste, such as peelings and cores, can be used but avoid cooked vegetables, and do not include meat, which will attract rats and other vermin.

Technique

Placing a few branches or twiggy material in the bottom of the bin will help to keep the contents aerated. Put in the material as it becomes available but avoid building up deep layers of any one material, especially grass cuttings. Mix them with other materials.

To help keep the heap warm, cover it with an old carpet or sheet of polythene (plastic). This also prevents excess water from chilling the contents as well as swamping all the air spaces. The lid should be kept on until the compost is required.

Every so often, add a layer of farmyard manure if you can get it because it will provide extra nitrogen to speed things up. Failing this, you can buy special compost accelerators. It is not essential to add manure or an accelerator, however – it just means waiting a couple of weeks longer for your compost.

Air is important, and this usually percolates through the side of the bin, so leave a few gaps between the timbers. If you use old pallets, these are usually crudely made, with plenty of gaps. The colder material around the edges takes longer to break down than that in the centre of the heap, so turn the compost around every so often. This also loosens the pile and allows air to circulate.

MAKING COMPOST

1 A simple compost bin, which should be about 1m/3ft square, can be made by nailing four flat pallets together. These bins are usually roughly made, which means that there will be plenty of air holes between the slats.

2 Pile the waste into the compost bin, making certain that there are no thick layers of the same material. Grass clippings, for example, will not rot down if the layer is too thick because the air cannot penetrate.

3 It is important to keep the compost bin covered with an old mat or a sheet of polythene (sheet vinyl or plastic). This will help to keep in the heat generated by the rotting process and it will also prevent the compost bin from getting too wet in bad weather.

4 Every so often turn the contents of the bin with a fork, partly to let in air and partly to move the outside material, which is slow to rot, into the centre so that the rotting process speeds up. It is easier if you have several bins and turn the compost from one bin into another.

5 When the bin is full, cover the surface with a layer of soil and use it to grow marrows (zucchini), pumpkins or cucumbers. If you want to use the contents as soon as possible, omit the soil and keep covered with polythene. The finished product *(inset, below)* is dark brown, crumbly and has a sweet, earthy smell, not a rotting one. It can be used straight away or left covered until required.

Fertilizers

You cannot go on taking things out of the soil without putting anything back. In nature plants return the nutrients they have taken from the soil when they die. In the garden the vegetables are removed and eaten, and the chain is broken. Compost and other organic materials help to redress the balance, but there may not be enough available to do the job properly and then fertilizers are needed.

ABOVE **The most natural way of adding nutrients to the soil is to rot down old plant material in a compost bin, and then return it to the soil.**

What plants require

The main foods required by plants are nitrogen (N), phosphorus (P) and potassium (K), with smaller quantities of magnesium (Mg), calcium (Ca) and sulphur (S). They also require small amounts of what are known as trace elements, including iron (Fe) and manganese (Mn).

Each of the main nutrients tends to be used by the plant for one specific function. Thus nitrogen is concerned with plant growth and is used for promoting the rapid growth of the green parts of the plant. You should, therefore, add nitrogen to help leafy plants such as cabbage but cut back on it with plants such as runner beans, because you do not want to promote lush leaves at the expense of flowers and beans. Phosphorus, usually in the form of phosphates, is used to create good root growth as well as helping with the ripening of fruits, while potassium, in the form of potash, which is used to promote flowering and formation of good fruit, is, for example, the main ingredient in tomato feed.

The natural way

The most natural way to add nutrients to the soil is to use compost and other organic matter. As we have already seen, such materials are important to the general structure of the soil, but they also feed it. Well-rotted farmyard manure and garden compost have been the main way that gardeners have traditionally fed their gardens. However, some of today's gardeners are unhappy with this method because they claim that you cannot know which fertilizer you are adding and in what quantity, because the quality of organic materials varies so much. Although they concede that organic material is useful for adding bulk, they prefer to use bought fertilizers to feed the soil.

Organic material normally contains less of the main nutrients than concentrated fertilizers, but it is often strong in trace elements, and although they may not contain such a strong concentration of nitrogen, they do release it over a longer period which is of great benefit. Because of its other benefits, farmyard manure and garden compost are still the best way of treating the soil.

Organic fertilizers

Synthetic, concentrated fertilizers are broken down into two groups: organic and inorganic. Organic fertilizers are made up of chemicals derived from naturally occurring organic materials. So bonemeal (ground-up bones) is quite strong in nitrogen and phosphates,

INORGANIC FERTILIZERS

Growmore (not available in the United States)

sulphate of ammonia

potash

superphosphate

making it a good fertilizer to promote growth, especially at the start of a plant's life. Bonemeal also has the advantage in that it breaks down slowly, gradually releasing the fertilizer over a long period. When you apply bonemeal, you may want to wear gloves. Other organic fertilizers include fish, blood and bone; hoof and horn; and seaweed meal.

Because they are derived from natural products without any modification, they are deemed "safe" by organic growers.

Inorganic fertilizers

These are fertilizers that have been made artificially, although they are frequently derived from natural rocks and minerals and the process may just involve crushing. They are concentrated and are usually soluble in water. This means that they are instantly available for the plant and are useful for giving a plant a push when it is required. They do, however, tend to wash out of the soil quickly and need to be replaced.

Some are general fertilizers, and might contain equal proportions of nitrogen, phosphorus and potassium, for example. Others are much more specific. Superphosphate, for example, is entirely used for supplying phosphorus, while potassium sulphate is added to the soil when potassium is required.

ORGANIC FERTILIZERS

blood

bonemeal

seaweed

fish/blood/bone

Increasing numbers of gardeners are turning against inorganic fertilizers, unaware that they are not as artificial as is generally believed. Many are not classified as organic simply because they are not derived from living things. Nevertheless, it is their concentrated form and the fact that they can be readily washed from the soil that lead many gardeners to object to their use.

Slow-release fertilizers

A modern trend is to coat the fertilizers so that they are released slowly into the soil. These are expensive in the short term, but because they do not leach away and do not need to be replaced as frequently, they can be considered more economic in the longer term. They are particularly useful for container planting, where constant watering is necessary (with its attendant rapid nutrient leaching).

LEFT **This kitchen garden is planted with a delightful mixture of herbs, vegetables and flowers, growing in well-fed beds.**

Digging and Breaking Down

Although it is a technique that is now being questioned by some gardeners, digging is still one of the main garden activities. It breaks up the soil, allowing the ingress of water and air, which are both important for plant growth. In addition, it also allows organic material to be incorporated deep down in the soil, right where the roots need it.

All weeds and their roots can be removed during digging, which also brings pests to the surface so that they can be destroyed. Also and importantly, it allows the gardener to keep an eye on the condition of the soil.

Single digging

The most frequently carried out method is single digging, of which there are two ways, one informal and the other formal. In the informal method the ground is usually already quite loose, and the gardener simply forks it over, turning it over and replacing it in the same position, hardly using any trench at all. This process is more frequently carried out on light or sandy soils.

Formal single digging is necessary on heavier soils and when there is organic material to be incorporated. First, a trench is dug across the width of the plot, and the earth taken from the trench is taken – in a wheelbarrow – to the other end of the bed. Compost or farmyard manure is put into the bottom of the trench and then another trench is dug. This time, the earth removed from the trench is put into the first trench to cover the organic material. This procedure is repeated down the length of the plot. When the final trench has been dug and organic material placed in it, it is refilled with the pile of soil taken from the first trench.

Further refinements can be applied. For example, the first trench can be dug so that it is two trenches wide. Dung is put in the bottom as usual, and then the next trench is dug but the soil is spread over the bottom of the previous two trenches, only half-filling them. This is then covered with another layer

ABOVE **After a winter exposed to the weather, most soils will readily break down into a fine tilth by using a rake. More recently turned soil, may need to be broken down with a heavier hoe first.**

of dung and then the fourth trench dug, filling up the first. Trenches three and four are treated in the same way, being filled first with the soil from trench five and then from trench six. This method makes a better distribution of the organic material through the soil.

Double digging

Double digging is the method that is employed to break up the subsoil, and it is useful on any new plot of ground as well as when deep beds are being prepared.

Dig the trench as before, taking the earth to the end of the plot. Then dig the soil in the bottom of the trench to the depth of a fork or spade, adding in organic material. Add more organic material on top and then dig the next trench, placing the soil into the first. Repeat until the end of the plot is reached. Take care that you do not bring any subsoil up to the top.

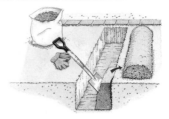
1 Start by digging a trench across the plot, putting the soil from the first trench to one side to be used later in the final trench.

2 Put a layer of manure in the bottom of the trench. Dig out the next trench and cover over the manure in the first trench with earth taken from the second trench.

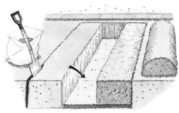
3 Repeat this process of adding manure to each trench and filling in with earth from the next, breaking up the soil as you go and keeping the surface as even as possible.

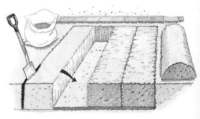
4 Continue down the length of the plot until you reach the final trench. This should be filled in with the earth taken from the first trench, which was set to one side.

DOUBLE DIGGING, METHOD ONE

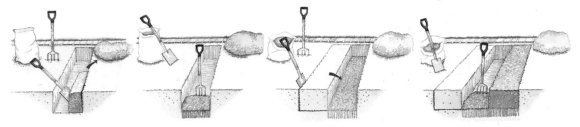

1 Dig a wide trench, placing the soil to one side to be used later when filling in the final trench.

2 Break up the soil at the bottom of the trench, adding manure to the soil as you proceed.

3 Dig the next trench, turning the soil over on top of the broken soil in the first trench.

4 Continue down the plot, ensuring that subsoil from the lower trench is not mixed with topsoil of the upper.

A method requiring more energy but giving better results is to dig out the first trench and then dig another below it, keeping the two soils separate. Dig out the top spit of the next trench and also put this to one side. Add organic material to the first double trench and dig the bottom spit of the second trench into it. Add more dung and then take the top spit of the third trench and place this on top of the new soil in the bottom of the first trench. Repeat down the plot and then fill in the remaining trenches with the reserved soil from the first ones.

Mechanical digging

It is possible to dig the soil using a mechanical rotavator (rototiller). These are, however, best used on large plots. One disadvantage of using a mechanical digger is that it cuts up weed roots into small pieces, and they are more difficult to remove by hand than with conventional digging.

Breaking down into a fine tilth

The best time to dig a heavy soil is in the autumn, then the winter frosts and rain will break it down for you. If clay soils are dug in the spring and allowed to dry out too much, they are difficult to break down because the clods set like concrete. A mechanical rotavator makes breaking the soil down easier, especially if the plot is large. For smaller plots, work on the soil when it is neither too wet nor too dry (experience will show you when), breaking it down, first with a large hoe and then with a rake. Shuffling along the surface with your feet will also help considerably, but do not do this if the ground is wet.

It is better to leave sandy soils until the spring because these do not need much breaking down. Raking the surface is usually all that is required.

Occasionally, the soil becomes too hard to break down. If this happens, water the soil with a sprinkler, leave it to dry slightly – so

ABOVE **For larger gardens with heavy soil, a rotavator (rototiller) will break down the soil into a fine tilth. Even a small one saves a lot of time, especially if the soil is too dry to break down with a rake.**

that it is no longer muddy – and then break it down. Alternatively, draw out a deep sowing row in the rough soil and fill it with potting compost (soil mix) and dig this in.

DOUBLE DIGGING, METHOD TWO

1 Keeping soil from each level separate, dig first trench two spits deep. Fork over trench. Dig second trench one spit deep.

2 Add organic material to the first double trench and dig the lower spit of the second trench into it.

3 Dig an upper third trench one spit deep, and place the soil on top of that already placed in the first trench.

4 Continue, ensuring topsoil and subsoil do not mix. Fill in remaining trenches with soil taken from first ones.

techniques

There are almost as many different ways of doing things in the garden as there are gardeners. In truth, no one way is better than any other – it depends very much on who is doing what and where it is being done. Something that works for you may not help a gardener just a few doors away down the road.

Having said that, there is a certain amount of common ground in most of the techniques used in the vegetable garden, and the procedures we discuss here should stand you in good stead, even if you eventually develop your own methods. In this section you will find helpful advice on general kitchen gardening techniques, including sowing seed, both outdoors and under glass; thinning and transplanting seedlings; and harvesting and storing. There is also guidance on the cultivation of herbs, from initial planting to final drying as well as on growing, supporting and pruning fruit trees and bushes. Detailed advice on the techniques to master for individual crops are covered in the later chapters on specific vegetables, herbs and fruit.

ABOVE **Greenhouses need more care and attention than the open garden. Factors such as good hygiene and the control of pests and diseases must be borne in mind.**

RIGHT **Most techniques involve working with nature, but a few are inevitably artificial. Terracotta rhubarb forcers, for example, are used to bring rhubarb crops to maturity faster than they would normally.**

Timing

There is an optimum time for most of the activities that are carried out in the garden, but precise timing is rarely crucial, and it does not matter if you cannot do something one week and have put it off to the next – or even later. Clay soils, for example, are best dug in autumn, but many gardeners never get around to it until spring.

Apart from social and business pressures that might upset your schedule, the weather and general garden conditions are likely to vary from year to year. When it comes to digging, for instance, a wet autumn may make it impossible for you to get onto the ground to dig it, and so you will have to wait until spring. When spring comes, you may want to get on with it and sow your carrots, but there is little point in doing this if the ground is still too cold, because carrots will not germinate until it has warmed up and any attempt to do so will end with wasted seeds.

It is, of course, wise to stick to the best timing if possible, particularly as there often comes a point when it is too late to do something. For example, there is little point in sowing most seeds after midsummer because they will not come to anything before autumn and winter set in.

Remember, though, that there is always another year. If things do go awry one year, there is always the next to look forward to.

Effort

Gardening can be strenuous, especially if you are elderly or not particularly fit. Do not overdo things, especially heavy tasks such as digging. Build up gradually, particularly after an idle winter. Many techniques and tools can be adapted for the disabled and elderly, but if things do become difficult, there is no shame in getting help of one sort or another.

Keeping tidy

When you are working in the garden, try to keep things tidy. Thinnings and weeds should always be removed from the beds to prevent the waste material promoting or harbouring disease. When you are harvesting produce, cut off and discard any fruit or vegetables that are rotten or diseased and do not leave them there to spread their problems. Many difficulties in the garden can be avoided by adopting techniques that result in a neat and tidy garden.

Sowing in the Open

Most vegetables and herbs can be sown directly into the open ground. The two main advantages of doing this are that no indoor facilities are required and the plants' growth is not delayed when they are planted out. Some plants also resent their roots being disturbed.

ABOVE **Some seed, beetroot (beets) in particular, benefits from an hour's soaking in tepid water before sowing.**

Soil requirements

The main requirement is that the soil should be broken down into a fine tilth – in other words, the soil crumbs should be small. The soil should be neither too wet nor too dry. If it is wet, cover it with cloches or polythene (plastic) to prevent it being further wetted and wait until it dries out a little before sowing. If the soil is too dry, then water the ground a short time before sowing; there should be sufficient water to soak in but not leave a sticky surface. The ground should also be warm. Seeds sown in cold ground will frequently just sit there until they rot. Ideally, the soil should be at a temperature of at least 7°C/45°F.

Seed requirements

Most of the seed that is available these days is of a high quality, especially when it comes from the major suppliers. The germination rate is usually good, although occasionally one gets an unsatisfactory batch. Non-germination, however, is usually due to some other factor, such as cold conditions. It is possible to keep your own seed, but only do this for non-F1 hybrids because F1s will not come true to type. Most seed is sold loose in packets, but seeds can be bought in other forms, and one of the most common is pelleted, when the seeds are coated with clay. The coating makes the seeds easier to handle and to sow. Increasingly, pre-germinated seeds and young seedlings are also becoming available. For most purposes, however, ordinary seeds will be suitable and certainly the cheapest.

Sowing in rows

The conventional way of sowing seeds is to do so in rows. Using a garden line for guidance, draw out a shallow drill in the fine soil with the corner of a hoe. If the ground is dry, water along the drill with a fine-rose watering can. Sow the seeds thinly. Mark the ends of the row with a label and a stick and draw the soil back over the drill with a rake. The

LEFT **Vegetables that are usually planted out, rather than sown where they are to grow, such as these cabbages, can still be sown in the open and then transplanted when they are large enough.**

SOWING SEED

1 Draw out a shallow drill with the corner of a draw hoe, using a garden line to ensure that it is straight.

2 If the soil is dry, water along the length of the drill and allow it to drain before sowing seed.

3 Sow the seed along the drill, sowing it as thinly as possible to reduce the amount of thinning necessary.

4 Put a label at the end of the row clearly showing what is in the row. Put a stick or another label at the far end. Do this before filling in the drill.

5 Rake the soil into the drill over the seed. Gently tamp down the soil along the row with the flat of the rake and then lightly rake over.

6 If the soil is heavy and is difficult to break into a fine tilth, draw out the drill and then line it with potting compost (soil mix).

depth of the drill depends on the size of the seeds, but most finer seeds should be sown at a depth of 1cm/½in. The seed packet usually gives the depth required.

Station sowing

With plants that grow quite large and therefore need to be spaced out in the row, it is wasteful to sow a continuous line of seeds. Station sowing involves sowing three seeds at distances that will be the eventual gap between plants – parsnip seeds, therefore, are sown at 20cm/8in intervals.

Wide rows

Some seeds, mainly peas and beans, are sown in wide rows – in effect, two rows are sown at once. A wide drill, 15cm/6in across, is made with the flat of the hoe. Two rows of peas or beans are sown, one down each side of the drill, and the soil is carefully raked back over the seeds so that they are not disturbed.

Broadcasting

This is the best method for sowing seeds in blocks. Rake the area to a fine tilth and scatter the seeds thinly but evenly over the surface. If the soil is dry, gently rake the seeds in and water with a fine-rose watering can.

Protecting

Fine earth is attractive to both birds and animals as a dust bath as well as a litter tray, and when it is used the seeds will be scattered far and wide. In addition, some birds find emerging seedlings an irresistible source of food. Protect the seeds by placing wire-netting guards along the rows. Alternatively, a few pea-sticks can be laid across the surface of the soil. Another possibility is to place short sticks in the ground and to twine cotton between them. This last method is the least convenient because the protection cannot be quickly removed and replaced to permit for hoeing and weeding.

Labelling

Before covering the seed with soil, mark the end of the rows with pegs and a label. Once the drill is filled in, it is difficult to see where it is. It may be some time before the seedlings emerge and the row can be easily disturbed by, for example, accidentally hoeing through it. Similarly, it is important to know what is sown where, so a label bearing the name and variety of the vegetable is important. Traditionally, many gardeners spike the seed packet on a peg but these quickly deteriorate and often blow away.

Sowing under Glass

Germinating seeds under glass is more tedious and time-consuming than sowing direct into the ground, but raising plants in this way has its advantages. It allows the gardener to grow reasonably sized plants that are ready to set out as soon as the weather allows, stealing a march on those sown in the soil by about two weeks. If there are pest problems, such as slugs or birds, the plants are better able to resist them if they are well grown when they are planted out than if they have to fight for their life as soon as they emerge through the soil.

ABOVE **There is a range of pots and trays now available that are suitable for sowing vegetable and herb seed.** *Clockwise from top left*: **individual cells or modules, a half tray, plastic pots, a fibrous pot and fibrous modules.**

Containers

Seeds can be sown in a variety of containers. Traditionally they were sown in wooden trays or flats. Some gardeners prefer to make their own, claiming that they are warmer and that they can be made deeper than the purchased equivalents. Plastic trays have, however, generally replaced the wooden varieties. They can be made of rigid plastic for multiple use or thin, flimsy plastic, and these are used only once before being thrown away.

Often, only a few plants may be required, and it is rather wasteful to sow a whole or half tray. A 9cm/3½in pot is usually sufficient.

More and more gardeners are using modular or cellular trays, in which one or two seeds are sown in a small cell. If both germinate, one is removed and the remaining seedling is allowed to develop without having to be pricked out. This method avoids a lot of root disturbance.

Even less root disturbance occurs if the seeds are sown in biodegradable fibrous modules. As soon as the seedling is big enough to be planted out, both pot and plant are inserted into the ground, and the pot allows the roots to grow through its sides into the surrounding earth.

Propagators

Propagators are glass or plastic boxes that help to keep the seed tray moist and in a warm atmosphere. The more expensive models have heating cables in them so that the temperature can be controlled. Although they are

desirable, they are by no means absolutely necessary. Cheap alternatives can also be made simply by slipping the tray into a polythene (plastic) bag and removing it as soon as the seeds have germinated. Plastic jars can also be cut down to fit over trays or pots.

SOWING IN BLOCKS

Fill the cellular block with compost (soil mix) and tap it on the table to firm it down. Sow one or two seeds in each cell. Cover with a light dusting of compost. Remove the weaker of the two seedlings after germination.

SOWING IN POTS

Fill the pot with a good seed compost (soil mix), tap it on the bench and sow one to three seeds in each pot. Once germinated, the weaker seedlings will be removed, leaving one to grow on.

SOWING IN TRAYS

1 Fill the seed tray with seed compost (soil mix) and tamp down the compost lightly to produce a level surface. Sow the seed thinly across the compost.

2 Cover with a thin layer of compost (soil mix), lightly firm down and label. Labelling is very important because the seedlings of many vegetables look the same.

WATERING IN

Water the trays or pots by standing them in a shallow tray or bowl of water so that the water comes halfway up the container. Remove the tray or pot as soon as the surface of the compost (soil mix) begins to moisten.

Heat

A source of heat is useful for the rapid germination of seeds. It can be provided in the form of a heated propagator, but most seeds will germinate in the ambient temperature of a warm greenhouse or conservatory, or even within the house.

Sowing seed

Fill the seed tray with a good quality seed or potting compost (soil mix). Gently firm down and sow the seeds thinly on the surface. Spread a thin layer of potting compost over the seeds so that they are just covered. Again, firm down lightly. Water by placing the seed

USING A PROPAGATOR

1 Place the seeds in a propagator. You can adjust the temperature of heated propagators like this. Seed packets should indicate the best temperature, but you may need to compromise if different seeds need different temperatures.

2 This propagator is unheated and should be kept in a warm position in a greenhouse or within the house. Start opening the vents once the seeds have germinated to begin the hardening-off process.

tray in a shallow bowl of water, so that the level of the water comes halfway up the sides of the seed tray. Once the surface of the compost shows signs of dampness, remove the tray and place it in a propagator or in a polythene (plastic) bag. A traditional alternative – and one that still works well – is to place a sheet of glass over the tray.

Subsequent treatment

As soon as the seeds begin to germinate, remove the lid from the propagator – or open the bag, depending on the method you are using – to let in air and after a couple of days remove the tray altogether. If you are

using a propagator, turn off the heat and open the vents over a few days and then remove the tray.

Once the seedlings are large enough to handle, prick them out into trays, individual pots or modules. Hold the seedlings by the seed-leaves and not by the stem or roots. Make sure they are well spaced in the trays – at least 5cm/2in apart – and keep them warm and watered.

As the time approaches to plant them out, gradually harden them off by exposing them to outdoor conditions for a little longer each day until they can be safely left out overnight. They are then ready to plant out.

USING A COLD FRAME

1 Once the trays of seedlings or pricked-out seedlings are ready to plant out, harden them off by placing in a cold frame which is opened a little wider each day to let in more air.

2 Finally leave the lights of the cold frame off altogether so that the plants become accustomed to outside light.

Thinning and Transplanting

Outdoor-sown seedlings inevitably grow too thickly, no matter how thinly you try to sow them. In order to grow properly, they will need thinning. Seeds are often sown in a row that will not be their ultimate cropping position. Leeks, for example, are grown in a seed row and later transplanted to their final positions.

Thinning distances
Beetroot (beets) 7.5–10cm/3–4in
Broad (fava) beans 23cm/9in
Carrots 7.5cm/3in
Dwarf French (bush green) beans 20cm/8in
Florence fennel 25cm/10in
Kohl rabi 20cm/8in
Lettuce 23cm/9in
Parsley 15cm/6in
Peas 5cm/2in
Parsnips 15–20cm/6–8in
Radishes 2.5–5cm/1–2in
Runner beans 25–30cm/10–12in
Salsify 15cm/6in
Scorzonera 15cm/6in
Spinach 15cm/6in
Spring onions (scallions) 5cm/2in
Swedes (rutabagas or yellow turnips) 30cm/12in
Swiss chard 30cm/12in
Turnips 15cm/6in

Why thin?

It is important that vegetables have enough space in which to develop. Plants that are too close together become drawn as they try to move to the light. In addition to not having room to develop, they become undernourished as they compete with their neighbours for moisture, nutrients and light.

Crops that are too tightly planted are more susceptible to disease because air cannot circulate freely around them, allowing fungal diseases, such as mildew, to get a hold. Half-starved plants are also more prone to disease than fully nourished ones. A little attention at this stage will pay dividends in producing healthy plants.

Thinning

The idea behind thinning is to remove all unwanted plants, leaving the best at regular intervals. Before you begin to thin, water the row to soften the earth and to make sure that the remaining plants have taken up enough water in case their roots are accidentally disturbed. Allow the water to soak in and the plants to take it up. If possible, water the evening before you plan to thin.

Go along the row, with a measuring stick if you are uncertain about the distances between the plants, removing the weaker seedlings and leaving one strong one at the correct planting distance for that variety – 15–20cm/6–8in for parsnips, for example. When you pull out the unwanted seedlings, gently press the ground around the one that is left so that the pulling motion does not disturb that one as well.

When the row is complete, gently water along its length so that soil is washed back around the roots of the remaining plants that may have been disturbed. Dispose of the unwanted seedlings on the compost heap.

Avoid thinning during hot or windy conditions because the remaining plants may become desiccated before their roots can become re-established if they have been disturbed. A slightly damp, overcast day is ideal.

In hot dry weather, you can snip the unwanted seedlings off with a pair of scissors so you do not disturb their neighbours' roots.

THINNING AND TRANSPLANTING SEEDLINGS

1 Water the row of seedlings, the night before if possible, but at least a few hours before transplanting.

2 Using a hand fork, dig up, rather than pull out, the excess plants. Only dig up the plants as you need them; do not dig them up all at once and leave them lying around.

3 Using a garden line to keep the row straight, and a measuring stick to get the distances equal, replant the seedlings using a trowel.

4 Gently firm in each plant and water around them. Rake the soil around the plants in order to tidy it up and to remove footprints and uneven soil.

RIGHT **Thinning vegetables to the correct distances ensures healthy, full-sized plants: shown are rows of onions, beetroot (beets), potatoes, carrots, spinach.**

Transplanting

Plants for transplanting can either be grown from seed sown in pots or trays, or from seed sown directly in the open ground. Seedlings that have been grown in containers should be pricked out first into individual pots, or widely spaced trays, so that each plant has room to develop. Harden them off if they have been grown under glass before transplanting them into the open ground.

Damp, overcast weather conditions are ideal for transplanting seedlings because the plants will not dry out quickly in a muggy atmosphere. Again, as with thinning, it is essential to water the plants first before transplanting them. This will give them sufficient moisture to keep them going until they have re-established their root systems.

Dig up just a few plants at a time – there is no point in leaving plants lying around on the ground where they can dry out. Discard any that are weak or undernourished, and never use any that are diseased. Using a line to make sure that the row is straight and a measuring stick in order to get the planting distances correct, plant at the same depth as in the seed bed, except where stated under individual vegetables – leeks, for example, are planted deeper. Gently firm in around each plant and water in.

THINNING SEEDLINGS IN SITU

When thinning a row of seedlings that have been sown in situ, water the row the night before or at least a few hours before. Remove the unwanted plants, leaving the recommended gap between each retained plant. Try not to disturb the plants that are left. Water the seedlings after thinning and remove all the discarded seedlings to the compost heap.

USING A DIBBER

Cabbages (shown here), onions and leeks are planted out using a dibber. This makes a hole in the ground into which the plant is slipped before the earth is firmed in around it.

Planting distances
Asparagus 30–38cm/12–15in
Aubergines (eggplants) 60cm/24in
Broccoli 60cm/24in
Brussels sprouts 50–75cm/20–30in
Cabbages 30–50cm/12–20in
Calabrese (Italian sprouting broccoli) 15–23cm/6–9in
Cauliflowers 50–75cm/20–30in
Celeriac (celery root) 30–38cm/12–15in
Celery 23–30cm/9–12in
Courgettes (zucchini) 60cm/24in
Cucumbers 60cm/24in
Garlic 15cm/6in
Globe artichokes 75cm/30in
Jerusalem artichokes 30cm/12in
Kale 60cm/24in
Leeks 15cm/6in
Marrows (zucchini) 60cm/24in
Onion sets 10cm/4in
Peppers 45–60cm/18–24in
Potatoes 30–38cm/12–15in
Pumpkins 90–180cm/36–72in
Rhubarb 75–90cm/30–36in
Runner beans 25–30cm/10–12in
Seakale 30cm/12in
Shallots 15–18cm/6–7in
Sweet corn (corn) 30cm/12in
Tomatoes 60cm/24in

Harvesting and Storing

The great moment comes when the vegetables are ready to harvest; nothing tastes quite like fresh vegetables that you have grown for yourself. However, not all the produce can be eaten at once and it is prudent to store some, especially for the winter months when fresh vegetables are at a premium.

ABOVE **Harvest root crops by levering up the root with a fork and pulling on the stems or leaves.**

Harvesting

Try to resist the temptation to harvest vegetables too soon. Until they have developed fully, their taste might not be matured and some might even be bitter. Traditionally, parsnips, celery and Brussels sprouts should not be harvested until they have experienced at least one frost, which makes them taste sweeter. There are some plants that can be harvested prematurely, however, in particular leafy crops. For example, young turnip tops are worth eating, while the tips of broad (fava) bean shoots can be tasty, long before the beans themselves have matured.

When you are harvesting do not simply pick the best vegetables. If you also come across any that are diseased or rotting, harvest these as well and compost them. Do not leave rotting vegetables on the plant or in the ground because they will spread their problems to healthy fruit or the spores may remain in the ground until the following year.

ABOVE **Some vegetables are harvested by cutting through the stems as and when they are required. Swiss chard, shown here, is a good example of this method of harvesting. The stem is cut close to the base. Some gardeners prefer to twist or snap the stems off at the base rather than cutting them.**

RIGHT **Quite a number of vegetables are picked. This usually entails snapping or cutting the stem just above the vegetable so that either part of the stalk remains or there is a complete break at the junction between vegetable and stalk. Here, runner beans are being harvested.**

There is no hard and fast rule about when or at what time of day to harvest, although taking the vegetable straight from the garden to the pot does, of course, give the freshest tasting dish. If possible, try to harvest when you want a vegetable, rather than leaving it lying around for a few days before using.

Storing

There are several ways of storing vegetables for later use. If you pick or dig up a vegetable and are unable to use it right away, it can usually be kept a few days before use. The best way of keeping these is to store them in a cool, dark place, preferably a cellar or cold shed. However, this is not always possible and a refrigerator is the next best thing.

The traditional way of storing root crops throughout winter is to dig them up, clean off any dirt and remove the leaves. Then they can be placed in trays of just-moist peat (peat moss or peat substitute) or sand. The vegetables are covered with more peat and, if the tray is deep enough, another layer of root crops is placed on top and again covered in peat. Carrots, beetroot (beets), celeriac (celery root), turnips, swedes (rutabagas or yellow turnips) and parsnips can all be stored in this way.

STORING ROOT CROPS

1 Most root crops can be stored in trays of just-moist sand or peat (peat moss or peat substitute). Place a layer of peat in the bottom of the tray and then lay a row of carrots on top. Cover these with more peat.

2 Place another layer of carrots on top and cover these with more peat. Repeat with more layers until the tray is full, topping off with a layer of peat.

Unless the weather is extremely cold, parsnips, celeriac (celery root), swedes (rutabagas or yellow turnips), carrots and beetroot (beets) can simply be left in the ground until they are required. However, if a deep frost is likely to occur, it is best to lift at least a few and store them inside because it is difficult to get them out of the ground once it has frozen. Although not strictly a root crop, leeks can also be left in the ground until they are needed.

Trays of root crops should be stored in a cool, but frost-free, shed or cellar. This is also one of the best places to store many other vegetables. Squashes, pumpkins and marrows (zucchini) can be stored on shelves or wire racks. Bulbous onions, shallots and garlic can be kept in trays or in net sacks. The important thing about storing all these vegetables is that they should not touch one another and that air should be able to circulate freely around them.

Brassicas are not so easy to store, but some of the solid cabbages can be harvested and hung in nets or placed on shelves in the same cool, frost-free shed until they are required. Stored in this way, they will stay sound for several months. Some brassicas are winter hardy and can be left where they are until required. Brussels sprouts are a good example of this.

Many vegetables will freeze reasonably well. To maintain good flavour they should first be blanched (placed in boiling water) for a few minutes, the length of time depending on the type of vegetable. Details can be found in good cookery books.

Although some vegetables do not freeze well this way, many can still be frozen, simply by cooking them first – Florence fennel, for example, can be cooked and puréed before freezing.

Another, more traditional way to store vegetables and fruit is to turn them into chutneys, pickles or some other sort of preserve. Fruit is delicious when bottled.

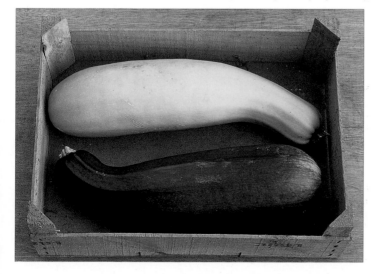

LEFT **Many vegetables, such as these marrows (zucchini), can be stored in trays. It is best if they are not touching one another.**

Planting Herbs

There is no basic difference between planting herbs and planting vegetables. However, since herbs are often grown in their own beds it is worth considering them separately. Even if you do not have the space to grow vegetables, it is usually possible to find at least a little room for a few herbs.

ABOVE **Plants such as mint that spread rapidly underground should be planted in a large bucket or flowerpot, about 30cm/12in across or more, which is then sunk into the ground. The rim of the pot should be level with the surface of the soil.**

Siting herbs

There are many reasons for growing herbs. They can be purely decorative or they can be medicinal, but within the context of this book they are culinary. Herbs for the kitchen are usually required instantly, with the cook dashing out in the middle of cooking to grab a handful, and so the most convenient site for this type of herb is as close to the kitchen door as possible. From a horticultural point of view, most herbs like to be in an open, sunny position.

Soil preparation

Herbs will grow in the same soil you have in your vegetable garden, and, like vegetables, they prefer a rich, moisture-retentive soil. Dig and prepare the ground thoroughly, adding plenty of well-rotted organic material. At the same time, remove any perennial weeds. This is particularly important around permanently planted herbs, such as chives, mint and sage, because there will not be an easy opportunity for removing the weeds if they reappear.

Sowing

Some herbs, such as parsley, can be sown directly into the ground. This makes a great deal of sense if you want to have a whole row or block of them. However, make sure that the soil is warm enough before you plant. In cold springs, wait until the soil warms up first, even if it means missing the theoretical first sowing date. For example, parsley will not germinate if the soil is too cold, and you will have to re-sow because the first sowing of seeds will invariably rot. Thin the resulting seedlings to the appropriate distances.

For small quantities of herbs or in cold springs, it is a good idea to sow the herbs under glass and plant them out once they are big enough. They can be sown in modules to reduce the amount of root disturbance. Thoroughly harden off before planting out.

Planting

When you are planting out, remember that herbs need space to grow and you should allow for their increase in size. This is particularly important with shrubby plants such as sage and rosemary, which can grow from small cuttings when first planted out to up to 1.2m/4ft or more across. In addition, when you are deciding what to plant where, put the taller ones to the north so that they do not overshadow the smaller ones.

Plant the herbs at the same depth in the soil that they were in their pots. Gently firm them in, water and tidy up the soil to remove footprints. Loosen the soil if it is compacted.

Wayward herbs

Some herbs, mint in particular, are rampant. If they are planted in a bed they will rapidly spread and soon invade other, nearby

LEFT **Some time before planting, give the plant a thorough soaking.**

PLANTING OUT

1 Using a trowel, dig a hole in the prepared ground that is slightly larger than the rootball of the plant.

2 Insert the plant so that the top of the rootball is level with the surface of the soil. Fill in the hole around the plant and firm down.

3 Water the plant and the soil immediately surrounding the rootball.

ABOVE **Planting herbs next to a path means that the delightful scent of fresh herbs is released when someone brushes past them.**

plants. One way to cope with this is to plant the mint in a bottomless bucket or large plastic flowerpot. Dig a large hole and then place the bucket or flowerpot into it so that the rim is level with the surface of the soil. Fill the bucket or flowerpot with the excavated soil and fill in the remaining hole around the edge of the pot with the rest of the soil. Plant the mint in the centre of the container and water. The questing roots will now be prevented from moving far because of the walls of the pot. Since the roots do not grow far down, they will not be able to exit through the bottom of the bucket or the holes in the pot, which will permit free drainage so that the container does not become waterlogged. Containers used in this way will become congested, and a piece of the mint should be replanted with fresh soil every year. Planting mint in a corner that is confined by paths is another way of keeping it in check.

Growing Herbs in Containers

Containers are the perfect way to ensure that herbs are in just the right amount of light or shade. The mature herbs can later be transferred to the garden, or kept conveniently close to hand in their pots on a patio or kitchen window sill. Planting in pots also gives scope for adding height and depth to a border, and a group of pots can form an attractive garden feature or balcony arrangement.

ABOVE **Herbs can be planted in a variety of containers. This wooden box has useful handles for moving the herbs to different locations.**

Choosing pots

Herbs can be grown in any form of container – even old coleslaw cartons, ice-cream cartons or plastic picnic boxes – but they will always look better and more at home if you choose an attractive container that has been properly designed for growing plants.

There are plenty to choose from – nurseries and garden centres stock them by the hundred – and they are no longer as expensive as they once were. Always try to choose one that is big enough for your needs.

Remember that plants need room to spread out their roots if they are to grow well and remain healthy, and if you are intending to grow several different types of herb you will need a large pot or several of them.

The shape does not matter too much as long as you do not choose an Ali Baba type pot, with a bulbous belly and a narrow neck, because the opening will not be large enough to get many herbs in (although such a pot could look beautiful with a single sage). Pot-bellied shapes work well if they

are designed like strawberry pots with openings in the side to take individual herbs. Window-boxes also make good herb containers. They can be used on the ground or mounted outside the kitchen window or simply on a nearby wall.

Whatever type of container you choose, make certain that it has drainage holes in the bottom so that excess water can drain away.

Planting the herbs

If the container is large, it is likely to be heavy once it is full of damp compost (soil mix), so, if possible, position it before you fill it. Cover the bottom of the container with irregularly shaped stones to help any excess water find its way to the drainage holes. Fill the pot with a good quality compost and firm this down lightly. Then plant the herbs, making sure that they are the same depth as they were in their original pots. Smooth over the top of the compost and

LEFT **Mints are very rampant, so it is a good idea to grow them in pots. Here, a selection of mints is growing in terracotta pots.**

adjust the level of the surface, removing or adding some to bring it just below the rim of the container. Water herbs thoroughly.

Maintenance

The biggest task is to keep the herbs well-watered. During the summer months, when it is hot and dry, the container is likely to need watering at least once a day and even twice a day in some circumstances. All this watering means that nutrients quickly leach from the soil, so it will be necessary to add a liquid feed to the watering at least once a week. As an alternative, a slow-release fertilizer can be added to the potting compost (soil mix) before the container is filled.

Re-potting

Herbs will not last forever in a container, and if you are to be sure of a continuous supply it will be necessary to re-pot at least once a year. Many herbs are best thrown away and new ones planted in any case, and this applies even to perennials. Sage and rosemary will eventually get large, and it is better to replace these with new plants every year or every second year at the most, unless you have a container large enough to keep them for longer.

Always wash out a container thoroughly and refill it with new compost (soil mix), adding the old soil to the vegetable garden.

ABOVE **Even if you only have a small garden, you can still make room for a large container planted with culinary herbs.**

PLANTING HERBS IN A CONTAINER

1 To ensure that no stagnant water lies in the bottom of the container, place a layer of irregularly shaped stones in the bottom. This will ensure good drainage.

2 Fill the container with a good potting compost (soil mix). Firm it down gently.

3 Plant the herbs by digging holes in the compost (soil mix) and then firming them in. Top up or reduce the amount of compost so that it is just below the rim of the container.

4 To ensure that the plants are kept fed, insert one or more fertilizer sticks into the compost, following the manufacturer's instructions on the packet.

5 Water the container thoroughly and place in the shade for a few days until the herbs have recovered and become established.

Harvesting and Storing Herbs

Many herbs are seasonal and are not available for cutting all year round. One way of overcoming this problem is to grow some indoors, where they will survive the winter, but this is not always convenient and a better solution is to dry and store as many different types of your herbs as you can.

ABOVE **Harvest herbs when they are at their peak, usually before they flower. Cut them on a dry day, avoiding times when they are wilting in the heat.**

Harvesting herbs

Many herbs, such as parsley, rosemary and sage, are harvested on a cut-and-come-again principle: you take just as much as you want, when you want. With care, you can have parsley all year round. Sage and rosemary, being evergreen shrubs, should present no problems. Most other herbs, however, die back in winter and are not available unless you harvest and store them.

The time to pick herbs for storing is when they are fresh and at their peak, and with most herbs this is before they come into flower. (This, of course, applies to leaf herbs; if you want the seeds, obviously you must let the plants flower.) If you wait until after flowering, the leaves on most herbs will be tired, and will have lost their freshness and lack the sweetness of younger plants. On some plants the lower leaves are best avoided, because these are old and past their best.

Avoid gathering herbs in the heat of the day, when the leaves may be limp. If you can, work early in the morning, as soon as any dew has disappeared. Do not harvest on wet days. It is easier to dry herbs if the whole stem is collected, so cut neatly with a pair of secateurs (pruners). Pick flowers on warm, dry days when they have just fully opened.

Seeds should also be collected on dry days and should be fully ripe before they are harvested. Tip the seeds into a paper bag or place the whole seedhead in the bag.

Root herbs, such as horseradish, should be harvested in autumn, once the above-ground parts begin to wither.

Drying herbs and flowers

The simplest way to dry any type of herb is to tie the stalks in small bunches and hang them in a warm, dark place where plenty of air can circulate. Although they can be hung in a light place, including indoors, do not place them in direct sunlight. An airing cupboard or a warm room is best, but kitchens and bathrooms, where there is a lot of steam, are not suitable. Do not put herbs into an oven, because they will dry too quickly. Individual leaves can be dried by placing them on mesh trays or sheets of muslin or on ordinary trays. Those with a mesh are preferable because air will circulate more freely around the leaves.

Do not dry different herbs in close proximity or you may find that they taint each other.

DRYING AND FREEZING HERBS

1 Pick seed just as it is ripening. At this stage it should readily come away from its stalks. Place it on a tray or muslin bag and leave the seed for a few days in a warm, dry place until it has completely dried.

2 Once herbs have been thoroughly dried, tip them into a glass jar with an airtight lid. Store in a cool, dry, dark place.

3 An alternative to drying is to freeze herbs. They can simply be packed into bags and frozen, or finely chopped and placed in ice-cube trays. Add water to the trays and freeze to produce ready-to-use cubes.

ABOVE **Oregano, which can be dried or frozen, is a useful herb for the kitchen.**

Drying roots

Roots should be cleaned and cut into small pieces and dried on a tray in the oven.

Storing

Do not attempt to store any herbs until they are completely dry. When they are dry, place them in airtight glass jars. Clear jars can be used if the herbs are to be kept in a cupboard, but dark glass is preferable for those to be left on open shelves. Keep the leaves whole if possible and crush them only just before use.

Freezing

A modern alternative to drying herbs is to freeze them. This has the advantage of keeping the plant's colour as well as being much quicker and easier to do. The cleaned herbs can be put into labelled polythene (plastic) bags and put directly into the freezer. Alternatively, the herbs can be finely chopped and placed in ice-cube trays. Add a little water to each and freeze. Individual frozen cubes can be added to dishes as required.

Infusions

Another possibility is to make flavoured oils and vinegars for using in cooking. A few sprigs of the herb are infused in a bottle of good-quality wine vinegar or in an olive or vegetable oil.

RIGHT **Herbs can be dried by tying them into bunches and hanging them in a warm, dry place such as near a stove or boiler. However, take care to avoid steamy places and direct sunlight.**

Growing Fruit Trees and Bushes

Fruit tends to be the poor relation in the garden, possibly because it can take up large amounts of space. However, fresh fruit is even more delightful than fresh vegetables and it need not take up as much space as you might think.

ABOVE **Strawberries can be grown in containers. If these are kept under glass, as here, then an early crop can be obtained.**

Where to grow your fruit

The traditional place to grow fruit is in a fruit garden, a separate area of the garden that is devoted to fruit. This has one especial advantage in that it can be completely protected in a fruit cage. Scattering the fruit over the whole garden means that individual plants have to be protected, which can be rather tedious.

Apart from the protection they require, however, there is no reason for keeping the fruit together. In a decorative kitchen garden, fruit can be mixed in with the vegetables, trees and standard bushes providing visual height in individual beds. Many fruit trees can also be grown along walls or fences, and they can be used as dividers or screens between various parts of the garden. If you have a small garden and want a shady tree to sit under, why not plant an apple tree rather than a species that is solely ornamental?

Choosing fruit

As long as it will grow in your garden, there is nothing to prevent you choosing whatever fruit you want. There is a slight complication in that some tree fruits need pollinators to make sure that the fruit is set, and this means that if you want a particular apple you may have to have another apple to act as a pollinator. This may not be necessary if your neighbour has a compatible tree.

Ground preparation

Most fruit trees and bushes are likely to remain in the ground for a long time and so it is important that the soil is thoroughly prepared. It is particularly important that all perennial weeds are removed. If any small piece is left in the ground it is bound to regrow and is likely to be difficult to extract from around the roots of the tree or bush without digging them up.

Another reason for preparing the ground thoroughly is to make sure that there is plenty of organic material tucked right down among the roots of the plants. This will help keep the soil moist as well as giving a continuous supply of nutrients until the plants are established. Once the tree and shrubs are planted, any organic material will have to be applied to the soil's surface and taken down by the worms. Double dig the soil if possible, incorporating as much well-rotted organic material as you can spare. Take this opportunity to make sure that all perennial weeds are removed. If the ground is heavy and it is

PLANTING A FRUIT TREE OR BUSH

When planting a fruit tree or bush, always ensure that it is planted at the same depth as it was in its container or in its nursery bed.

TYING IN A NEWLY PLANTED TREE

Using tree ties, ensure that a newly planted tree is firmly anchored to a stake. Attach the tie approximately 30cm/12in above the ground.

ABOVE **Even apple trees can be grown in containers. However, it is essential to water them every day, and at least twice on hot dry days.**

likely to be difficult to remove the weeds, spraying some time before digging may be the only answer to cleaning the soil.

Planting

As long as the weather is neither too wet nor too cold the best time to plant fruit trees and bushes is between late autumn and mid-spring. If bare-rooted plants are delivered when it is impossible to plant, heel them into a spare piece of the vegetable garden until they can be planted in their permanent position. Container-grown plants can be planted at other times of the year, but they need more attention to make sure that they survive.

Fruit trees and bushes should be planted to the same depth as they were in their pots or nursery bed when you purchased them. If a tree needs staking, place the stake in

TOP-DRESSING FRUIT BUSHES

In the autumn, and again in the spring, top-dress fruit bushes with a layer of well-rotted organic material such as farmyard manure.

MULCHING STRAWBERRIES

Strawberries can be grown through a black polythene (plastic) mulch. This not only protects the fruit from mud-splashes, but also reduces the need for weeding and watering.

the ground before planting. Water the plants in thoroughly and keep them watered in dry weather until they are firmly established. Apply a mulch around the base of the plant in order to help preserve moisture as well as to keep the weeds down. Remove any weeds that do appear.

Try to keep a record of what you have planted. Fruit trees and bushes often outlive any label that comes with them, and it is often annoying when asked for the variety of an apple or raspberry, for example, when you cannot remember. A notebook with details of the variety, where you purchased the plant as well as the date on which you planted it, will be of future interest.

Supporting Fruit Trees and Shrubs

Once they are established, some fruit shrubs and most trees are free-standing, but most benefit from, and some require, permanent support. If this is provided adequately and properly from the start, these supports should last many years.

This apple tree is being supported by wires in a very decorative manner.

Wall and fence fruit

Several types of trees and shrubs can be trained flat against walls or fences. The effects created can be decorative. These plants will need some means of holding them against the wall, and this usually takes the form of wires. To make sure that the framework lasts as long as possible use a galvanized wire, which will not corrode. The wire is held in place by vine eyes, of which there are several types available. Some are flat, metal spikes, which are hammered into the brickwork, while others are screw eyes, which are screwed into wall plugs that have been inserted into holes in the brick or stonework of the wall. They can be screwed directly into wooden fences. The eyes are placed 60–90cm/ 2–3ft apart and a wire led through the hole in each one. The wire is secured at the end eyes by pulling it back and twisting it around itself or by using a tensioning screw that can be tightened to tension the wire. The wires should be parallel to each other and 30–45cm/12–18in apart.

Free-standing wirework

Berried fruit – like raspberries, blackberries and the various hybrid berries – and grapes need a permanent framework. They are grown in the open, and it is necessary to build a structure that will carry the supporting wires. The end posts are the most important part of the structure because they take a strain in one direction only, and if they are not secured properly they can be pulled from the ground. Each post should be treated with a preservative to prolong its life. The end posts should be sunk into the ground by at least 60cm/ 24in and braced with another post set at an angle. Intermediate posts, every 2m/6ft or so, are set to a similar depth but do not need bracing. Galvanized wire is stretched along the length of the row, at 30cm/12in intervals, the first wire being 60cm/24in from the ground. These wires should be as taut as possible. They can be fixed with staples, or holes can be drilled in the posts and eye-bolts inserted, which can be used to tension the wire by tightening the nut on the outside of the end posts.

Individual support

Trees need individual support when they are first planted. In exposed positions some shrub fruit, especially standards, will also benefit from being supported.

SUPPORTING A TREE AGAINST A WALL ....

1 To support trees against walls, use wires held by vine eyes. Depending on the type of vine eye, either knock them into the wall or drill and plug before screwing them in.

2 Pass galvanized wire through the holes in the eyes and fasten to the end ones, keeping the wire as tight as possible.

The stake should be inserted before the tree is planted so that there is no chance of damaging the roots. Although the stake should be knocked well into the ground, there need only be about 45cm/18in above ground. Current practice is to support trees low down, at about 30cm/12in above the ground, so that the lower part of the tree and, more importantly, the rootball, are held in place, while the top is allowed to move freely, gaining strength as it does so.

Tie the tree to the stake, using a proper tree tie that will provide good support, but at the same time not cut into or chafe the trunk of the tree. It is important that you check at least twice a year that the tie is not too tight and cutting into the growing trunk. Adjust the tie if necessary.

If the tree is already in position, place the stake at an angle to the trunk so that it enters the ground some way from its base in order to avoid damaging the tree's roots. Alternatively, insert two posts, each some distance from, and on either side of, the trunk. Fix a crossbar between these two posts, and then tie the tree to this.

BELOW **The branches of small apple trees can be trained to spread by tying them down with string tied to the trunk.**

STAKING FRUIT

1 Knock a stout post well into the ground at the end of the row. An alternative is to dig a hole and insert the post before refilling and ramming down the earth.

2 Knock another post at a 45° angle to the vertical to act as a support to the upright post. Nail it firmly so that the upright post is rigid and will not be pulled by tight wires.

3 Fasten the wires around one end post and pull tight along the row stapling it to each post. Keep the wire as taut as possible. If necessary, use eye-bolts on the end posts to tension the wire.

4 Fasten the canes – in this case raspberry canes – to the wire with string or plant ties. Space the canes out evenly along the wire so that the maximum amount of light reaches the leaves.

Pruning Fruit Trees and Bushes

Pruning is a subject that terrifies many gardeners. Indeed, many gardeners fail to prune at all, to the detriment of the tree or the bush and to their subsequent crops. Like so many other things connected with gardening it is largely a question of experience. Once you have practised it a couple of times, you will be able to do it without any trouble at all.

Basic pruning cuts

Although trees and shrubs need different methods of pruning and training, the pruning cuts are the same in all instances. Always cut a stem just above a bud and make sure that the cut is angled away from the bud.

Branches that are large enough to be cut with a saw are usually cut across the branch at right angles. If the branch is thick and heavy and likely to break, thereby splitting the wood before the cut is complete, the sawing is done in three separate stages. The first cut is made on the underside of the branch, 5cm/2in from the final cutting position. The second cut is made slightly further out along the branch, this time from above, by sawing down until the branch splits along to the first cut and is then severed. The final cut can be made straight through from the top because there is now no weight to cause splitting.

Shapes

There are so many different ways of pruning and training fruit trees and bushes that it is impossible to explain every case here. Detailed pruning advice is given for individual fruits in the Fruit section

Rootstocks

The rootstock on which a fruit tree grows affects the size and rate of growth of the tree. It is important that you get the right stock for the type of tree you want to grow. Always check with the supplier that the tree or bush is suitable for your needs.

ABOVE **A standard apple tree is a particularly good shape for a traditional garden. It also provides shade in the summer.**

Fruit Tree and Bush Shapes

Standard trees are full-sized trees with a natural shape. These need space as they can grow large, but they create good shade for sitting under.

Half-standard trees are similar to standard trees, but, as the name implies, they are smaller.

Bush trees are much smaller than standards but are still quite large for a small garden. The trees are quite short but bushy with an open centre.

Spindle-bush trees are short – to 2.1m/7ft high – and cone shaped, with a central leader and side branches that are tied down to make them spread.

Dwarf pyramid trees are short growing and pruned into a pyramid shape. In general, more branches are retained than in the similarly shaped spindle-bush trees.

Fan trees or bushes are trained so that the branches are in a two-dimensional fan, radiating from the top of a short trunk. They are grown against a wall, a fence or post-and-wire supports.

Espalier trees or bushes are trained flat against a wall, a fence or post-and-wire supports. They have a main trunk and parallel branches coming from it at right angles.

Cordon trees or bushes consist of a single main stem. They are usually trained at 45° to the ground, but they can be also be vertical.

Double cordon trees or bushes are similar to ordinary cordons, except two shoots are trained vertically, forming a U-shape.

Triple cordons are similar to ordinary cordons, except three stems are trained vertically.

Standard bushes are grafted onto a single tall stem to give it a "lollipop" appearance.

ABOVE **Pears are the perfect fruit to grow in all manner of decorative shapes. Here, the pear is being trained into a crown shape.**

TOP LEFT **An espaliered pear tree on wire supports. Many other fruit trees can be trained in the same decorative way.**

OPPOSITE PAGE, TOP **This pear tree has been beautifully trained into a fan. The fan is supported on wires, but it could also be grown against a wall.**

Good and Bad Pruning Cuts

1 A good pruning cut is made just above a strong bud, about 3mm/⅛in above the bud. It should be a slanting cut, with the higher end above the bud. The bud should generally be outward bound from the plant rather than inward; the latter will throw its shoot into the plant, crossing and rubbing against others, which should be avoided. This is an easy technique and you can practise it on any stem.

2 If the stem has buds or leaves opposite each other, make the cut horizontal, about 3mm/⅛in above the buds.

3 Always use a sharp pair of secateurs (pruners). Blunt ones will produce a ragged or bruised cut, which is likely to introduce disease into the plant.

4 Do not cut too far above a bud. The piece of stem above the bud is likely to die back and the stem may well die back even further, causing the loss of the whole stem.

5 Do not cut too close to the bud otherwise the bud might be damaged by the secateurs (pruners) or disease might enter. Too close a cut is likely to cause the stem to die back to the next bud.

6 It is bad practice to slope the cut towards the bud as this makes the stem above the bud too long, which is likely to cause dieback. It also sheds rain on to the bud, which may cause problems.

Protecting Fruit

Gardeners are not the only animals to like fruit. Many others, birds in particular, do so as well, and the only way to make sure that there is enough left for the gardener to enjoy is to protect the fruit bushes and trees in some way. The only practical way to do this is to put some form of physical barrier between the predators and the fruit.

Fruit cages

There is no doubt that the easiest way to protect fruit is with a complete cage. The advantage of this is that it covers the area completely and that the gardener can walk around within it, maintaining the bushes or harvesting the fruit. When individual protection is provided, each cover has to be removed in turn, which can be tiresome, especially if netting snags on branches.

The only problem with caging on a large scale is that it can be expensive. If you have every intention of leaving the fruit cage where it is, it might be more economical in the long term to build a cage with long-lasting materials. Use thick posts and make the covering from galvanized wire netting, which, although more expensive than plastic, will outlive many replacements of its plastic equivalent.

Ready-made fruit cages are expensive but they still probably work out cheaper than making one of your own, unless, of course, you have access to free materials, such as posts. Fruit cages are supplied in kit form and are easy to erect; they can usually be ordered to whatever size you require. Make sure that there are no gaps in the

ABOVE **A tunnel of wire netting can be used to protect low-growing strawberries. The netting can be in short sections for easy removal and storage.**

netting and that it is well pegged down or buried at the base because birds have a knack of finding the smallest hole to squeeze through.

A homemade fruit cage is time-consuming to construct, but you can make it fit any shape and cover any area you want. Metal posts, such as scaffolding poles, will last for ever but most gardeners find that wooden poles are more practical. They should be sturdy and treated at their base with preservative. Each should be let into the ground by about 60cm/24in for security, because the netting will act as a sail, putting great pressure on the posts in strong winds.

The covering can be plastic netting, but galvanized wire netting will last longer and be less likely to tear accidentally. Some gardeners like to remove the top covering to allow birds in to eat pests when the fruit is not actually ripening, and if you want to do this, use wire sides and a plastic netting for the top. Another reason for being able to remove the top covering in winter, especially if it is plastic, is that a heavy fall of snow can

LEFT **A fruit cage is expensive but it is the only really effective way of protecting fruit from birds.**

ABOVE **Strawberries can be protected against frost with cloches.**

LEFT **Fruit trees and bushes trained against a wall or fence can be protected with a home-made frame, as seen here. A similar frame can be covered with polythene (plastic) to protect the blossom from frosts.**

Draped netting

There is no satisfactory way of protecting taller, free-growing subjects, such as fruit bushes or trees. Draping them with netting is the only possible method, but gaps are usually left and the netting snags on twigs and shoots

If a fruit is growing against a wall or fence, then the netting can be held away from the plant by building a simple frame, and this can also be covered with polythene (plastic) in the spring in order to protect the blossom against frost.

Non-netting protection

Netting is the only satisfactory way to protect fruit crops in the garden. Commercial methods, such as bangers, are impracticable in a domestic garden. Humming wires have a limited success but do not really work. Covering the bushes with threads may keep the birds off but they make harvesting awkward and they are difficult to remove for pruning.

The traditional scarecrow makes a good feature in the garden, but it has no success in deterring birds and animals. Plastic birds of prey or owls at strategic points often work well for a while, but birds soon get used to them.

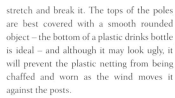

stretch and break it. The tops of the poles are best covered with a smooth rounded object – the bottom of a plastic drinks bottle is ideal – and although it may look ugly, it will prevent the plastic netting from being chaffed and worn as the wind moves it against the posts.

Make a door wide enough to get a wheel-barrow through and make certain that it fits well, or birds will get in.

Low-level protection

It is easier to provide protection for individual crops when low-level protection is required because less material is needed. The simplest method is to bend some wire-netting into an inverted U-shape and peg it to the ground with wires. This works well for strawberries. Alternatively, put short stakes in the ground at intervals all round and in the middle of the crop and drape plastic netting over this.

Harvesting and Storing Fruit

The best fruit is always the crop you pick and pop straight into your mouth. Given kind weather and a certain amount of skill on the gardener's part, however, there should be sufficient fruit not only to supply the kitchen but also to store for later use.

Harvesting

Fruit should be properly ripe before it is harvested for immediate use. There is little point in picking it early and leaving it to ripen – it will always ripen better on the stem. Fruit for storing should be mature and ripe – but do not pick at the very peak of ripeness, aim for just a little before. This is a matter of judgement and will come with experience. The time to pick is when the fruit comes away easily in the hand. Apples, for example, will come free with a little twist of the wrist, while raspberries will come away when twisted with the fingers.

With the exception of cane fruit, such as raspberries and blackberries, most fruit is picked with the stalks left on. Normally fruit is picked individually, but the various types of currant and grapes are usually picked in bunches. Pick fruit during dry weather and be careful not to bruise or otherwise damage it.

Storing

On the whole, the only types of fruit that can be satisfactorily stored without some method of preservation are apples, pears and quinces, and it is worth remembering that some varieties of fruit store better than others. 'Cox's Orange Pippin' apples, for example, can be kept until spring, but 'Beauty of Bath' apples have to be eaten right away, because they last not much longer than a week. As a general rule, early maturing apples do not store, but later ones do.

ABOVE **Apples are removed with a twist of the wrist. All fruits, other than cane fruit such as raspberries and blackberries, are picked with the stalks left on.**

Keep only fruit that is in perfect condition and throw out any that are marked or beginning to rot. Place the apples or pears in trays separated with paper so that they do not touch each other. Place the trays in a cool, dark place. Check periodically and throw out any fruit that is beginning to rot. Some apples will shrivel in storage and it is better to wrap these individually in greaseproof paper or to place several in a polythene (plastic) bag that has a few small holes in it.

ABOVE AND LEFT **Soft fruit, such as strawberries, raspberries and gooseberries should be carefully picked between thumb and finger. The fruit may then be placed in small individual containers so that they are not squashed or bruised.**

RIGHT **A filbert tree (*Corylus maxima*) is a rare but
welcome sight in the garden. The variety shown
here is 'Purpurea'.**

Do not place quinces close to apples and
pears because the strong aroma will taint the
other fruit. Store quinces in open trays.

Freezing

It is possible to freeze most fruit. However,
although the taste will remain, many will
lose their "solid" appearance when thawed
and are, therefore, better used for cooking
than for eating raw. Soft fruits are the
easiest to freeze, but it is also possible to
freeze apples, although it is best to cut
them up or even cook and purée them
before freezing.

Again, only choose sound fruit. Place
the fruit on trays so that they are not
touching each other and then put them in
the freezer. Once frozen, they can be put
into a bag. The fruit can be put straight
into a bag before freezing, but they are
likely to stick together and so the whole
batch will have to be used at once. If you
have no room for trays, split the fruit up
into small usable quantities and place each
batch of fruit in an individual bag.

Preserving

Freezing is a modern method of preserving
fruit, but there are also a number of traditional ways. Some fruits, such as apples and
pears, can be dried while others, such as
plums and gooseberries, can be bottled.
Another way is to turn the fruit into chutneys or jams. All these methods are dealt
with in good cookery books.

ABOVE **Apples, pears and quinces can be stored in
trays in a cool place. It is best if they are laid on
paper so that the individual fruits do not touch.
The length of storage time depends on the variety.**

ABOVE **With the exception of apples, pears and
quinces, most fruit cannot be kept for any length
of time without some form of preserving. The
simplest method of preserving fruit is to freeze it.**

Propagation

While most gardeners do not have much space to increase their stock, and many do not need to replace their tree fruit, they need to know how to propagate soft fruits, so that they can be replaced from time to time. The techniques involved are all fairly simple to master.

ABOVE **This strawberry plant is producing plenty of runners, which root to produce a number of different plants.**

Hardwood cuttings

Currants, gooseberries, blueberries and grape vines are usually increased by taking hardwood cuttings. This process does not need any propagators or other equipment other than a pair of secateurs (pruners) or a sharp knife.

The best time for taking hardwood cuttings is autumn, preferably early autumn. Select a few shoots that have grown during the previous year and are now firm and well-ripened. They should be straight and about 30cm/12in long.

Choose a sheltered site, away from drying winds and hot sun. Make a narrow trench by inserting a spade into the soil and pushing it to one side to open up a narrow V-shaped slit. If the soil is heavy, trickle some clean sharp sand into the bottom of the slit and insert the cuttings. Place them about 15cm/6in apart, planting them so that about half of the cutting is below ground. Place the spade into the ground about 10cm/4in away from the initial slit and lever it so that the slit closes up, firmly holding the cuttings. Firm down the soil gently with your feet.

By the next autumn the cuttings should have rooted. They can be dug up and transplanted to their final positions or moved to a nursery bed for another year.

Layering

Blackberries and hybrid berries are best increased by the simple process of layering, as are strawberries, although the latter are usually obliging enough to do it themselves, leaving the gardener to transplant the new plants.

At some time during the growing season choose a healthy blackberry cane that is long enough to touch the ground. At the point where the tip makes contact with the soil, dig a hole about 10cm/4in deep. Place the tip in it and bury it by replacing the soil. If it is in an exposed position and it is possible that the cane will be blown or knocked out of the ground, you can secure it with a peg, although this is not normally necessary. By late autumn the tip will have rooted. Cut the new plant from its parent shoot, about 30cm/12in from the ground. Dig up the young plant and transplant it to its fruiting position.

If you want to grow a few new plants in pots, perhaps for selling, the young plant can be transplanted directly into a pot. However, it is possible to cut out this stage by burying the tip of the parent cane into a pot of potting compost (soil mix) instead of a hole in the ground; it will root just as easily. The pot can be let into the ground, which will prevent it from being knocked over and it will not dry out as quickly as it would if left standing on the ground.

Strawberries can be treated in a similar way. After fruiting they send out runners, which will drop roots at intervals along their length to produce new plants. To make sure that they root, you can peg them down or cover a short length of runner with soil, but

LAYERING

1 Blackberries, hybrid berries and strawberries can all be increased by layering. Choose a healthy shoot, dig a hole near the tip and then bury it.

2 After a short period the tip will have produced roots. It can then be cut from the parent plant and replanted where required.

3 If you would like to have potted specimens, then bury a flowerpot in the ground, fill it with compost (soil mix) and bury the tip in this.

this is usually unnecessary as the plant will root itself quite naturally. Again, the runners can be pegged into pots of compost (soil mix) if you want ready-potted plants.

Division

Raspberries are usually increased by division. It is a simple matter to lift some of the suckers that emerge a little way from the parent plant. In the autumn dig up a healthy, strong-growing sucker and cut through the root that is still attached to the main clump. Replant this in its fruiting position. It is advisable never to divide diseased plants for replanting. If you are in any doubt, it is always better to start from scratch, using certified disease-free stock that has been sold by a reputable nursery.

Methods of Propagation
Division Blackberries, hybrid berries, raspberries and strawberries
Layering Blackberries, hybrid berries and strawberries
Hardwood Cuttings Blackcurrants, gooseberries, grapes, red currants and white currants
Semi-ripe Cuttings
Blueberries
Grafting Tree fruits

TAKING HARDWOOD CUTTTINGS

1 Take the hardwood cuttings in the autumn, with each cutting measuring approximately 30cm/12in in length. Cut the cutting off just below a bud.

2 Dig a slit trench by pushing a spade into the ground and levering it backwards and forwards. If the ground is heavier, open the slit a bit more and part fill it with some clean sharp sand.

3 Place the cuttings vertically in the trench at about 15cm (6in) intervals.

4 Dig the spade in a short distance from the trench and lever it so that the slit closes up.

5 Firm down the soil around the cuttings with your foot and generally tidy up the surface of the soil with a rake.

common
problems

Nothing is ever straightforward in the garden – perhaps if it were, many gardeners would give up through sheer boredom. Nature always throws in a few problems just to keep us on our toes. The weather is rarely consistent: it is either too wet or too dry, too hot or too cold. You turn your back for a few moments, and weeds seem to sprout up everywhere. Just when everything looks perfect, plagues of pests and diseases arrive. The gardener has a lot to contend with.

On the other hand, the situation is rarely as bad as many chemical companies would have you believe. Many of the problems are such that you can probably live with them, while others need only minor attention. Chemicals are only usually needed as a last resort.

RIGHT **This informal vegetable garden, with its rows of onions, carrots, marrows (zucchini), spinach and beans, is a tribute to good garden hygiene.**

Getting it in perspective

If the problems encountered by gardeners were insurmountable, no one would ever grow any vegetables at all. It cannot be denied that there are problems, but they often seem worse than they really are, particularly if you believe the literature issued by the chemical companies. Most of the problems that occur in the garden can be overcome by simple means that cost little in terms of either time or money. Many of the difficulties are insignificant and can, unless you are fastidious to the extreme, be ignored. A bit of rust on the leeks in a wet year doesn't look nice but it will not do a great deal of harm. A few minutes' contemplative hoeing will see off most of the weeds, and a sudden outbreak of caterpillars can soon be picked off by hand.

Do not let the thought of pests and diseases put you off in any way. An occurrence of either to the extent that serious action is needed is rare. Most gardeners find they survive season after season without any trouble. Anyway, if the worst comes to the worst, you can always give up and start afresh next year.

ABOVE **Mulching with a layer of grass cuttings helps to preserve the moisture in the soil. You will need to water the ground before applying the mulch.**

Be prepared

If you exercise a little forethought and adopt a good routine, you will be able to pre-empt many of the problems that might occur. Always practise good hygiene. Never leave rotten vegetables on the plants or in the ground. Remove them to the compost heap. Don't leave piles of weeds lying about, but put them on the compost heap or, if they are pernicious, burn them. Keep a close eye on your crops and take action as soon as possible if you see problems beginning to appear. Take out the tips of broad (fava) beans, for example, before they can be infested with blackfly. Cover your brassicas with fleece to keep off butterflies, and hence the caterpillars. If you notice one or two greenfly, crush them with your fingers before they can start breeding. Don't wait until they have multiplied and you have to resort to chemicals to control them.

ABOVE **Weeds use up a great deal of moisture and nutrients, and crowd out young plants, making them drawn and sickly. Weeds can also harbour disease.**

Hoe as part of a regular routine. If you allow weeds to get too large, they will take longer to remove. Make your compost in such as way that it gets hot enough to destroy all weed seeds and fungal spores.

Stake peas and beans early, rather than leaving them until they are a tangled mass. Put up windbreaks in exposed areas, instead of waiting for things to blow over. Mulch to preserve moisture so that the soil does not dry out and you have to water. Foresight saves a lot of time and frustration.

Chemical control

An increasing number of gardeners are becoming aware of the benefits of organic gardening and are avoiding the use of chemicals. There are times when chemicals can be useful, but these are less frequent than the large companies that manufacture them would have us believe. A weed-infested garden can probably only be cleared with chemicals, but if this is carried out

BELOW **A good mixed garden, with plenty of varieties of flowers and vegetables, is less likely to have problems than one restricted to a monoculture.**

properly, it should need to be done only once, and all subsequent control can be done by hand. Using chemicals on just one occasion will probably do no permanent harm to the soil, but do not become dependent on herbicides and reach for the spray every time you see a weed – that is not what gardening is about. You will end up creating a desert and a polluted one at that.

If you do use chemicals make sure that you follow the manufacturer's instructions. Take the necessary safety precautions and thoroughly wash all equipment. Never leave chemicals or associated equipment where children can get at them.

Weather Problems

We cannot control the weather; we simply have to take what nature throws at us. Nevertheless, there are some ways in which we can limit the worst of its effects.

Wind

Winds can be destructive. Not only can they knock over and break plants, but also wind-rock can cause a plant to move about so that it becomes loose in the soil or it can create a hole around the point at which the plant enters the soil. This fills with stagnant water, and the plant can rot. A dry or hot wind can remove moisture from leaves, making them wilt. Cold winds can create wind-burn, which

BELOW **A hedge provides excellent protection from the wind. It allows some air to filter through, thus reducing the turbulence that occurs with solid features such as walls.**

shrivels leaves. Winds can also make it unpleasant to work in the garden, frequently making the gardener not only uncomfortable but also irritable – not the best of moods to produce a good vegetable garden.

A long catalogue of woes, but the wind can be tamed to a large degree by creating windbreaks of some sort. By far the best defence is a hedge, which filters the wind, cutting down its speed considerably but at the same time not creating turbulence. A wall, on the other hand, stops the wind dead, but it escapes over the top and creates turbulence on the far side, and this can be more destructive than the wind itself. An

ABOVE **A maximum/minimum thermometer is ideal for keeping track of the temperature both in the open garden and inside a greenhouse.**

alternative to a hedge is a form of plastic netting that is designed especially to be used as a windbreak. This is not the most beautiful of materials, but it is extremely functional.

TOP **Newspaper makes an excellent temporary insulation against sudden frosts in spring. Drop several layers, one on top of the other, to create air pockets. Do not leave on during the day.**

ABOVE **Fleece has a similar function to newspaper. It is very light and will not harm the plants. Unlike newspaper, it can be left on during the day as light penetrates though it.**

RIGHT **If a frost pocket is caused by a thick hedge, stopping cold air rolling down a hill, cut a hole in the base so that the air can pass through and continue down the hill away from the garden.**

Make sure that the poles supporting it are anchored securely because the netting will act as a sail and exert enormous pressure on its supports.

As a rule, a hedge or windbreak netting will create a "wind shadow" of about ten times the height of the barrier. In other words, a hedge 2m/6ft high will create a relatively wind-free area of about 20m/60ft from its base. The degree of protection decreases the further you get from the hedge, and at 20m/60ft from the hedge the decrease in wind speed is minimal.

Turbulence is reduced considerably by the use of double hedges or two rows of windbreak. Set a few yards apart, these give far greater protection than a single barrier.

Frost

There are two aspects to frost. The first is general winter cold; the second is those sudden unseasonable frosts that can wreak havoc among tender, newly put-out plants.

Winter cold is not generally too much of a problem in the vegetable garden because most of the things left in the garden are hardy. In particularly cold areas or in very cold spells, it is a good idea to give protection to some of the permanent crops, such as globe artichokes, by covering them with straw.

There is more of a problem if the garden is a cold one and the soil does not warm up until late in the spring. If your garden is like this, you will find it impossible to start gardening until then, and this makes early crops difficult to grow. There are several things you can do to help, however. If your vegetable garden is in a frost hollow – caused by cold air being trapped within it – it may be possible to "drain" it. Make a hole in the hedge or fence at the lowest point of the garden so that the air can flow through and continue down the slope. Alternatively, hedges may be placed higher up the slope to deflect the cold air as it moves downhill. Covering the soil with black polythene (plastic) or cloches will help warm up and dry out the soil so that you can start work on it earlier.

Sudden frosts can be a nightmare, especially if they are preceded by a warm spell that brings plants into early growth. Keep an ear or eye on the weather forecasts and cover tender plants if frost threatens. Use cloches, fleece or even newspaper.

ABOVE **Some plants, such as globe artichokes, are hardy but can be damaged by severe weather. They can be covered with straw to give them extra protection.**

ABOVE **Filling a box with straw makes a good form of insulation that can be removed and replaced. It also prevents the straw being blown about.**

ABOVE **Cloches produce longer-term protection than straw. They can be used to protect crops through the winter or as temporary cover in spring whenever frosts threaten.**

Drought

Few vegetables and fruit will grow without adequate moisture. Many plants will grow in dry conditions, but they quickly bolt (run to seed) and tend to be tough and often taste bitter. A constant supply of water is necessary so that growth is steady and uninterrupted. Irregular supplies of water will lead to irregular growth and many vegetables and fruit, in particular, will split.

ABOVE **The best way to water a vegetable garden is with a watering can. Water can then be applied to exactly the right spot and in the right quantity with little water being wasted. However, watering by hand is both time-consuming and heavy work.**

Maintaining reserves

Throughout this book there is an emphasis on adding as much organic material as possible to the soil. Once again, this advice has to be repeated. Any free moisture in ordinary soil is likely to drain away or evaporate from the surface. However, fibrous material around the plant's roots will hold moisture in the same way as a cloth or a sponge. If there is excess moisture it will drain away, so that the plant is not standing in stagnant water, but enough will be retained to supply the plant's roots over a considerable time. Even if the water supply depends on irregular rain showers, the slow release will help to mitigate the dry periods.

Working as much organic material as possible into the soil is one way of pre-empting a dry summer. Add it to the soil when it is dug or, if you are using a non-digging, deep-bed system, add it as a top-dressing. Do this every year so that the water-retaining quality of the soil improves.

Keeping water in

One way that moisture is lost from the soil is through evaporation from the surface. Hot sun and drying winds quickly take their toll on the soil and can dry it to a surprising depth, simply because more is drawn upwards to replace what has been lost nearer the surface. Covering the soil with a mulch helps to preserve this moisture.

ABOVE **A dribble hose is a good watering method because the hose is laid along the row of plants and it only waters the immediate area. The water slowly seeps out of the pipe, which means that it does not flood the area, but sinks well into the soil.**

LEFT **Place water butts beneath as many rooves as possible to catch the water as it runs off. It is the purest form of water to use and, being at ambient temperature, it does not chill the plants. It will also save water and, in most gardens, the money spent on water bills.**

RIGHT **Mulching with a layer of grass cuttings helps to preserve the moisture in the soil. Water before mulching and do not use too thick a layer as this may heat up and burn the plant – 7.5cm/3in is sufficient.**

Organic mulches are the best ones to use because they not only act as a barrier, but also eventually break down and are taken into the soil, much to its benefit. A mulch acts as a barrier partly because moisture does not evaporate from it quite as quickly as it does from ordinary soil, and partly because it acts as a thermal barrier, preventing the soil from getting too warm and thus speeding up the drying process.

Non-organic mulches – polythene (plastic), for example – prevent even greater loss as little moisture finds its way through, but, of course, it is not as easy for water to penetrate in the first place. Those to whom the aesthetic qualities of the kitchen garden are important may find that polythene looks ugly and will prefer to use an organic mulch.

It is important that the ground is thoroughly watered before any mulch is applied. If the ground is left dry the mulch will prevent it from getting wet unless a very large quantity of water is supplied.

Watering

Water is an expensive commodity – and becoming increasingly expensive in some areas – so you should use it only where and when it is really needed. Avoid, if possible, using sprinklers that waste large quantities of water on paths and other non-productive ground. If you have the time and strength use a watering can, supplying water to the base of individual plants. If you do this, you can be sure that the water goes where it is most needed. Sprinklers are especially use-

ful when there is a large area of produce to cover or if watering by hand is difficult for physical reasons.

One efficient way of supplying water is to use a drip hose. This is a hosepipe (garden hose) with holes in it. It is laid along the line of plants and water constantly dribbles out. There is not enough water to flood the soil, but there is sufficient to provide a constant supply to the plants. If the ground is mulched, lay the pipe under the mulch. These hoses are best left on for several hours until the soil has taken up sufficient moisture, and then turned off, but there are gardens where they can be left on permanently. The system works best with permanent plantings, such as fruit bushes.

Whatever method you use, make certain that the ground is thoroughly soaked. A sprinkling of water on the surface will do little other than lay the dust. To be effective, a watering should supply at least the equivalent of 2.5cm/1in of rain.

LEFT **Black polythene (plastic) mulch is not attractive, but it is effective in reducing the water lost through evaporation. Special horticultural mulch can also be bought which allows water to pass through into the ground but prevents it escaping again.**

Weed Control

Many people are put off gardening simply because they do not like the idea of weeding. However, there are two points that they probably never consider. The first is that in a well-maintained garden there is far less weeding to do than they might think, and, second, weeding can be a rather relaxing, even therapeutic, task.

ABOVE **Avoid using chemical weedkillers in the vegetable garden. If necessary, use them to kill persistent weeds when initially preparing the plot. Always follow the instructions on the packet.**

Keep it clean

Weeds in the right place can be a good thing, but the right place is not the vegetable garden. Weeds take nutrients and moisture from the soil, depriving the vegetables of their share. They can grow tall, smothering or drawing up the vegetables so that they do not grow properly. Many weeds harbour diseases, particularly rusts, and pass these on to your crops. So keep your kitchen garden clear of weeds if you want to produce the best crops.

Good preparation

One way to reduce the amount of weeding is to prepare the ground thoroughly in the first place. If all perennial weeds are removed, either by hand or with weedkillers, the only problem to cope with are new perennial and annual weeds that germinate from seeds. These are not much of a problem as long as they are hoed off soon after they have appeared. If you remove them before they can run to seed, gradually the number of seeds left in the soil – and hence the number of germinating weeds – will be reduced.

Keeping on top

As long as you keep on top of weeds they are not a problem. It is when you let things slip that it all becomes a chore. Hoe off weed seedlings as they appear and it will only take a few minutes of your time. Allow them to become fully grown and it will take hours to sort things out.

Hoeing

The method of hoeing is often a matter of personal preference. If you have a draw or swan-neck hoe, you scrape the weeds off by drawing the hoe towards you. If you have a plate or Dutch hoe, you push it forwards, slicing off the weeds. If you have a three-pronged cultivator, you pull it through the top layer of soil, disturbing the roots of the weeds. In dry weather a hoe of either kind is best because you do not want to open the soil too much or water will evaporate. In wetter weather, however, the cultivator can be extremely useful because it opens the soil and allows the water to drain through.

Close work

Weeds do not always conveniently grow between the rows; they also grow in them where it is not as easy to hoe. With well-spaced

BELOW **For delicate hoeing around plants that may be easily damaged, a small one-handed hoe, known as an onion hoe, can be used. It is a form of draw hoe.**

ABOVE **It is not always possible to hoe without damaging the vegetables, or because the weeds are too well advanced. Weeding with a hand fork is then the best alternative.**

TOP **A push, plate or Dutch hoe is pushed forward, slicing either on or just below the surface, cutting off the weeds.**

ABOVE **A cultivator is a form of three-pronged hoe that is drawn between the rows of vegetables. This loosens the earth and with it any seedlings that have just germinated. As their roots are loose in the soil they cannot pick up moisture, and so die. This method is not as good in wet weather because the rain replants the weeds.**

LEFT **Hoeing is the traditional way of keeping a vegetable garden free of weeds. A draw hoe or swan-neck hoe is pulled towards the gardener in a series of chopping movements.**

crops, such as cabbages, it is possible to hoe around them, but this is impossible with vegetables such as carrots, and here you will have to weed by hand. Sometimes there is space to use an onion hoe, a small hoe with a short handle, which is held in one hand.

When you are working close to vegetables be careful not to disturb them. If a vegetable is disturbed when weeding nearby, firm down the soil and water in afterwards.

Non-digging methods
Gardening lore says that one year's weed seed means seven years' hard-work, spent removing the resulting seedlings. What actually happens is that the seeds get mixed with the soil and germinate only when they come to the surface – one year's worth of weed seeds, therefore, will continue to be a nuisance until they have all been used up. However, if you do not bring the seeds to the surface in the first place they cannot germinate, and in non-digging methods only the surface layer is disturbed and the store of weed seeds is quickly used up. In consequence, if you regularly scrape off any weeds that appear, then the amount of work will soon be reduced because the only new weeds will be those blown in on the wind – the rest will be left underground, out of harm's way.

Pests and Diseases

Some gardeners get terribly worried about pests and diseases, but in reality they are rarely a real problem. Common sense and good management mean that you should be able to go for years without feeling the need to reach for the spray gun.

Gardening books always include long lists of pests and diseases and make it look as if these problems are lurking around every corner, just waiting to burst in on your garden and ruin your crops. In fact, it is unlikely that most gardeners will ever see a fraction of these during his or her lifetime, and, if they do, they are probably not really worth worrying about.

A mixed garden

One of the best ways of keeping the garden pest free is to grow a wide range of crops. If you only grow carrots and carrot root fly turns up and devastates your crop, you have nothing left. However, if you grow 20 different types of vegetables, you are only going to lose a twentieth of your total crop, which is relatively insignificant.

A mixed garden, which contains plenty of flowers – particularly the old-fashioned varieties – will attract a host of wildlife such as ladybirds, hoverflies and plenty of other predators, which will attack any pests that arrive in the garden. I have a large cottage garden with several large flower gardens within it and I am rarely troubled by even such common pests as aphids. Indeed, I cannot actually remember the last time any chemicals were used on my garden, not because I am against using chemical treatments, but because it has just not been necessary to do so.

ABOVE **Rabbits can devastate a garden overnight, leaving nothing but chewed off stumps as a result of their visit.**

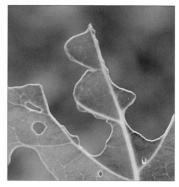

ABOVE **Birds are one of the worst pests in the garden. Here large bites have been taken out of a brassica.**

LEFT **Nets can be used to guard your crops against rabbits and rodents.**

Animals

There is one type of pest that is very difficult to control – mammals. They can rarely be killed and are difficult to deter. The only real action that you can take is preventative, and this means building a barricade around your garden. Wire netting, which will keep out most animals, should be partially buried in the ground to prevent burrowing species, such as rabbits, getting underneath. For the more athletic species, such as deer, the barrier will need to be at least 2.4m/8ft high if you are to prevent them from jumping over it. Fortunately, there is no need to take action unless you live in an area where these pests are a problem. You will rarely be troubled, for example, if you garden in a town.

Birds

While only relatively few gardeners have deer to contend with, birds are everywhere, and even if things are quiet one day, a large flock of pigeons can appear the next, even in a town. The only real recourse against pigeons is to net everything. A fruit cage that is tall enough to allow the gardener in is the best,

ABOVE **Damage to trees can be prevented by using wire guards.**

RIGHT **Birds and butterflies can be kept at bay with fine-meshed nets.**

ABOVE **Insect damage can cause a wide range of problems. Aphids, like these, not only distort and kill plants by sucking the sap from leaves and stems, but can also introduce diseases.**

ABOVE **The caterpillar stage in the development of butterflies and moths causes a great deal of damage to leaves, especially to members of the cabbage family.**

ABOVE **Mechanical methods are often easier and cause less harm than using chemicals. Here, fleece is used to cover brassicas to prevent butterflies from laying eggs.**

but this is expensive. Low level netting can be used as temporary protection when crops are at their most vulnerable.

Bird scarers are also a possibility, but they are not especially effective. Humming tapes are probably the most effective solution, but they do not always work.

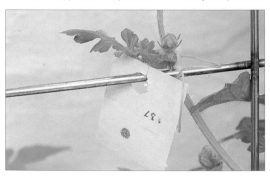

LEFT **Biological controls are an increasingly successful way to fight pests. They are mainly used in greenhouses, but others are now becoming available for the open garden. The control insects are released, here from a sachet, in order to attack the pests.**

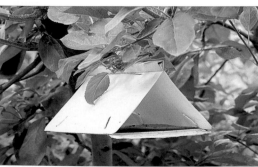

LEFT **Sticky traps are another form of non-spray control that is becoming popular for a wide range of pests. Here, pheromones attract insect pests to the trap, where they get stuck. Other sticky traps consist of sheets of yellow plastic covered with a non-drying glue. These are mainly used in greenhouses.**

In addition to eating fruit, buds and leaf vegetables, birds can also cause damage to crops by dust-bathing in the seedbeds of the garden. These can be covered with netting as a deterrent. The birds are usually also deterred if several pea-sticks are laid temporarily on the bed.

Insects

A wide range of insect pests can attack vegetables. Some of these, such as aphids, attack virtually anything; others, such as carrot fly, restrict themselves to one type of crop. Many pests can be deterred by taking simple precautions. Cabbage root fly, for example, can be deterred by placing a piece of roofing felt or plastic on the ground around the plant to prevent the adults from laying their eggs next to the stem. Black fly can be a pest of broad (fava) beans, but if you remove their favourite part of the plant, the succulent tips, before they appear, the blackfly usually do not stop. Small outbreaks of insects can usually be removed by hand before they get out of control.

If the worst comes to the worst, you can use a chemical control. There are types that are safe to use with vegetables, but it is essential to read the instructions on the packaging, especially any advice about safety. Use chemicals only when and where they are needed; do not automatically drench everything. Make sure that spray or powder does not drift onto other plants, especially those that may be ready to be harvested.

Caterpillars

There are three ways of dealing with caterpillars. The first is preventative. Cover the plants with fleece or small-mesh netting so that butterflies and moths cannot lay their

eggs. The second is to check susceptible plants regularly and remove any eggs or caterpillars by hand. You may miss a few, but this usually keeps the problem within reasonable bounds. The third is to use chemicals. Again, be certain that they are suitable for vegetables and follow the instructions scrupulously.

Slugs and snails

Mollusc are probably the gardener's worst enemy. There are many traditional ways of ridding the garden of them, including using containers of beer sunk into the beds, but one of the most effective ways is to go out after dark with a torch (flashlight) and round up as many as you can see – and you will be surprised how many you will find. Kill them by putting them in a container of water with added washing-up liquid, or capture and release them on waste ground away from your garden. Doing this for a few nights should help to keep the problem under control.

If you must, you can use slug bait. There are organic baits available if you prefer, but they do not seem to be as effective as the non-organic type. Always follow the manufacturer's instructions to the letter and do not leave either bait or dead slugs around because they may be eaten by wildlife. Biological control is available, but it is expensive, the supply is erratic, and it does not always work; but things should improve on this front.

Diseases

Good housekeeping can prevent many diseases. Remove diseased or rotting material as soon as you see it. Deter aphids, which are often the carriers of disease, and, as a matter of practice, do not use the same ground two years running for the same crop. Wet, ill-drained soil may be the cause of some diseases, so improving the condition of the soil can be an important factor in keeping disease at bay. Healthy, well-fed and watered plants are less likely to fall prey to disease. Never buy, or accept as gifts, diseased plants.

Many modern hybrids are less susceptible to certain diseases than some of the older ones, so choose your varieties with care, if you are worried about possible diseases.

Some diseases can be treated with chemicals, but if there is any doubt, dig up the affected plants and burn them as soon as possible. If you do use chemicals, be careful and follow all instructions, especially the safety ones. Store chemicals well out of the reach of young children.

Burning is the only solution for plants suffering from viral diseases, such as mosaic virus on marrows (zucchini) and cucumbers or on spinach, because there is no known cure. Burning vegetables may seem a waste, but it is far better to safeguard the unaffected plants as well as to prevent spores from getting into the soil. If this does happen, next year's plants might be affected as well. To avoid this, use a rotational system of growing crops.

Remember not to put diseased plants on the compost heap. In theory, the compost should get hot enough to kill off any spores, but you can never be quite certain that all parts of the heap are sufficiently hot, and you might end up spreading the disease over the whole garden.

BELOW **Many of the diseases that affect vegetables are fungal ones, such as this rust on leeks.**

vegetables

Vegetables are the mainstay of any kitchen garden. The quantities and varieties as well as the way in which the crops are laid out will be determined by the preferences of the gardener. However, there are a few principles that apply to the growing of each type of vegetable, and these are described in this section of the book.

The gardener is spoilt for choice when it comes to the range of varieties available. At first it will be a question of experimenting to find the varieties whose taste you prefer as well as those that are best suited to the soil and climate in your garden. Once they have identified these varieties, many gardeners tend to stick with them. There is no harm in this, although it pays to be adventurous and to try not only a few new varieties, but also some types of vegetable that you have not grown before.

As well as buying seed, many gardeners collect their own. In this way they are certain to continue using the varieties that do well in their garden, especially if they collect seed from the best plants each time. F1 hybrids will not come true and it is not worth collecting seed from them, but it is worth experimenting with ordinary open-pollinated seed. Some plant seeds, like beans and peas, are easy to collect, but other plants, such as carrots, are biennial and do not set seed until the second year. Leaving plants in the ground for two years takes up valuable space and so it may not be worth it for these. Experiment, it will add to the fun of gardening, especially if you end up with your own strain of vegetables.

BULB VEGETABLES

Onions
Allium cepa

Onions are one of the oldest vegetables. They were grown by the Ancient Egyptians over 5,000 years ago and were probably eaten long before that. Their actual origins are not known, but they probably first grew in the mountainous regions of Central Asia. As well as adding flavour to food, they have long been known for their health-giving properties.

ABOVE **A good crop of onions growing in a block in a raised bed.**

Traditionally, the large, round onions that are mainly used for cooking are grown from sets, which are small bulbs that have started their life during the previous season when they were sown as seed by seed merchants. They are harvested at the end of their first season, when they are approximately 1–2.5cm/ ½–1in in diameter. They are then either sold loose or, as is more frequently the case these days, they are pre-packaged and bought by weight or, less often, by number.

Some varieties can be grown from seed as long as they are sown early enough, and this usually means sowing under glass in midwinter in order to get a sufficiently long growing season. Another group, known as Japanese onions, has been developed for sowing as seed or for planting out as sets in autumn for harvesting earlier than sets planted out in spring.

Smaller bulb onions are either shallots or pickling onions. Pickling onions are small, round onions that are grown from seed.

There are over one hundred different varieties of onion available. They can be broken down into three basic types according to colour: golden-brown, red and white. Most are round, but some varieties are torpedo-shaped. The main criteria – unless you are growing for showing, when uniformity and appearance are important – are taste and storage qualities. Golden varieties are generally best for storing, but the reds and whites provide, respectively, sweeter and milder flavours.

Cultivation

Onions should be planted in an open position in a light soil that has been manured during the previous autumn. Plant the sets out in early spring.

Some varieties are heat treated, which prevents them from bolting, and they can be planted out later, in mid- to late spring when the soil is warmer. Plant them at 10cm/4in intervals in rows that are spaced about 30cm/12in apart. Plant with a dibber and cover the bulbs so that only the tips are showing.

Spring-sown seed can be sown in trays under glass in midwinter. Harden off and plant out in rows in mid-spring. Sow Japanese onions directly in beds in late summer or plant out as sets in early autumn.

Keep the plants weed free. There is generally no need to water unless the summer is particularly dry.

LEFT **The leaves of these onions are beginning to brown and have been moved to one side in order to speed up this process. This also allows maximum sunlight to reach the bulbs. Although not necessary, arranging the leaves in this way gives a satisfying beauty to a practical task.**

Cultivation

Sets
Planting time early spring (most varieties);
early summer (overwintering varieties)
Planting distance 10cm/4in
Distance between rows 25–30cm/10–12in
Harvesting late summer (most varieties);
midsummer (overwintering varieties)
Seed
Sowing time midwinter (under glass)
Sowing distance sow thinly
Sowing depth 1cm/½in
Distance between rows 25–30cm/10–12in
Thinning distance 5–10cm/2–4in
Harvesting late summer

RIGHT **Onions should be stored in trays in a frost-free shed.**

Harvesting

Onion bulbs can be lifted at any point in their growth for immediate use. However, for storage they must be fully developed, and the foliage should be beginning to die back. This is usually in late summer (midsummer for Japanese onions). As the foliage begins to turn yellow, lift each bulb slightly with a fork so that the roots start to break. Two weeks later carefully lift the bulbs. Clean off any soil and place them in a sunny, dry place to finish drying. A greenhouse is ideal, but if they are placed outside, move them under cover at night or if rain threatens.

Storage

Tie the onions into ropes or place them in net bags or on trays. Store them in a cool but frost-free place, such as a cellar, garage or shed. Check regularly, throwing out any that show signs of rotting.

Pests and diseases

The main pest is onion fly, whose maggots eat the onions, turning the leaves yellow and eventually killing them. Sets are less susceptible to onion fly than seed-grown onions are. Burn or destroy any affected bulbs. Onion eelworm produce distorted leaves. Again, burn or destroy affected plants.

Various fungal diseases, such as neck rot and white rot, can affect the bulbs. Destroy all infected bulbs.

Varieties

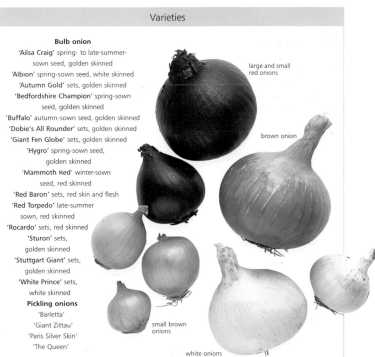

Bulb onion
'Ailsa Craig' spring- to late-summer-sown seed, golden skinned
'Albion' spring-sown seed, white skinned
'Autumn Gold' sets, golden skinned
'Bedfordshire Champion' spring-sown seed, golden skinned
'Buffalo' autumn-sown seed, golden skinned
'Dobie's All Rounder' sets, golden skinned
'Giant Fen Globe' sets, golden skinned
'Hygro' spring-sown seed, golden skinned
'Mammoth Red' winter-sown seed, red skinned
'Red Baron' sets, red skin and flesh
'Red Torpedo' late-summer sown, red skinned
'Rocardo' sets, red skinned
'Sturon' sets, golden skinned
'Stuttgart Giant' sets, golden skinned
'White Prince' sets, white skinned
Pickling onions
'Barletta'
'Giant Zittau'
'Paris Silver Skin'
'The Queen'

large and small red onions

brown onion

small brown onions

white onions

Shallots

Allium cepa Aggregatum Group

Shallots have been grown for almost as long as onions. They were originally named scallions after Ascalon (Ashqelon) in Israel, the place from where the Greeks thought the vegetable originated, but shallots probably originally came from Central Asia.

Shallots are widely used in cooking, especially in France, where small onions are preferred. Although they lack the strong smell of onions and do not make your eyes water, the taste is often more intense yet sweeter than that of onions, and they are used where delicate flavours are needed. The leaves are sometimes used as a substitute for chives, and in country areas shallots are often used as a substitute for pickling onions.

Shallots are a small form of onion, but instead of growing as single bulbs they tend to grow in bunches or clusters. The shapes and colours of shallots vary considerably, and France in particular has a great number of cultivars. Some are torpedo-shaped, others are rounded. The colour varies from yellows through browns to reds, and flavours range from delicate to strong.

Cultivation

An open, sunny position is required for growing shallots, and a light soil, which has been dug and manured during the previous autumn, is preferable. In the northern hemisphere the traditional day for planting shallots in many regions is

Plant the shallot bulbs in rows at 15–18cm/6–7in intervals with 30cm/12in between each row. Using a dibber or trowel, bury the bulbs so that only the tips are showing.

Boxing Day, but this is too early for most areas, and late winter or early spring is a better time. Set them out in rows, planting the individual bulbs at 15–18cm/6–7in intervals. Use a dibber or trowel, and bury the bulbs so that only the tips are showing. The rows should be 30cm/12in apart.

Keep weeded. Water in early summer if necessary.

Harvesting

When the foliage shrivels in midsummer, ease the shallots from the soil with a fork. Place them on staging in a greenhouse or on racks of wire netting to dry. Once the leaves have completely dried, remove any

LEFT **Rows of shallots with garlic growing in the background.**

BELOW **Shallots drying on netting in the sunshine before being stored.**

dirt and dead foliage and break them up into individual bulbs before leaving to dry further.

Storage

Place shallots on wire racks or trays or in netting bags. Store them in a dark, cool but frost-free place, such as a cellar or garage. They should keep through the winter. Check on them regularly and throw out any that show signs of rotting.

Pests and diseases

On the whole, shallots are relatively trouble free, but they may succumb to the same problems in terms of pests and diseases as onions. The main pest is likely to be onion eelworm, which produces distorted leaves. Onion fly may also be a problem. They lay their eggs in the bulbs, and the maggots then go on to eat the shallots, turning the leaves yellow and eventually killing them. Companion planting with parsley is a

ABOVE **A vigorous crop of young shallots with the individual bulbs just beginning to form.**

traditional deterrent. In both cases you will have to burn or destroy any infected bulbs.

Various fungal diseases, such as neck rot and white rot, can affect shallots. Burn or destroy all infected bulbs.

Cultivation

Planting time late winter to early spring
Planting distance 15–18cm/6–7in
Planting depth just below the surface
Distance between rows 30cm/12in
Harvesting midsummer

Varieties

'Atlantic' yellow skinned
'Delicato' red skinned
'Dutch Red' red skinned
'Dutch Yellow' yellow skinned
'Giant Red' red skinned
'Giant Yellow' yellow skinned
'Golden Gourmet' yellow skinned
'Hâtive de Niort' brown skinned
'Pikant' yellow skinned
'Sante' yellow skinned
'Success' red-brown skinned
'Topper' yellow skinned

shallots

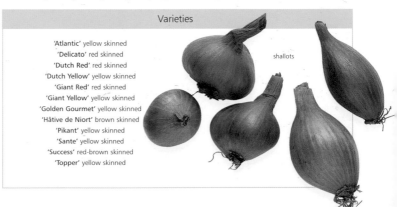

Garlic
Allium sativum

Garlic is a very individual form of onion, characterized by its distinctive smell and flavour. It is widely used throughout the world for cooking and medicinal purposes and has been so for thousands of years. It is thought to have originated in Central Asia, but it can no longer be found in the wild. Even in cultivation it has ceased to set seed, and existing cultivars are thought to be very old indeed.

ABOVE **Young garlic in spring before the bulbs begin to form.**

Garlic forms a bulb made up of numerous individual cloves. There are several different cultivars available worldwide, but they are very similar, the main differences being taste and pungency. The skins are usually white but can be tinged to a lesser or greater extent with purple. The only other differences are the size and number of cloves, hardiness and storage qualities. Garden-grown garlic is often bigger and more pungent than purchased bulbs.

Most seed merchants sell one or two varieties, sometimes just listed as "garlic bulbs". It is possible to plant bulbs purchased through a greengrocer or super-market, but sometimes these have been "treated" and fail to sprout or, if they do sprout, produce distorted leaves. It is, however, worth trying if you find a variety you particularly like.

BELOW **This is a healthy crop of garlic plants. Unlike onions, the garlic bulbs form out of sight below the ground.**

PLANTING

1 Use a dibber to make holes in the ground for each clove, at 10–15cm/ 4–6in intervals. A line of string will help you to keep the row straight.

2 Plant the cloves just below the surface, firming them in so that they are covered to their own height with soil.

RIGHT **Garlic can be started off by planting the cloves in individual pots.**

Cultivation

A sunny open position is required and, as with other members of the onion family, a light soil is preferred. Use soil that has been manured for a previous crop or, if you are planting in spring, dig in the manure in the preceding autumn.

If possible plant in mid- to late autumn. In colder districts, however, and in heavy cold soils it is better to wait until spring. Remove the outer skin and break the bulbs into individual cloves. Use a dibber to plant the cloves at 10–15cm/4–6in intervals, burying them so that they are covered to about their own height with soil. Alternatively, draw out a drill about 5cm/2in deep and plant the cloves in this at 10–15cm/4–6in intervals. Allow 30cm/12in between each row.

Keep well weeded, but avoid damaging the bulbs with the hoe.

Harvesting

Lift the bulbs when the leaves have turned yellow. Spread them out in a sunny place, preferably under cover – on greenhouse staging is ideal. When they have dried out thoroughly, remove any dirt and any long roots. If you are plaiting them or tying them in bunches, the leaves will need to be left on. If you are keeping them in net bags or trays, remove the dead foliage, leaving about 2.5cm/1in of stem.

Storage

Tie the stems together so that the garlic can be hung in bunches. A more sophisticated method is to plait the leaves together so that a chain of garlic is formed. Although these ropes of garlic are decorative, resist the temptation to hang them in the kitchen because the warmth and moist air will soon bring them into growth. Hang them in a cool, but frost-free, shed or cellar. Alternatively, place the garlic in trays and keep them in a similar position.

Pests and diseases

Garlic is relatively pest free. It can, however, suffer from various fungal or viral diseases. If the problem is a minor attack of rust, it can be ignored. If it is anything else, you will have to remove the bulbs, and burn or destroy them.

LEFT **A simple way of "stringing" garlic is to thread a stiff wire through the dry necks of the bulbs. The bulbs can also be tied on string.**

garlic

Varieties

Frequently just listed as garlic.
'Long Keeper'
'Long Keeper Improved'
'Marshall's Mediterranean'

Cultivation

Planting time mid-autumn (milder areas);
early spring (cold areas)
Planting distance 10–15cm/4–6in
Planting depth twice height of the clove
Distance between rows 30cm/12in
Harvesting mid- to late summer

Spring Onions (Scallions)
Allium cepa

Spring onions (scallions) are small onions that are eaten fresh; they are not dried. They produce small bulbs that are little more than a slight swelling at the base of the stem. The bulb and the base of the stem is white; the cylindrical leaves are green. A young form of large, bulbous onions, they originate from the same part of the world, Central Asia. They are called spring onions (scallions) because they are ready to eat in spring, unlike other onions, which do not mature until later in the year.

The Welsh onion is similar to spring onions (scallions) but derives from a different species, *Allium fistulosum*. It has little to do with Wales, since it has been introduced to the West only relatively recently, although it has been in cultivation in China since prehistoric times. It found its way westwards through Russia in the early 17th century, possibly picking up its name from the German *welsche* (foreign) on the way. Welsh onions are somewhat coarser in appearance than spring onions. They are perennials, rather like coarse chives, and the foliage can be used in the same way as that of chives.

Bunching onions are similar again and have been derived from Welsh onions. These can be used as annuals, like spring onions (scallions), or as perennials, like Welsh onions.

Spring onions (scallions) can be used in cooking but they are more frequently eaten raw, especially in salads. The leaves can be used as a substitute for chives, and the onions themselves are often used as a garnish. Welsh and bunching onions are used in much the same ways.

Many gardeners use shallots for pickling. However, there is also a special type of pickling onion (also called a cocktail onion) that can be grown. These are similar to spring onions (scallions) except that the bulb develops more fully. They are small, white-skinned onions. Like spring onions, they are grown from seed sown in the spring and are usually ready for harvesting after two months. They are treated in the same manner as spring onions and can be left unthinned for smaller bulbs or thinned for larger ones. The smaller ones can be used as a substitute for bulbous spring onions. Although usually pickled they can be stored like other bulbous onions.

Cultivation
Like the rest of the family, spring onions (scallions) need an open, sunny site. The soil should preferably be light, but they will grow in most soils as long as they are manured. Dig in manure in autumn for spring sowing. Sow the seed in spring and then at three-week intervals for a succession. Late summer sowings can be overwintered under cloches for an early spring crop.

Sow thinly in drills 1cm/½in deep and 15–20cm/6–8in apart. If sown thinly enough, there should be no need to thin. This is important because the smell of bruised plants that is caused by thinning attracts onion fly.

Spring onions (scallions) should be grown quickly or they become tough, so they will need watering in dry weather. Welsh onions are grown in the same way

ABOVE **Spring onions (scallions) can be pencil-slim or have a slight swelling at the base, forming a small bulb.**

but should be left in situ – only the leaves are cropped. Lift and divide every few years when the clumps get congested.

Harvesting
Spring onions (scallions) are ready for use at about eight weeks from sowing. Simply pull them from the ground. If the soil is compacted, they can be eased out with a hand fork.

Storage
Spring onions (scallions) cannot be stored for more than a few days. Keep in a cool place or in a refrigerator. The leaves can be chopped

THINNING

Although it is advisable to avoid thinning spring onions (scallions) where possible, it is often necessary to thin out congested rows.

HARVESTING

Spring onions (scallions) can be harvested either by pulling them from the ground by hand or, as is shown here, by gently forking them out.

and frozen, either in bags or in ice cubes, for use in winter in the same way as chives.

Pests and diseases

The main pest is onion fly, whose maggots eat the onions, turning the leaves yellow and eventually killing them. The dangerous period is when the onions are damaged by thinning or weeding because the flies smell the odour that is given off. Burn or destroy any affected onions. Onion eelworm produces distorted leaves. Again, burn or destroy affected plants.

Various fungal diseases can affect spring onions (scallions) but because their life is so short any diseased plants should be destroyed and a fresh start made in a new position in the garden.

ABOVE **Spring onions (scallions) that have been newly harvested.**

Cultivation

Sowing time early spring
Sowing distance sow thinly
Sowing depth 1cm/½in
Distance between rows 15–20cm/6–8in
Thinning distance avoid thinning if possible
Successional sowing three-week intervals
Harvesting eight weeks after sowing

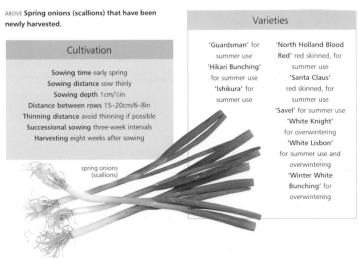

spring onions (scallions)

Varieties

'Guardsman' for summer use
'Hikari Bunching' for summer use
'Ishikura' for summer use

'North Holland Blood Red' red skinned, for summer use
'Santa Claus' red skinned, for summer use
'Savel' for summer use
'White Knight' for overwintering
'White Lisbon' for summer use and overwintering
'Winter White Bunching' for overwintering

Leeks
Allium porrum

Like most forms of onion, leeks have been grown since ancient times. They were probably derived from Allium ampeloprasum, which grows in the Near East and in countries of the Mediterranean littoral. Its traditional connection with Wales arose because Welshmen were said to have worn leeks in their hats in a battle against the Saxons in AD640 to distinguish them from their enemies.

Although leeks belong to the onion family, they do not have such a pronounced basal swelling nor the pungent flavour and smell of the other culinary members of the genus. They consist of cylinders of tightly wrapped leaves, white where they have been blanched and green above soil level. It is the white section that is mainly used. Unlike the other culinary onions, which are mainly used as flavourings, leeks are used as a vegetable in their own right in a wide range of dishes and soups. They can also be used, of course, as a simple vegetable accompaniment.

A wide range of varieties is available, some are hardier than others (those with bluer leaves tend to be hardier), and some are

1 Make a hole with a dibber and drop the plant in. Do not fill in the hole.

BELOW **A good block of leeks, with their rich green leaves, looks decorative in its own right.**

2 Fill each hole along the row with water.

ready earlier, while others stand better until spring. Some varieties have been bred specifically for their appearance on the show bench.

Cultivation

Leeks like an open, sunny position and a rich, fertile soil that is reasonably free draining. Dig well-rotted organic compost into the soil in autumn for planting in spring. Leeks like a long growing season, so start them off by sowing in nursery-bed rows in early to mid-spring. Sow thinly in drills 1cm/½in deep and 15cm/6in apart if you need more than one row. Transplant

Cultivation

Sowing time early to mid-spring
Sowing distance sow thinly
Sowing depth 1cm/½in
Distance between sown rows 15cm/6in
Planting distance 15cm/6in
Distance between planted rows 30cm/12in
Harvesting early autumn to late spring

when the seedlings are 15–20cm/6–8in high, which will be two or three months after sowing. Water the row the day before lifting and then dig out in batches with a hand fork. Plant into their permanent rows using a dibber. The plants should be 15cm/6in apart and the rows should be 30cm/12in apart. Make a hole about 15cm/6in deep and drop the leek in so that about 5cm/2in of the leaves show above the soil. Do not fill in the hole with soil, but fill it with water. This will wash sufficient soil around the roots.

As the leeks grow, earth (hill) them up by pulling soil up around the stems to blanch them. Alternatively, plant the leeks in the bottom of a trench and gradually fill the trench as the leeks grow. Keep weeded and watered in the early stages of growth.

Harvesting

Leeks can be lifted for use at any time between early autumn and late spring. Dig them out with a fork. Autumn varieties are not as hardy and should be harvested before midwinter.

Storage

Leeks are generally hardy and can be left in the ground until they are required. In cold areas they can be covered over with a cloche. They are best used fresh from the ground, but they can be dug several days before use and kept in a cool place. There is no method of storing leeks out of the ground. If the piece of ground they occupy is needed for some other purpose in the spring, then they can be lifted and heeled in elsewhere until they are needed. Simply dig a trench and insert the leeks to the same depth as they were in their original planting position. Dig them up as and when they are required.

EARTHING (HILLING) UP

Earth up the plants as they grow in order to blanch the stems. Alternatively, plant the leeks in a trench and fill it in as the plants grow.

Pests and diseases

Leeks are not usually troubled by pests and diseases. Rust is the most likely problem. Infected plants can be burned or destroyed; if the rust is not too severe it can be ignored, although it is best to plant leeks elsewhere for the next year. Other onion pests and diseases may occasionally be a problem; destroy any affected plants.

Varieties

Autumn
'Albinstar'
'Autumn Giant Startrack'
'Autumn Mammoth-Argenta'
'Elephant'
'Pancho'
Mid-season
'Carentan'
'Cortina'
'Grenvilliers-Splendid'
'King Richard'
Winter
'Alaska'
'Giant Winter-Cantalina'
'Giant Winter-Royal Favourite'
'Giant Winter-3'
'Kajak'
'Musselburgh'
'Wila'
'Yates Empire'

HARVESTING

Harvest the leeks by digging under them with a fork. As you do this, pull them from the ground with the other hand.

leeks

LEAF VEGETABLES

Cabbages
Brassica oleracea Capitata Group

Cabbage has been in cultivation for 3,000 years or so, but the cabbage as we know it today is a comparatively recent development, probably dating from the Middle Ages. Cabbage can be found growing in the wild throughout Europe, from Britain to Spain, but the wild form is more akin to broccoli than the hearted varieties with which we are now familiar.

Cabbages come in various forms, mainly depending on the time of year they are harvested – spring, summer, autumn and winter varieties are self-evidently named. These are all hearting cabbages, although spring cabbage is also available as "greens", which are loose heads of green leaves, unlike the typical tight heads of blanched leaves. There are also a few other winter varieties, which are sometimes considered separately, such as the savoys (with their distinctive, crinkly leaves), hybrids between the savoys and winter cabbages and 'January King'. The most distinctive of this group of cabbages is the red cabbage.

Some people have been put off cabbage by having to eat overcooked leaves, but it has always remained a staple winter vegetable for gardeners, especially in country areas, and nowadays it is enjoying a revival in popularity as people increasingly appreciate its culinary potential.

Cultivation
Cabbages do best in an open, sunny site in a soil that is fertile but reasonably free draining. They do not like a soil that is too acid, and acid soil may need liming to bring it to pH6.5–7. This should be done immediately after digging and before planting. Most gardeners sow cabbages in nursery beds and transplant them; others prefer to sow them in trays under glass; still others buy them as young plants from nurseries and garden centres. The methods are basically the same for all types; it is just the timing that varies.

Thinly sow seed in shallow drills about 1cm/½in deep. Thin seedlings if necessary to prevent them from becoming drawn. After about five weeks, when they have four or five leaves, transplant them to their final position. Final spacing depends on the type and size (see Cultivation). Plant using a dibber or trowel and firm the soil in well around the roots. Water well and keep watered until they have become established.

Spring cabbages can be sown in situ and initially thinned to 10cm/4in. In spring thin again to 30–38cm/12–15in.

Hoe regularly and keep free of weeds. Draw up some soil around the stems of overwintering varieties. Remove any dead leaves.

Harvesting
Cut the hearting cabbages when they have become firm. Use a knife to cut through the stem, just below the firm head but inside

ABOVE **This is a very well-grown specimen that would do as well on the show bench as it will on the kitchen table.**

any loose leaves. Savoy cabbages taste better if they are harvested after they have experienced at least one frost. The leaves of spring cabbages are cut as required, a few being left to heart up if required.

Storage
Most cabbages are winter hardy and can be left where they are until required. Those with solid heads can be cut and stored in a cool place, where they will keep for a couple of months. Some varieties of red cabbages may not be as hardy and can be harvested in early winter and stored.

PROTECTING YOUNG CABBAGES

Young cabbages need protecting from birds. Wire guards are light and easy to erect. They are also easy to store if they are made in short sections.

PREVENTING CABBAGE ROOT FLY

Cabbage root fly can be kept at bay by placing a felt or plastic collar around the base of the cabbage in order to stop the fly laying its eggs.

Cultivation

Spring cabbage
Sowing time late summer
Sowing distance sow thinly
Sowing depth 1cm/½in
Distance between sown rows 15cm/6in
Planting distance 30–38cm/12–15in
Distance between planted rows 50–60cm/20–24in
Harvesting spring

Summer cabbage
Sowing time early to mid-spring
Sowing distance sow thinly
Sowing depth 1cm/½in
Distance between sown rows 15cm/6in
Planting distance 35cm/14in
Distance between planted rows 60cm/24in
Harvesting midsummer onwards

Autumn cabbage
Sowing time late spring
Sowing distance sow thinly
Sowing depth 1cm/½in
Distance between sown rows 15cm/6in
Planting distance 50cm/20in
Distance between planted rows 60–75cm/24–30in
Harvesting autumn

Winter cabbage
Sowing time late spring
Sowing distance sow thinly
Sowing depth 1cm/½in
Distance between sown rows 15cm/6in
Planting distance 50cm/20in
Distance between planted rows 60–75cm/24–30in
Harvesting winter

Varieties

Spring cabbage
'April'
'Durham Early'
'Greensleeves'
'January King'
'Offenham 1-Myatt's'
'Offenham Compacta'
'Pixie'
'Spring Hero'

Summer cabbage
'Castello'
'Derby Day'
'Hispi'
'Minicole'
'Primo'
'Quickstep'

Autumn cabbage
'Autoro'
'Bingo'
'Castello'
'Minnicole'
'Rapier'
'Winnigstadt'

Winter cabbage and savoys
'Best of All'
'Capriccio'
'Celtic'
'Christmas Drumhead'
'Duncan'
'Hidena'
'Ice Queen'
'January King'
'Novusa'
'Ormskirk 1-Ormskirk Late'
'Tundra'
'Wivoy'

Red cabbage
'Kissendrup'
'Metro'
'Red Drumhead'
'Red Dutch'
'Ruby Ball'
'Vesta'

red cabbage

loose-leaf cabbage

Pests and diseases

Cabbage root fly are a nuisance, but they can be deterred by placing a collar of roofing felt or a similar material around the plant's stem. This prevents the adults from laying their eggs near the plant. Caterpillars are another problem. Cover the plants with netting or fleece to stop butterflies laying their eggs. Caterpillars can be removed by hand, but if you decide to spray, follow the manufacturer's instructions. Flea beetles make small holes in young leaves and should be prevented by dusting with the appropriate chemical. Slugs and snails should be controlled. The most serious disease is club root, which causes the roots to swell up. Any affected plants should be burned or destroyed. Liming helps to deter club root, as does growing cabbages in a different bed each year.

RIGHT **A block of cabbages in very good condition.**

Brussels Sprouts

Brassica oleracea Gemmifera Group

Cultivation
Sowing time early to mid-spring
Sowing distance sow thinly
Sowing depth 1cm/½in
Distance between sown rows 15cm/6in
Planting-out time when 13cm/5in high
Planting distance 50-75cm/20-30in
Distance between planted rows 75cm/30in
Harvesting mid-autumn to spring

Brussels sprouts are so called because they are thought to have originated in Belgium, where they are recorded as growing in the mid-18th century. By the beginning of the 19th century they had spread to France and Britain. Even after 200 years of cultivation, Brussels sprouts still seem to be an acquired taste. Not everybody likes them, and children in particular seem to find that they have too strong a taste. When cooked properly, however, they are a very tasty and valuable part of winter meals, and few would consider their Christmas dinner complete without a bowl of them.

Brussels sprouts are usually categorized according to season: early, mid and late. If plants are grown from each group, there can be a continuous crop from autumn right through to spring.

The sprouts themselves are the tight buds that form where the leaves join the main stem. As well as the sprouts, the succulent tops of the plants can be harvested once the sprouts are finished. The size of the plant varies according to cultivar, and some that have been bred as dwarf or compact plants are best suited to smaller gardens where space is at a premium. Another intriguing type is the red-leaved variety, 'Rubine', which is ideal for decorative kitchen gardens.

ABOVE **These Brussels sprouts are just beginning to develop. Soon the lower leaves will be removed, exposing the sprouts.**

Cultivation

An open position is required, but it should be protected from strong winds. The ground should be manured in autumn and limed if necessary to bring the acidity to within pH6.5–7. The seed can be sown in the open ground or started in trays under cover. For a late-summer picking, the seed should be sown in late winter or early spring – soil and weather conditions would generally mean that these seeds should be sown inside. For the more usual autumn-onwards harvest, sow in the open in early to mid-spring. Sow the earliest varieties first and the latest a few weeks later to make sure that they crop successfully. Sow thinly in shallow drills (see Cultivation). Plant out in the final position about five weeks after sowing, when the plants are about 13cm/5in tall. Plant the taller varieties at 75cm/30in intervals and the dwarfer forms at 50cm/20in intervals, with 75cm/30in between rows. Use a dibber or a trowel and firm the soil lightly around the plant. Water well.

Keep the plants well watered until they are established. Because there is such a large amount of space between plants they can be intercropped with a fast-growing crop such as radishes or lettuces. Keep the weeds down. If the site is exposed, stake the plants against the wind, and drawing soil up around the stems also helps. Remove the bottom leaves as they turn yellow.

Harvesting

Harvest when the Brussels sprouts are large enough to pick but while they are still tight. Start at the bottom of the plant, picking a few off each plant and snapping off each one with a downward twist. Move up the stems as the sprouts fill out. When all the sprouts are removed, pick the loose heads or tops and cook them as greens. Most gardeners prefer not to start harvesting until after the first frosts because this improves the flavour. As you harvest, remove any sprouts that have "blown" – that is, those that have not formed tight sprouts but are just a loose collection of leaves – and put them on the compost heap.

BELOW **Here, purple-leaved Brussels sprouts make an impromptu, but striking, combination with** *Dahlia* **'Bishop of Llandaff' on the other side of the fence.**

Storage

Brussels sprouts are hardy and can be left on the stems until they are required. They cannot be stored after picking for any length of time unless they are frozen. Freeze early maturing varieties before the weather damages the outer leaves. Choose only good quality, uniform sprouts for freezing.

Pests and diseases

Brussels sprouts are prone to the same problems as cabbages. The worst problem is clubroot. Aphids will also take shelter in the tightly packed sprouts.

ABOVE **This healthy block of Brussels sprouts has been planted with red cabbages to create a highly decorative effect.**

Brussels sprouts

Varieties	
Early	'Mallard'
'Lancelot'	'Roger'
'Oliver'	**Late**
'Peer Gynt'	'Fortress'
Mid-season	'Icarus'
'Bedford Fillbasket'	'Sheriff'
'Citadel'	'Trafalgar'
'Evesham Special'	'Widgeon'

Broccoli
Brassica oleracea Cymosa Group

Broccoli was developed from the wild cabbage in the 17th century in Italy, from where it spread through the rest of Europe. It is also known as sprouting broccoli or purple sprouting broccoli. Calabrese (Italian sprouting broccoli) and romanesco (Roman broccoli) are very closely related, but in the garden and kitchen they are considered separately because they grow at a different time of year and are cultivated in a slightly different way. In the past, gardeners also referred to winter cauliflowers as broccoli, and in some areas they may still do so.

Cultivation
Sowing time mid-spring
Sowing distance sow thinly
Sowing depth 1cm/½in
Distance between sown rows 15cm/6in
Planting-out time when 13cm/5in high
Planting distance 60cm/24in
Distance between planted rows 60–75cm/24–30in
Harvesting late winter to mid-spring

It is the flower shoots of broccoli that are gathered and eaten, just as the buds are forming and before the yellow of the opening flowers is seen. The flower-heads appear both at the top of the plant and as side shoots. In most varieties the flower-buds are purple – hence one of the alternative names, purple sprouting – but there are also creamy-white varieties, on which the flower-buds appear like miniature cauliflowers. The purple varieties are generally considered to be hardier than the white forms. There is one variety – 'Nine Star Perennial' – which, as its name suggests, is perennial in habit. If all the heads are picked each year it should last up to about five years, producing white heads each year.

In addition to the flower-heads, the stalk just below the buds and their associated leaves can also be eaten. Even more stalk may be eaten if the tougher outside is first removed.

The harvesting period for broccoli varies slightly, but it fills the "hungry" gap between late winter – 'Rudolph' is one of the earliest varieties – and mid-spring, when fresh vegetables are at a premium. The problem is that they are large plants and occupy the land for the best part of the year. Use the space between plants when they are first planted out for cultivating catch crops such as radishes. Each plant usually produces plenty of shoots and if space is very limited, it is worth growing just a couple of plants.

Cultivation
An open position is required, preferably one not buffeted by strong winds. The ground should be reasonably rich as well as manured in autumn and limed if necessary to bring the acidity to pH6.5–7. The seed can be sown in spring in the open ground or started in modules or trays under cover. Sow thinly in shallow drills 1cm/½in deep. If necessary, thin to 5cm/2in apart. Transplant the young broccoli when they are about 13cm/5in high. Water the row of plants the day before transplanting. Plant out the young broccoli at 60cm/24in intervals with the same distance between rows, using a dibber or trowel. Firm them in well with your heel and water.

Keep watered until they are established. Remove any weeds as soon as you notice them. In windy areas it may be necessary to stake the plants to prevent wind-rock. Earthing (hilling) up the stems will also help.

Harvesting
Depending on variety, harvesting starts in late winter to mid-spring. Snap or cut off the shoots as they begin to bud up but before they come into flower. Shoots should be about 15cm/6in long. Pick the shoots from all parts of the plant. Do not allow any to come into flower, or they will quickly run to seed and exhaust the plant.

Storage
Broccoli is perfectly hardy and should be left on the plant until required. It will not keep for more than a few days after picking, although it can be stood in a jug of water to keep it fresh or placed in a cool place such as a refrigerator. It can be stored for longer periods by freezing, a good way of coping with excess heads, which should always be picked and not left on the plant to flower.

Pests and diseases
Broccoli is susceptible to the same problems as cabbages.

LEFT **This purple-sprouting broccoli is now ready for cutting.**

Varieties	
'Claret' late season	'Purple Sprouting' mid- to late season
'Early Purple Sprouting' early to late season	'Rudolph' early season
'Nine Star Perennial' mid-season	'White Sprouting' mid- to late season

broccoli

Calabrese (Italian Sprouting Broccoli)

Brassica oleracea Italica Group

Although calabrese (Italian sprouting broccoli) is in many ways very similar to broccoli, it is usually considered as a separate vegetable. Its origins are the same: it originated in the countries of the eastern Mediterranean littoral and in Italy, before moving to the rest of Europe. It is sometimes known as Italian broccoli or American broccoli. A similar vegetable, which is usually bracketed with calabrese, is Romanesco (Roman broccoli).

Unlike broccoli, calabrese (Italian sprouting broccoli) is quick growing but not very hardy, and it is grown so that the edible heads, which are much larger than those of broccoli, are produced in late summer and autumn. Calabrese forms a large central head, rather like a loose cauliflower, and when this is picked, side shoots develop, each carrying a slightly smaller head. Not all varieties seem capable of producing side shoots, however, and these varieties are finished once the main head is picked. The colour is different from broccoli in that it has a blue-green tinge. Another major difference to broccoli is that it is important that growth should not be checked so it is sown where it is to grow and not transplanted.

Romanesco (Roman broccoli), which is sometimes known as green cauliflower, is similar to calabrese (Italian sprouting broccoli) and is, in fact, often listed as a variety of calabrese. The main difference is that it is hardier and can be grown to produce heads from late autumn into early winter, covering

at least part of the gap between calabrese and broccoli. Unlike calabrese and broccoli, romanesco only produces a single head and is then finished. The shape of the head is also different. It is distinctly conical-shaped, with little eruptions over the surface, creating further small whorls or pinnacles. It is an attractive plant, with yellowish, lime-green buds.

Cultivation

Sow in an open site in a fertile soil that has either been manured for a previous crop or manured during autumn digging. It is important to sow calabrese (Italian sprouting broccoli) and romanesco (Roman broccoli) where they are to mature, because they do not transplant well. Station sow in shallow drills about 1cm/½in deep at 30cm/12in intervals. Sow three seeds at each station. Rows should be 30cm/12in apart. Seeds can be sown closer together but this results in smaller heads. After germination, remove surplus seedlings so that only one, the strongest, remains at each station.

Keep well watered, especially in dry spells, so that the plants' growth is not checked. Keep them free of weeds.

Harvesting

Depending on variety, calabrese (Italian sprouting broccoli) is ready for harvesting from summer until well into autumn, usually 10–12 weeks after sowing. Romanesco (Roman broccoli) is ready from late autumn to the turn of the year or even later if protected with cloches.

Calabrese (Italian sprouting broccoli) first produces a single head, which should be cut while it is still tightly closed. Some varieties will subsequently produce side shoots with smaller heads. Romanesco (Roman broccoli) produces only one head, and when this is harvested the plant can be disposed of.

STATION SOWING

Calabrese (Italian sprouting broccoli) needs to be sown where it is to grow. Station sow the seed at intervals of 30cm/12in.

Cultivation
Calabrese (Italian sprouting broccoli)
Sowing time successional sowings from mid- to early summer
Sowing distance station sow at 30cm/12in
Sowing depth 1cm/½in
Distance between sown rows 30cm/12in
Harvesting late summer to autumn
Romanesco (Roman broccoli)
Sowing time early summer
Sowing distance station sow at 30cm/12in
Sowing depth 1cm/½in
Distance between sown rows 30cm/12in
Harvesting late autumn early winter (later if protected)

Storage

Neither calabrese (Italian sprouting broccoli) nor romanesco (Roman broccoli) keeps for more than a few days in a cool place and both are best eaten straight from the plant. They can be preserved for longer by freezing.

Pests and diseases

Both vegetables are susceptible to the same problems as cabbages.

Varieties	
Calabrese (Italian sprouting broccoli)	'Ramosa'
	'Trixie'
'Caravel'	**Romanesco**
'Corvet'	**(Roman broccoli)**
'Green Comet'	'Romanesco'
'Mercedes'	'Temple'

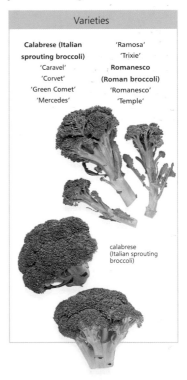

calabrese (Italian sprouting broccoli)

Kale

Brassica oleracea Acephala Group

Because kale is a leafy, rather than a headed, brassica, it is much closer than many of the others to the original wild cabbage, and it is, therefore, probably one of the oldest forms. There are several different types, because the name is used to refer to any leafy brassica, including a whole group of coloured varieties that are used purely as ornamental plants. The main edible group is the curly kales, which are also known as borecoles. Another group, particularly popular in the southern United States, is the plain-leaved collards.

It is important that kale plants are kept growing, so make sure that you do not let the soil dry out. Water well, as and when required.

Although kale is one of the least favourite of brassicas as far as culinary uses are concerned, it does fill the period in midwinter when there are very few fresh vegetables around. Kales are very hardy and withstand winter weather well, and they will also tolerate wet and even poor soil conditions.

The edible varieties are decorative and are often grown for that attribute rather than for their flavour. The leaves of the traditional curly kale are so curled that they

look like froth. In recent times the dark, narrow-leaved 'Nero di Toscana' (palm-tree cabbage) has become very popular for its visual qualities, and it is frequently seen in decorative potagers. In addition, there are some non-edible forms that are used purely as decoration both in the kitchen garden and in flower borders. Ornamental kales come in a wonderful range of purple, pinks, reds and creamy-whites. They are at their best in the winter when there is very little else of interest in the garden.

The leaves of kale are eaten, especially the young leaves from the centre of the

plant. Some of the resistance to eating kale arises from the fact that some kales are used as cattle and sheep fodder in winter. Some people dislike its strong flavour, which can be rather bitter if the leaves are not cooked properly. Cooked well, however, kale makes a very good winter dish and is well worth growing.

BELOW **This informal vegetable garden includes a block of young curly kale plants.**

Cultivation

Kale needs an open situation in which to grow. Although it prefers a fertile soil, it will grow in poorer soils than most other cabbages. If possible, however, incorporate manure when digging in autumn. Thinly sow the seed in late spring in the open ground in drills that are about 1cm/½in deep and 20cm/8in apart. Thin if necessary so that the young plants are about 5cm/2in apart. Transplant to their final positions when they are about 13cm/5in high. The final planting distances vary depending on the variety – for smaller varieties 45cm/18in will do, but the largest may need to be 60cm/24in apart. Allow 60cm/24in between the rows.

Kale needs to be kept steadily growing because it is slow to recover from any checks. It is, therefore, necessary to water during dry spells, especially when the plants are young. Weed regularly and remove any yellowing leaves.

Harvesting

With curly varieties, harvesting can begin in autumn and continue through winter and into spring. Pick the young leaves but do not strip plants, which will take time to recover. It is better to remove just a few leaves from each plant. In spring pick the emerging shoots before they come into flower. Leaves and shoots are picked simply by snapping them off.

Storage

Kale is extremely hardy, and the leaves can be left on the plants until required. It cannot be stored for any length of time, although it can be frozen for use between spring and the first of the summer vegetables.

Pests and diseases

Kale is generally the most pest free of all the brassicas, but it is still prone to the same problems as cabbages. Caterpillars can be a particular problem with autumn-picked varieties, especially because they hide within the curly leaves. Treatment with a spray or powder may help if it gets into the creases. Soaking the leaves in salted water before you cook them is a good way to remove caterpillars.

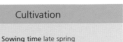

Cultivation

Sowing time late spring
Sowing distance sow thinly
Sowing depth 1cm/½in
Distance between sown rows 20cm/8in
Planting-out time when 13cm/5in high
Planting distance 45–60cm/18–24in
Distance between planted rows 60cm/24in
Harvesting autumn to mid-spring

HARVESTING

Narrow-leaved black kale is being harvested here by removing the younger, more succulent leaves.

Varieties

'Cottagers'
'Dwarf Blue Curled Scotch'
'Dwarf Green Curled'
'Fribor'
'Frosty'
'Hungry Gap'
'Nero di Toscana'
'Pentland Brig'
'Tall Green Curled'
'Thousandhead'

curly kale

Cauliflowers

Brassica oleracea Botrytis Group

Cauliflowers are not the easiest of crops to grow, but they are one of the most rewarding, both in a sense of achievement and in the eating. Like so many of our vegetables, their origins are rather obscure. The Romans are thought to have cultivated a type of cauliflower, but the vegetable as we know it today originated in the countries at the eastern end of the Mediterranean at a much later date. It was introduced into Italy in the late 15th century and finally reached Britain about a hundred years later. However it was another two hundred years before it came to be widely grown.

Cauliflowers are characterized by their large, dome-shaped heads of creamy-white flowers (which are generally known as "curds"). When well-grown, these should be tight, evenly shaped and unblemished. The typical cauliflower has creamy-white curds, but there are also other colours for those who want something a bit different. Purple is the most common alternative colour, but there are also various shades of green and orange, although most of these are not true cauliflowers but hybrids, often produced using broccoli. The heads are usually 15–20cm/6–8in across, but there are now modern hybrids, often known as mini-cauliflowers, which develop very quickly and have heads to only 10cm/4in or less across.

Cauliflowers must be firmed in well when they are planted. Plants in loose soil run to seed quickly.

For those with the space to grow them there are cauliflowers for almost every season of the year. The only gap comes in winter, because most of the so-called winter cauliflower are not, in fact, ready until spring.

Cauliflowers can be awkward to grow, but, with care and attention, all gardeners should be able to produce good-quality crops. The main factor is to make sure that the plants' growth is not checked, because this causes irregular and undersized curds. An irregular water supply can be one cause. Late transplanting may be another. The one aspect that is difficult for the gardener to control is high summer temperatures, which are not conducive to growing good cauliflowers, since they prefer cool conditions. In hot areas you may have to abandon the idea of summer cauliflowers and concentrate on winter varieties.

Cultivation

Cauliflowers should be planted in an open, sunny position. To grow cauliflowers well it is essential that you have a fertile soil, preferably manured during digging in autumn. The manure is important, because the soil should be moisture-retentive so that the plants are not checked during dry

LEFT **Harvest the cauliflower by cutting the stem with a sharp knife just below the first ring of leaves.**

periods. The soil must not be too acid; if possible adjust the pH level to 6.5–7 by liming in autumn.

Cauliflowers can be sown in the open ground or in modules or trays. They should be sown thinly in shallow drills about 1cm/½in deep and 20cm/8in apart. For the timing for the various seasons, check the Cultivation box. If necessary, thin the seedlings to about 5cm/2in apart. Transplant them when they have five leaves, which should be about six weeks after sowing. Water the rows of seedlings on the day and then transplant them using a dibber or trowel. Firm the soil around the plant down well with your heel. The planting distances vary from 50–75cm/ 20–30in, depending on the variety. compare Varieties with Cultivation box.

Keep cauliflowers well watered, especially in warm, dry spells. Once the curds begin to form, snap the larger outside leaves down over them to protect them. This will prevent discoloration.

Harvesting

The curds are ready when they form an even dome shape. Summer and autumn varieties mature in about 16 weeks from sowing and winter ones in about 40 weeks. Mini varieties are ready in about 15 weeks. When they are ready, cut through the stem with a sharp knife just below the head, leaving one or two leaves around the curd to protect it on its way to the kitchen. If you are storing them for a while, cut them so

PREVENTING SUN SCORCH........................

Protect the curds from discoloration by the sun by covering them with the inner leaves.

that they have a short length of stem from which you can hang them. If the leaves are occasionally sprayed with water, they will keep for several weeks in cool conditions.

Storage

In general, it is best to leave the cauliflowers on the plants until they are required, but they can be cut and placed in a cool place for up to three weeks. They store best if they are hung upside down, otherwise cauliflowers will freeze well.

Pests and diseases

Cauliflowers are susceptible to the same problems as cabbages.

cauliflower

Cultivation
Early summer
Sowing time midwinter
Sowing position under glass
Planting-out time spring, when 13cm/5in high
Planting distance 50cm/20in
Distance between planted rows 60cm/24in
Harvesting early to midsummer
Summer
Sowing time mid-spring
Sowing distance sow thinly
Sowing depth 1cm/½in
Distance between sown rows 20cm/8in
Planting-out time early summer, when 13cm/5in high
Planting distance 60cm/24in
Distance between planted rows 60–75cm/24–30in
Harvesting late summer
Autumn
Sowing time late spring
Sowing distance sow thinly
Sowing depth 1cm/½in
Distance between sown rows 20cm/8in
Planting-out time early summer, when 13cm/5in high
Planting distance 60cm/24in
Distance between planted rows 60–75cm/24–30in
Harvesting autumn
Winter
Sowing time late spring
Sowing distance sow thinly
Sowing depth 1cm/½in
Distance between sown rows 20cm/8in
Planting-out time summer, when 13cm/5in high
Planting distance 70–75cm/28–30in
Distance between planted rows 60–75cm/24–30in
Harvesting late winter to early spring
Mini-cauliflowers
Sowing time spring
Sowing distance station sow 15cm/6in
Sowing depth 1cm/½in
Distance between sown rows 45cm/18in
Harvesting late summer to autumn

Varieties		
Early summer and summer	**Late summer and autumn**	**Winter**
'All Year Round'	'All Year Round'	'Arcade'
'Alpha'	'Autumn Glory'	'Cappacio'
'Mayflower'	'Castlegrant'	'Early Feltham'
'Montana'	'Dok Elgon'	'Jerome'
'Snow Crown'	'Plana'	'Purple Cape'
'Snowball A'	'Violet Queen'	**Mini-cauliflowers**
'White Summer'	'Wallaby'	'Candid Charm'
		'Mini-Cauliflower King'

Spinach
Spinacia oleracea

Spinach is the bane of most children and many adults, and yet when it is cooked properly it is a magnificent vegetable and a key ingredient in many classic and modern dishes. Spinach is related to the beetroots (beets) and chards and not to the cabbages or lettuces, to which it bears a superficial resemblance. It was first cultivated in Asia by the Persians, and it spread along the trade routes to China and eventually to Spain by the 11th century. It was five centuries later that it arrived in Britain.

Spinach is really a plant for a cool climate. It dislikes hot, dry summers, when it will very quickly go to seed, often before it is fully developed and ready to harvest. However, if you make sure that your plants are properly watered and that you select cultivars that suit your area, you can produce a crop that should last for two or three weeks and, with successional cropping, this can be extended considerably.

The plants look rather like a loose lettuce, with stalked leaves rising from a central stem. When the plant bolts, this stem quickly elongates. Supplying the plant with plenty of moisture and nourishment can postpone the tendency to bolt.

Alternatives to spinach

Spinach has a relatively short life, especially in hot, dry summers, when it is likely to bolt, and so many gardeners (erroneously one can't help feeling) think it is not worth growing. There are other vegetables that are cooked in the same way as spinach and have the advantage of having a longer season. These are generally known as "perpetual spinach", and the chief of them is Swiss chard. Another good alternative is New Zealand spinach (*Tetragonia tetragonioides*), which is not related botanically to spinach but makes a good substitute, both in the garden and kitchen. It is grown as an annual, but unlike true spinach it can be picked throughout the summer months and also way into autumn. Sow in trays or modules under glass and plant out after the danger of frosts has passed. Alternatively, station sow at 45cm/18in intervals in shallow drills, 1cm/½in deep, where they are to grow, again after the last frosts. It is more tolerant of drought than spinach but it does best if

HARVESTING

Spinach is a very easy crop to harvest. When you require some, simply cut away the young leaves with a pair of sharp scissors.

LEFT **This beautifully maintained walled potager includes a healthy crop of spinach.**

watered during dry periods. Pinch out the tip to make it bush out and harvest the leaves when they are big enough. Carry on doing this for as long as the plants last. Do not allow them to set seed or they may self-sow and possibly keep coming up for several years.

The young leaves of red orache or red mountain spinach (*Atriplex hortensis*) can also be used in the same way. In spring, sow seed where they are to grow either in shallow drills or by broadcasting. Thin to 30cm/12in apart. It is worth growing in a potager for its decorative qualities alone.

Cultivation

Grow spinach in an open, sunny position but preferably one that does not get too hot. The soil should be fertile and contain as much organic material as possible so that it is moisture retentive. Permanently wet soils should be avoided, however. Dig in manure or compost in autumn.

Thinly sow the seed in early spring, with successional sowings at two-week intervals through to late spring. It is better to sow several short or part-rows at intervals than one long one if there is the possibility that most of the plants will run to seed before they are harvested. Sow in shallow drills, about 1cm/½in deep and 30cm/12in apart. As soon as the seedlings are big enough to handle, thin them out to 15cm/6in apart. Keep well watered and keep weeds under control.

A crop for overwintering can be sown in late summer or early autumn. This will benefit from being covered with cloches from autumn onwards. The cloches will not only protect the plants, but will keep the leaves tender.

Harvesting

Start harvesting as soon as the leaves are big enough, which is usually 8–12 weeks after sowing. Don't strip the plant, but just take a few leaves to start with and until the plants are mature. Break or cut the stems, but avoid pulling because this may loosen the plant and precipitate bolting. Continue harvesting until the plants start to run to seed – when the central stem starts to elongate. When harvesting winter spinach, do not overpick.

Storage

Spinach should be picked and used as fresh as possible because it does not store. The leaves can, however, be frozen.

Pests and diseases

Spinach should be grown so fast that there can be few problems (apart from bolting) and, in any case, there is little time for the gardener to satisfactorily correct any problems that do occur. The best solution in this case is to scrap the affected plants and start again.

To avoid slug damage, clear the ground of slugs before sowing and at regular intervals thereafter.

The most likely diseases to affect spinach are downy mildew (choose resistant varieties) and spinach blight. Destroy the affected plants.

Varieties	
Summer	**Winter**
'Bloomsdale'	'Broad-leafed Prickly'
'King of Denmark'	'Norvak'
'Long Standing'	'Sigmaleaf'
'Medana'	'Symphony'
'Monopa'	
'Melody'	
'Triathlon'	

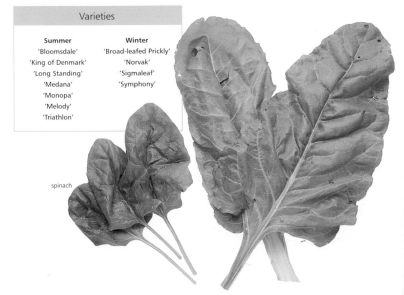

spinach

Swiss Chard
Beta vulgaris Cicla Group

Swiss chard has a number of alternative names, including chard and seakale beet. The red-stemmed forms are additionally known as rhubarb chard, red chard or ruby chard. Spinach beet or perpetual spinach is essentially the same but has thinner stems. Although it is called Swiss chard, the plant originates from around the Mediterranean and dates back long before the modern state of Switzerland was thought of. Both the Greeks and Romans grew chard including red-stemmed forms. Although not grown much in England until recently, it has been around since at least the 16th century.

ABOVE **The vibrant colour of the stems of Swiss chard can be relied upon to make a strong decorative statement in the kitchen garden.**

Swiss chard has large, glossy, dark green leaves on wide creamy-white stalks. Both parts can be eaten, although they are often cooked separately, because the stems take much longer than the leaves. Ruby chard is similar, but the stems are a brilliant red and the leaves are a deep purple-green in some varieties and green in others. A third variant are those with striped stems, which can be in a range of colours, including red, yellow and orange. All three versions are very decorative and can be used in any ornamental scheme. Unlike some other brightly coloured vegetables – ornamental kale, for example – these chards are eminently edible as well as being decorative.

Perpetual spinach is relatively dull in comparison. It has smaller, less shiny leaves and stems that have no ornamental value at all. However, it makes a very good alternative to spinach. Both are easy to grow and maintain and produce an abundance of leaves for harvesting over a long period. Both can be used as a straightforward vegetable dish or combined with ingredients to make something a bit more special.

Cultivation

Swiss chard and perpetual spinach need an open site and a fertile soil. Manure the soil while digging it in the autumn. Station sow the chard in spring in shallow drills 1cm/½in deep and 38cm/15in apart. The stations should be 45cm/18in apart for larger plants, although for smaller plants they can be closer together. For perpetual spinach the intervals should be 30cm/12in. Germination is rapid, within a few days. Thin out unwanted seedlings at each station. A sowing can be made in late summer to provide a crop that goes on until the following summer, thus together with the spring sowing, providing leaves all year round.

Water and keep weed free. Both can be sown in trays or modules and planted out when they have reached an adequate size, at the same intervals as above. In very cold areas it may be necessary to give the plants protection of cloches or fleece, but they are generally hardy enough to need no protection.

Harvesting

Both forms, the Swiss chard and perpetual spinach, are perpetual in that once they have matured (usually 8–12 weeks after sowing) leaves can be cut from them as you wish, right through from summer until the following spring when they are likely to start running to seed (Swiss chard in seed is a very decorative vegetable indeed, so do not be in too much of a hurry to get rid of it unless you desperately need the space). Snap or cut off the leaves at the

WINTER PROTECTION

In cold areas Swiss chard needs some form of winter protection. Any form of cloche or portable cold frame can be used.

HARVESTING

Swiss chard is harvested by cutting the stalks at the base with a sharp knife. Like perpetual spinach, it can be harvested from summer until the following spring.

base of the plant. Take the leaves as soon as they are big enough and continue to harvest them so that the outer leaves do not get too large and coarse.

Storage

Neither Swiss chard nor perpetual spinach stores well and should be cooked straight from the plant. Both can be frozen if necessary.

Pests and diseases

On the whole, both Swiss chard and perpetual spinach are pest and disease free. However, it is difficult to grow perfect Swiss chard (the leaves always seem to have holes in them), but while this may be

a problem on the show bench, once cut up in the kitchen, no one will notice, so it isn't something to worry too much about. Slugs, earwigs, caterpillars, flea beetles and birds may all be to blame, but apart from getting rid of the slugs there is little need for

ABOVE **This row of mixed colour Swiss chard is ready for harvesting.**

action. If planted too close together they may suffer from downy mildew, especially in a damp season.

ABOVE **A perfect specimen of Swiss chard, clearly showing the white ribs that can be cooked separately from the leaves.**

Varieties

Swiss chard	Perpetual spinach
'Argentata' deep green leaves, silvery white stems	No varieties normally simply listed as "Perpetual Spinach" or "Leaf Beet".
'Bright Lights' dark green leaves, red, pink, orange, creamy silver and yellow stems	
'Charlotte' purple-red leaves, bright red stems	
'Feurio' red leaves, red stems	
'Fordhook Giant' deep green leaves, white stems	
'Lucullus' pale green, ruffled leaves, white stems	
'Rainbow Chard' red, pink, orange, creamy silver or yellow stems.	
Sometimes listed simply as "Swiss Chard" (with white stems) or "Rhubarb Chard" (with red stems) with no varietal name given.	

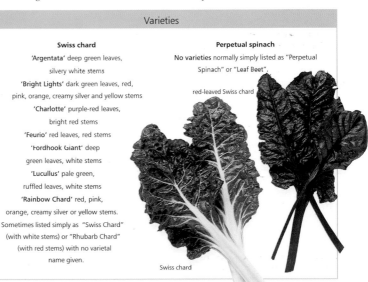

red-leaved Swiss chard

Swiss chard

Chinese Cabbage
Brassica rapa var. *pekinensis*

Chinese cabbage is rather like a cos (romaine) lettuce, with crisp, crunchy leaves that can be eaten either raw or cooked. It is also a convenient name under which to group several other oriental greens, such as pak choi (bok choy) and mizuna, in which gardeners are becoming increasingly interested.

Chinese cabbage has been developed over centuries, particulary in China, since it was first recorded in the 5th century. It had reached America by the end of the 19th century but had to wait until the last decades of the 20th century before it arrived in Europe.

The original Chinese cabbages were loose headed, but the varieties we grow today are mainly hard headed and mostly derive from cultivars raised in Japan. They are tightly packed with dense leaves, which are a very pale creamy-yellow, blanched through lack of light, and sweet tasting. They last well if kept cool after harvesting, and one head seems to last several days of liberal helpings as a salad leaf. It can also be cooked, but its delicate flavour can be lost or overpowered by stronger flavours if the cook is not careful. Not many new vegetables have been introduced into gardens in the last couple of hundred years, but this one is most welcome.

Other new introductions have also appeared from the Far East, although they are perhaps not as popular as Chinese cabbage. Pak choi (bok choy; *Brassica rapa* var. *chinensis*) is one such. The common varieties are looser headed than the more commonly grown forms of Chinese cabbage and look more like a small Swiss chard, with dark green leaves and wide white stems. There is more flavour in pak choi (bok choy) than in Chinese leaves. They can be used raw or cooked.

Another plant that is creating increasing interest is mizuna (*Brassica rapa* var. *nipposinica*), which originated in Japan. This is unlike other greens in that the leaves are feathery, which makes them

ABOVE **Young pak choi (bok choy) planted in a block, ready for harvesting. They can be cut on a cut-and-come-again basis.**

useful for the decorative kitchen garden as well as the purely productive one. They, too, can be cooked or used in salads.

Cultivation

As with most vegetables, Chinese cabbage and other oriental greens like an open position and a fertile soil that is moisture retentive. Dig in plenty of well-rotted organic material during autumn digging. They do not do well on poor soils. Sowing in the open is best because they resent disturbance, which may cause bolting. They will also bolt if sown too early. Sow in early to midsummer in shallow drills 1cm/½in deep and 25cm/10in apart. Station sow the seed at 30cm/12in intervals, or sow thinly and thin to that distance. Take care not to disturb the roots too much when transplanting, and to avoid this, seed can be sown in modules. Keep weeded and well watered at all times.

LEFT **Like the original Chinese cabbages, this specimen is loose-headed.**

Cultivation

Chinese cabbage
Sowing time early summer
Sowing distance station sow at 30cm/12in
Sowing depth 1cm/½in
Distance between sown rows 25cm/10in
Harvesting late summer to late autumn

Pak choi (bok choy)
Sowing time late spring
Sowing distance thinly
Sowing depth 1cm/½in
Distance between sown rows
15cm/8in–45cm/18in
Harvesting summer to late autumn

Mizuna
Sowing time spring
Sowing distance thinly
Sowing depth 1cm/½in
Distance between sown rows 38cm/15in
Thinning distance 15–45cm/6–18in
Harvesting summer to winter

RIGHT **The hard-headed Chinese cabbage is derived mainly from cultivars raised in Japan.**

Similar sowing conditions prevail for pak choi (bok choy), which can be sown a bit earlier as it is slightly less prone to bolt. Sowing distances vary from about 15cm/6in for smaller varieties to 45cm/18in for the larger. Mizuna, which does not bolt, can be sown at any time during the season, and it can be easily transplanted from seed trays if so desired. The spacing is the same as for pak choi. It can be harvested in winter from a late summer sowing, although it does best with some form of winter protection.

Harvesting

Chinese cabbage is ready to harvest after about seven weeks and can be cut as required through until late autumn. It can also be cut on a cut-and-come-again basis at a much earlier stage. However, it is more usual to remove the whole head by cutting just below the lowest leaves. If the stump is left in the ground, more leaves may develop, and these can be harvested as required.

Leaves of pak choi (bok choy) can be cut at any stage once they are big enough, usually after about three weeks. Whole heads can be removed when ready and the stumps left to reshoot. Flower-heads can also be eaten. Mizuna leaves can be cut at any stage from three weeks onwards, although the older leaves are not as succulent. The flower stalks can be eaten.

Storage

Chinese cabbage and other oriental greens should be used fresh from the garden.

Pests and diseases

The main pests are likely to be slugs, snails and caterpillars. Apart from these, there are usually not too many problems, although Chinese cabbage and the other oriental greens can be prone to any of the cabbage diseases.

Varieties

Chinese cabbage
'China Express'
'Eskimo'
'Harmony'
'Jade Pagoda'
'Kasumi'
'Mariko'
'Michihili'
'Tip Top'

Pak choi (bok choy)
Frequently listed simply as pak choi/bok choy.
'Joi Choi'
'Mei Quing'
'Shanghei'
'Tai-Sai'

Mizuna
Usually listed simply as mizuna greens.

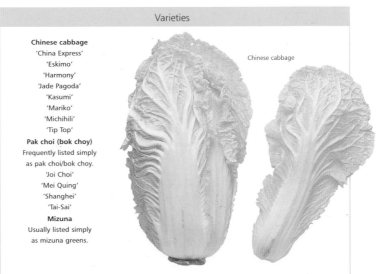

Chinese cabbage

Chinese cabbage

Lettuce
Latuca sativa

Lettuce is an odd vegetable, which is as often used for decorative purposes as for taste and nutrition. Shop-bought lettuces have much to answer for in this respect, as are the oft-repeated scare stories about their being full of chemicals. Home-grown lettuces not only have flavour, but you also know what they have been fed on. Another advantage of growing your own lettuces is that you can grow several different types and colours so that you can make a really attractive salad – and, of course, they are fresh. You can pick just as many leaves as you want right at the last minute.

ABOVE **A block of developing lettuces shows how decorative this varied crop can be.**

Lettuces have been popular for a long time and were even depicted in carvings and paintings in Ancient Egypt. They were popular among the Romans, who are reputed to have introduced them to Britain. The original lettuces were probably quite bitter and needed blanching to make them palatable, much like endives today.

Modern gardeners are fortunate in having so many different types as well as a wide range of varieties. The main type is the cabbage or headed lettuce. These are either loose balls of soft leaves – butterhead lettuces – or those with much firmer, crinkly-edged leaves – crispheads. Cos or romaine lettuces are more upright and have long, crisp leaves and a succulent heart. Then there are the loose-leaved or non-heading varieties, which do not produce a heart but just a mass of loose, individual leaves. These lettuces are very good when you want to be able to take leaves as and when you require them. There has recently been a great deal of interest in these cut-and-come-again lettuces, and many new varieties have appeared. This method of growing lettuces is far from new, however.

The mainstay of salads, lettuce is usually eaten raw, although an increasing number of recipes include cooked lettuce. Lettuce leaves are also widely used as a garnish, for which the coloured forms of the loose-leaved varieties are particularly useful. There is now quite a wide range of red- and bronze-leaved forms, as well as green forms with decorative leaves.

Lettuces are not difficult to grow and, in theory, can be harvested all year round, but some type of protection is required for winter varieties. They grow relatively quickly and will be ready from 5 to 12 weeks after sowing, depending on the variety. This means that they can be grown among slower growing crops or used to replace another crop that has already been harvested.

Cultivation

Lettuces need an open, sunny position, although light, partial shade during the heat of the day can be an advantage in hot areas or during hot summers. The soil needs to be fertile and, preferably, moisture retentive, and this is best achieved by incorporating plenty of manure during the autumn dig. Lettuces can be sown straight in the ground or grown in trays and transplanted. It is a good idea to sow a short row of lettuces and then, instead of throwing away the thinnings, to transplant them to make up the rest of the row. The advantage of this is that the transplants will take a few days to settle down and will produce a slightly later crop than the sown plants. If the whole row is sown at once, the lettuces will mature at the same time, which will probably mean that many are wasted.

Transplanting is difficult after midsummer, because lettuces often rapidly run to seed.

Start early sowings in trays or modules under glass in late winter or early spring. Plant these out under cloches or in cold frames to get an early crop. Seed can be sown directly in the soil from early spring onwards. Sow in shallow drills 1cm/½in deep, each row about 30cm/12in apart. Thin the lettuces to 15–30cm/6–12in apart, depending on the size of the variety. Transplanted lettuces should be planted at the same distances. Keep the soil moist and do not allow the plants' growth to be checked or they will rapidly run to seed. Sowings after midsummer will provide lettuces for autumn and early winter, but cover them with cloches when necessary from around mid-autumn. Special winter varieties can be overwintered under cloches or grown in greenhouses or in cold frames.

Harvesting

Lettuces can be harvested whole or leaves can be taken from the plants as required. The loose-leaved varieties are usually picked leaf by leaf, but cabbage-type varieties can be picked in the same way if you wish. Hearted varieties are usually ready for harvesting as soon as they feel plump and firm. Do not leave them too long in the

HARVESTING

Harvest lettuces when the "heart" feels firm.

ground after maturing or they may bolt. Pull the whole lettuce from the ground or cut below the bottom leaves if you want the plant to resprout. Loose-leaved varieties mature earlier, and leaves can be picked as soon as they are large enough, which is usually from about seven weeks after sowing.

Storage

Whole lettuces can be kept in a refrigerator for a short time, but they are best used straight from the garden.

Pests and diseases

Slugs and greenfly (aphids) are two of the worst problems and should be dealt with by your preferred methods. Other pests can include root aphids and cutworms.

The main disease is downy mildew, and lettuces also tend to suffer from a few other fungal diseases. These occur mainly in wet seasons and are best avoided by making sure that individual lettuces are not planted too close together. This will ensure that there is plenty of air movement around the

ABOVE **A block of decorative lettuces, showing the rich variety of colours available.**

plants. If pests or diseases do get out of control, do not spend a lot of time and money on chemical control. Simply get rid of the plants and start again.

Cultivation
Sowing time late winter (under glass) to early spring onwards
Sowing distance thinly
Sowing depth 1cm/½in
Distance between sown rows 30cm/12in
Thinning distance 15–30cm/6–12in
Harvesting early summer onwards

Varieties			
Butterhead	**Cos**	'Lobjoits Green Cos'	'Lollo Rosso'
'Avondefiance'	'Balloon'	'Paris White'	'Red Fire'
'Buttercrunch'	'Bubbles'	'Wallop'	'Red Sails'
'Continuity'	'Corsair'	**Loose-leaved**	'Redina'
'Dolly'	'Little Gem'	'Cerise'	'Salad Bowl'
'Hilde II'		'Cocarde'	**Winter**
'Musette'		'Frisby'	'Arctic King'
'Sabine'			'Kellys'
'Tom Thumb'			'Novita'
Crisphead			'Valdor'
'Avoncrisp'			'Winter Density'
'Beatrice'			
'Iceberg'			
'Lake Nayah'			
'Malika'			
'Minetto'			
'Saladin'			
'Warpath'			
'Webb's Wonderful'			

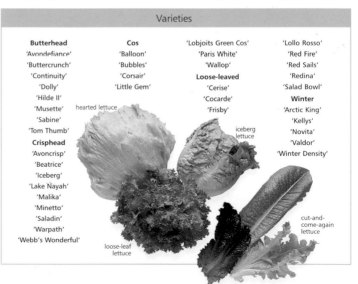

hearted lettuce

iceberg lettuce

loose-leaf lettuce

cut-and-come-again lettuce

Salad Leaves

*Although lettuces, perhaps supplemented by leaves such as endives
and chicory, provide the traditional greenery for most salads,
there is an increasing number of small leaves that play their part.
Some are available during the winter months, when lettuce from the
garden may be scarce, and as well as adding bulk, each adds an
individual flavour to pep up the overall interest of the salad. The two
most important of these salad leaves are rocket (arugula; Eruca
vesicaria), which is also known as salad rocket, rucola and Italian
cress, and lamb's lettuce (mâche; Valerianella locusta), which is
also known as corn salad.*

ABOVE **Chinese leaf mustard, in this case the variety
is 'Red Giant', will add a zing to any salad with
its pungent flavour.**

Neither rocket (arugula) nor lamb's
lettuce (mâche) is new – indeed, both
have been eaten for centuries – but their
popularity seems to be on the increase,
particularly in the United States, where
numerous varieties are available. The choice
is also increasing in Europe, where it has
always been particularly popular in France,
from where many of the varieties come.

Young rocket (arugula) leaves have a
sharp taste, and the older the leaves, the
hotter and spicier the taste. They are usually
eaten raw in salads, but older leaves are
sometimes cooked, and the flowers can be
eaten too. They make an excellent winter
crop. Lamb's lettuce (mâche) is also used as
a winter crop. The leaves are milder than
those of rocket, and it is also much slower
growing, taking up to 12
weeks before being ready to
cut, compared with three
weeks for rocket.

Several other leaves can
be grown, each needing
similar cultivation to rocket
(arugula) and lamb's lettuce
(mâche). The leaves of land
cress (*Barbarea verna*) have a
similar flavour to watercress.
Mustard (*Brassica hirta*) and the similar
tasting salad rape (*Brassica napus*) are also
worth growing. Cress (*Lepidium sativum*),
also known as garden or curly cress, can be
grown to complement the other leaves, and
winter purslane (*Claytonia perfoliata*) is
another mild leaf for the salad bowl.

Cultivation

All these salad leaves are plants for a cool
climate and will rapidly run to seed in
hotter areas. Because of this and because
other salad materials are scarce at that
time, they are mainly grown for autumn
and winter use. In cooler areas they can be
sown in spring for summer use. Although
they are hardy, they need to be protected by
cloches to be at their best.

Both rocket (arugula) and lamb's lettuce
(mâche) are sown in late summer; rocket
can also be sown in early autumn. Sow in
drills 1cm/½in deep and 30cm/12in apart.
Thin the resulting seedlings to 15cm/6in
apart for rocket and 10cm/4in for lamb's
lettuce. Keep lettuces watered if the
weather is dry. Cover with cloches in late
autumn or early winter.

LEFT **Land cress, often known as upland cress, is
similar in taste to watercress and is often used as
a land-grown substitute. This makes a welcome
contribution to most salads.**

Cultivation

Rocket (arugula)
Sowing time late summer to early autumn
Sowing distance thinly
Sowing depth 1cm/½in
Distance between sown rows 30cm/12in
Thinning distance 15cm/6in
Harvesting late autumn onwards
Lamb's lettuce (mâche)
Sowing time late summer
Sowing distance thinly
Sowing depth 1cm/½in
Distance between sown rows 30cm/12in
Thinning distance 10cm/4in
Harvesting winter

Harvesting

Either pick individual leaves or cut off the lot as soon as they are large enough. They will sprout again.

Storage

Both plants should be picked as required because they will not store.

Pests and diseases

Both plants should be free of both pests and diseases, although rocket (arugula) may be attacked by flea beetle. If the tell-tale marks appear on the leaves, dust with derris.

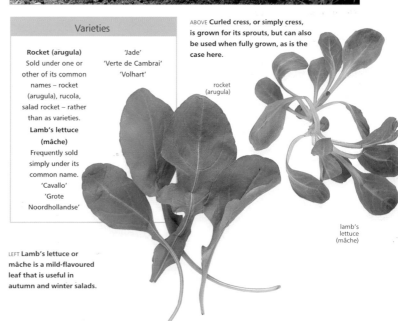

Varieties

Rocket (arugula)
Sold under one or other of its common names – rocket (arugula), rucola, salad rocket – rather than as varieties.
Lamb's lettuce (mâche)
Frequently sold simply under its common name.
'Cavallo'
'Grote Noordhollandse'

'Jade'
'Verte de Cambrai'
'Volhart'

ABOVE **Curled cress, or simply cress, is grown for its sprouts, but can also be used when fully grown, as is the case here.**

rocket (arugula)

lamb's lettuce (mâche)

LEFT **Lamb's lettuce or mâche is a mild-flavoured leaf that is useful in autumn and winter salads.**

Endives
Cichorium endivia

Endives and chicory (Cichorium intybus) are very closely related. So close, in fact that they can often be confused. The confusion is not helped by the fact that in France endive refers to what an English-speaking gardener would call chicory, while chicorée frisée is, in fact, the frilly-leaved form of endive. When it comes to growing them in the garden, however, there is rarely any confusion.

There are two main types of endive. Curly endive is a flat-growing plant with frilly leaves; it is not very hardy and is mainly grown as a summer salad vegetable. Batavian endive or escarole is a more upright plant, with broad, wavy (rather than frilly) leaves. It is much hardier than curly endive and is, therefore, the type to choose for winter growing, although in milder areas both can be grown. Both types are annuals, unlike chicory which is a perennial.

Endives have been used as a salad vegetable for many centuries – in fact, civilizations as far back as the Ancient Egyptians are known to have enjoyed them. They are thought to have originated somewhere in the Near East but have long been grown in southern Europe, before eventually moving northwards.

They are still not cultivated as widely as lettuces, probably because they have a rather bitter taste, which deters many people from growing them. The flavour can be dramatically improved, however, by blanching the leaves and the bitterness is more intense in hot conditions, so it is worth remembering that summer varieties are likely to have a sharper taste than the winter ones. This bitter taste contrasts well with other flavours in a mixed leaf salad.

One advantage that endives have over lettuce is that some varieties can be used in winter when lettuces are scarce. In summer, particularly in late summer,

ABOVE **These curly-leaved endives, whose foliage creates a textured effect, have been grown in a block rather than in rows.**

endives have the added advantage that they are less likely to bolt in dry weather, and they are also less prone to diseases, making them a reliable choice all the year round for the vegetable garden.

Cultivation
Endives generally prefer an open, sunny position, but in very hot areas they will benefit from a little light shade. The soil should be fertile and moisture retentive. Both curly-leaved and broad-leaved forms can be sown in open soil from spring onwards, and broad-leaved forms can also be sown in late summer for winter cropping. Sow in shallow drills 1cm/½in deep and 38cm/15in apart. When the seedlings appear, thin them to 25cm/10in apart for curly varieties and 38cm/15in for broad-leaved forms. Make sure that the soil does not dry out because it is very important not to check their growth.

LEFT **Broad-leaved endives or escaroles are more cold-tolerant than the curly-leaved varieties.**

Cover the winter varieties with cloches at the onset of winter. Alternatively, they can be grown in a greenhouse or covered cold frame.

Curly-leaved forms can be blanched by slipping a porous pot (terracotta is best) over the plant for about a week in summer or for up to three weeks in the colder weather of autumn and winter. Cover only a few plants at a time because they do not keep for long under these conditions. Place the cover over them when the leaves of the plant are dry. The taller broad-leaved varieties can also be covered, but it is often enough simply to tie the plant with raffia or soft string so that the outer leaves exclude the light from the inner ones.

Harvesting

Cut the blanched plants as required. Both can either be cut complete or just a few leaves can be used. The cut stalks will reshoot.

Storage

Neither form stores well and should be cut as required.

Pests and diseases

On the whole both forms of endive are trouble free. The most likely problem to occur will be attacks from slugs and snails, especially during the blanching process. Place a few slug pellets under the cover or lift it regularly and remove any slugs or snails that you find.

TOP **The leaves of endives can be used in salads or cooked. Unblanched leaves like these are more bitter than blanched ones.**

ABOVE **Blanching makes the leaves of endives taste sweeter. A plate laid over the centre of the plant is one way to achieve this.**

Varieties

Curly-leaved	Broad-leaved
'De Ruffec'	'Batavian'
'Frisée de Namur'	Broad-leaved'
'Green Curled'	'Batavian Green'
'Monaco'	'Cornet de Bordeaux'
'Moss Curled'	'Full Heart Italian'
'Riccia Pancalieri'	'Golda'
'Wallone'	'Stratego'

curly-leaved endive

Chicory
Cichorium intybus

Although it is very closely related to the endive, chicory is quite distinct, both in the kitchen and the garden. Both vegetables are salad leaves, both can be bitter and both are useful as winter vegetables, but whereas endive is an annual, chicory is a perennial, even though it is often grown as an annual.

ABOVE **The Witloof or Belgian chicories are mainly grown for their chicons, but the leaves can also be eaten.**

Chicory dates from at least Roman times, when it was eaten as a salad leaf and a cooked vegetable. It has always been most widely used in Italy, which still grows more varieties than most countries. Left unharvested, chicory produces blue dandelion-like flowers, which set plenty of seed. The seeds spread easily, and chicory has become naturalized in many places, including North America, where it did not formerly grow.

As with endive and lettuce, the name chicory is, in fact, used to describe several distinct types. The best known is probably Witloof or Belgian chicory, which has green edible leaves but is grown mainly for the tight-leaved shoot or "chicon". This is produced in winter by blanching and can be used raw in salads or cooked.

Another type is the sugar loaf chicory, which has an upright head, looking rather like a cos (romaine) lettuce. Its large outer leaves envelop the inner ones, so that these are blanched naturally and thus lose some of their bitterness. Sugar loaf chicory is usually harvested from late summer onwards and can be used as a winter crop if given protection.

Radicchio or red-leaved chicory is another group. Unlike the sugar loaf type, this is a low-growing plant, but again, the outer leaves protect the tight, crisp heart, thus blanching it naturally and improving the taste. As well as flavour, radicchio adds colour to winter salads. It is harvested in the autumn and on through winter if given protection.

Traditionally, chicory has also been grown for its root, which has been used, roasted and ground, to bulk up coffee. Today few gardeners grow chicory for this purpose, although there is no reason why they should not.

Although it is not a chicory, dandelion (*Taraxacum officinale*) is often treated and eaten in exactly the same way, with the blanched leaves providing salad material. Sow in spring, removing any flower-heads that subsequently appear. Early in the following spring, cover and blanch the leaves. Keep the plants for another year or discard and start again.

Cultivation

Grow chicory in an open, sunny position. Although it will grow in any soil, it does best in fertile ground, into which manure has been incorporated during the previous autumn. Sow Witloof chicory in late spring or early summer in drills 1cm/½in deep and 30cm/12in apart. Thin the subsequent seedlings to about 15cm/6in. Remove any flowering stems.

To blanch chicory cut off all the leaves in late autumn and cover the remaining stumps with 15cm/6in of free-draining soil or compost (soil mix). The chicons are ready to pick as they appear. To blanch them indoors, lift a few roots from late autumn onwards. Cut off the leaves and trim back the base of the roots so that they fit into a 23cm/9in pot. Put three or four roots in the pot and fill with damp compost so that just the tops show. Cover with another pot or a bucket and place in a dark, preferably warm place. The chicons should be ready in about three weeks. Cut and cover again to get a second crop.

Sow sugar loaf from spring to late summer in 1cm/½in drills set 30cm/12in apart. Thin to 25cm/10in. Do not allow soil to dry out.

Radicchio can be sown in a similar way from early to midsummer. Thinning should be the same, although some of the larger

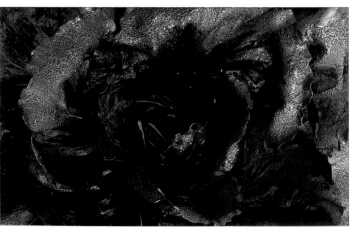

LEFT **Radicchio or red-leaved chicory produces a tight, self-blanching head that can be eaten like a lettuce.**

ABOVE **Radicchio chicories do not need the same care as Witloof or Belgian chicories.**

varieties may need more space. Protect with cloches once winter arrives.

Harvesting

Chicons should be cut complete when they are about 15cm/6in long. Harvest individual leaves of other forms as required or remove the complete head. The inner leaves are always the sweetest.

Storage

Chicory does not store well, so cut as needed. They can be kept for a few days in a refrigerator but wrap them so that no light reaches them or they will turn green and become bitter.

Pests and diseases

Slugs and snails are likely to be the only problem.

Cultivation

Witloof
Sowing time spring to early summer
Sowing distance thinly
Sowing depth 1cm/½in
Distance between sown rows 30cm/12in
Thinning distance 15cm/6in
Harvesting late autumn and winter

Sugar loaf
Sowing time spring to summer
Sowing distance thinly
Sowing depth 1cm/½in
Distance between sown rows 30cm/12in
Thinning distance 25cm/10in
Harvesting autumn

Radicchio
Sowing time early to midsummer
Sowing distance thinly
Sowing depth 1cm/½in
Distance between sown rows 38cm/15in
Thinning distance 25–30cm/10–12in
Harvesting late autumn to winter

Varieties

Witloof
'Normato'
'Witloof'
'Witloof Zoom'
Sugar loaf
'Bianca di Milano'
'Crystal Head'
'Poncho'
'Snowflake'

'Sugar Loaf'
'Winter Fare'
Radicchio
'Cesare'
'Medusa'
'Palla Rossa Zorzi Precoce'
'Rossa di Treviso'
'Rossa di Verona'

Witloof chicons

ROOT CROPS

Parsnips
Pastinaca sativa

Parsnips were developed in Europe from the widespread wild parsnip. It is possible that the Greeks and Romans cultivated them, but there is confusion over whether they were referring to parsnips or carrots in their writings. However, parsnips were certainly being eaten in Europe in the Middle Ages, although they subsequently went into something of a decline (except as cattle food), and it is principally in Britain where they remain popular. Parsnips have always been part of country fare, but they are now regaining a rightful place as vegetables for discerning palates.

ABOVE **Parsnips can be left in the ground until they are required.**

There is not much to see of the parsnip above ground, except for its inedible leaves. It is the large, swollen root that is the part that is eaten. Some varieties, especially when they are in light, fertile soil, can grow very big, to 45cm/18in or even longer. For most purposes, however, smaller roots are more than adequate.

There are more than 30 different varieties of parsnip. They differ little from each other, although some are more resistant to canker, while others have less hard cores. Certainly, none is more decorative than any other, either in the garden or on the plate. Ultimately, your choice of variety will be based on which grows best for you and which taste you prefer, although, in truth, there is not a great deal of difference.

Cultivation
An open, sunny position is required. Parsnips can be grown in heavy soils, but they prefer light ones, and although they do best in a fertile soil, do not sow them on freshly manured ground (the parsnips fork). Sow in soil that was manured the previous season or dug in the autumn. Always use fresh seed; last year's is unlikely to germinate. The seed should be station sown at 15–20cm/6–8in intervals in 1cm/½in drills. The rows should be 30cm/12in apart. Do not sow too early – the soil should be at least 7°C/45°F – but they do need a long growing season, so sow as soon as you can. Parsnips are slow to germinate so sow a few radishes between the stations of parsnips. These will appear quickly and mark the line of the rows, making it easier to hoe without accidentally disturbing the germinating parsnips.

In heavy or stony soils the parsnips may fork and produce stunted growth, rather than the desired conical shape. To avoid this, make holes with a crowbar at each sowing station, moving it in a circle to make an inverted conical hole in the ground. Fill this with potting compost (soil mix) or good loam and sow the seeds in this.

Thin the seeds to one to each station as soon as they are big enough to handle. Keep

PLANTING IN STONY GROUND

1 At the required sowing intervals, make an inverted conical hole with a crowbar.

2 Fill the hole with potting compost (soil mix) and sow in the centre, covering the seed with more compost.

Cultivation

Sowing time early spring
Sowing distance station sow at 15–20cm/6–8in
Sowing depth 1cm/½in
Distance between sown rows 30cm/12in
Harvesting late autumn until spring

free from weeds. Water in dry spells because sudden rain after a prolonged dry spell may cause the roots to split. In very cold climates cover the rows of parsnips with straw during the winter.

Harvesting

Parsnips can be harvested from autumn onwards. Although they can be harvested before the leaves die back, most gardeners wait for this. Many gardeners also wait until after the first frosts, because these make parsnips taste sweeter. Dig the roots from the ground with a fork. In heavy soil or if the parsnips have deep roots, take care or the fork may slash through the flesh rather than lifting it out of the ground.

Storage

Parsnips are very hardy and should be left in the ground until they are required. If a frosty spell is forecast, however, it can be a good idea to lift a few while you can still get them out of the ground, and place them in trays of just-moist peat (peat moss) or sand until they are required. They are a late crop and may be harvested in spring well beyond the time that the ground may require preparing for the next crops. The parsnips can be dug up and temporarily heeled into another piece of ground or stored in sand or peat as described.

Pests and diseases

Parsnips can be attacked by such pests as celery fly or carrot flies, but on the whole they are usually pest free.

Parsnips are also prone to canker, but you can help reduce the chances of this occurring by choosing one of the increasing number of varieties that have been grown with a resistance to this problem.

SOWING

Parsnips are best station sown in groups of three, eventually reducing the seedlings to one by thinning out the weakest.

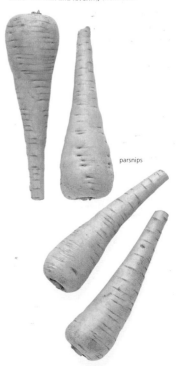

ABOVE **Harvest parsnips by digging a fork well under the root and levering them out.**

parsnips

Varieties

'Avonresister' small, some canker resistance	Improved' long-rooted
	'Intermediate' small
'Bayonet' long-rooted, some canker resistance	'Tender and True' long-rooted, some canker resistance
'Cobham Improved Marrow' medium	
'Gladiator' long-rooted, some canker resistance	'White Gem' medium, long-rooted
'Hollow Crown'	'White Spear' long-rooted

Carrots
Daucus carota

Many people may wonder if it is worth growing carrots when they are so cheap to buy. The answer must be an emphatic "yes". Fresh carrots, whether old or young, that are taken straight from the ground before being cooked taste infinitely better than shop-bought ones; there is no comparison. You may have to put up with them being covered in mud and perhaps with slug and carrot fly holes in them, but this is a minor consideration compared with the superior taste.

Wild carrots appear throughout Europe and well into Asia. The exact origin of domestic carrots is rather obscure, but they probably originated in the countries of the eastern Mediterranean, possibly even in Afghanistan. The original domesticated ones were various colours, including white, yellow, purple and red, and carrots of these colours are currently being re-bred and will soon be re-introduced by seed merchants. The orange ones, with which we are all familiar, were developed in Holland and France at a much later date.

The edible part of the carrot is below ground, while above are the attractive filigree leaves. Although mainly grown for the kitchen, they are well worth growing as purely decorative plants.

Although carrots bought in supermarkets are more or less identical, there is a lot of variety available to the gardener. Not only are there early carrots (often grown in

frames) that are round, looking almost like radishes, there are some that are long and tapered. Others are just as long but are cylindrical, with parallel sides and a rounded end. Shorter varieties are best for immediate use, while the longer ones are better for storing over winter. Although the other colours are being bred, the majority of carrots are the familiar orange, but there are a few pale yellow and creamy-white forms available.

Cultivation

Choose an open, sunny position. Carrots will grow in heavier soils, but they do best in light ground – sandy soils are perfect. The soil should be free from stones and fresh manure because both will cause the carrots to fork. If the soil is stony, make individual holes with a crowbar, fill them with compost (soil mix) and sow into these. Avoid freshly manured soil by using a plot that was manured for a previous crop or by manuring in the autumn. Sow very thinly in drills 1cm/½in deep and set 15–20cm/6–8in apart. Sow under cloches in late winter or in the open from early spring, but not before the soil has warmed up to at least 7°C/45°F. Sow successionally, with the last sowing in early summer.

When the seedlings appear, thin the earliest to 8cm/3in and the maincrop to 5–8cm/2–3in apart, depending on the size of carrot required. It is best to thin on a muggy, windless evening in order to avoid attracting carrot fly. For the same reason, remove all thinnings and bury them in the compost heap. Weed regularly but avoid disturbing the young carrots – a mulch of grass cuttings will help keep weeds down. It will also help to keep the soil moist. Water in dry weather.

THINNING

Thin the carrots only if necessary. Do so on a still, muggy evening to prevent the smell of the carrots travelling and betraying their presence to carrot root flies. Water after thinning.

SOWING WITH SAND

Carrots must be sown thinly. To help with this mix the seed with a little silver sand and "sow" the mixture.

Harvesting

Harvesting can begin at a very early stage as the thinnings can be very delicious, although they are rather tedious to clean. Early carrots can be dug up from late spring onwards, approximately seven weeks after sowing. Maincrop carrots take a bit longer and are ready from ten weeks onwards. Shorter varieties can be pulled, but longer ones and those that have been grown in heavier soils will need digging out with a fork.

HARVESTING

Shorter varieties can be pulled out by hand, but longer ones and those grown on heavier soils will need digging out with a fork. Try to avoid piercing the roots with the tines of the fork.

Storage

Carrots are usually left in the ground until they are required. They may even be left in the ground over winter unless there are a lot of slugs or the winter is very harsh. Instead, they can be lifted, cleaned and placed in a tray of just-moist sand or peat (peat moss).

Pests and diseases

The worst pest is undoubtedly carrot fly, the maggots of which burrow into the carrots. There are an increasing number of varieties that are resistant to this pest and these may be worth trying. Be careful when thinning, because the flies are attracted by smell, and the bruising of any part of the carrot will release the tell-tale odour. Planting garlic nearby is a traditional way of disguising the smell. Another, cumbersome but success-ful, method is to erect a fine mesh barrier, up to 90cm/3ft high, around the carrots. This deflects the flies, which fly quite close to the ground.

The principal disease from which carrots are likely to suffer is violet root rot, in which, as its name suggests, the root rots, becoming a violet colour. Burn or destroy all affected plants and make sure that you do not use the same ground for carrots for at least a couple of years.

ABOVE **A flourishing row of carrots, coming to maturity. These will be ready for harvesting a few at a time, whenever required for the kitchen.**

carrots

Cultivation

Sowing time early spring and successively to early summer
Sowing distance very thinly
Sowing depth 1cm/½in
Distance between sown rows 15–20cm/6–8in
Thinning distance 5–8cm/2–3in
Harvesting late spring onwards

Varieties

Early	'Chantenay Red Cored'
'Amsterdam Forcing 3'	tapered
cylindrical	'Favourite' stump-rooted
'Amsterdam	'Fly Away' cylindrical
Sweetheart' cylindrical	'Ingot' cylindrical
'Early Nantes'	James Scarlet
stump-rooted	Intermediate' tapered
'Rondo' round	'Nantes' stump-rooted
Maincrop	'Nantes Express'
'Autumn King'	stump-rooted
cylindrical	'St Valery' tapered

Beetroot (Beets)
Beta vulgaris

Beetroot (beets) originated around the shores of the Mediterranean and was spread northwards into the rest of Europe by the Romans. Once the Romans reached northern and eastern Europe, the vegetable seems to have been taken to heart, and many of the recipes in use today come from these areas.

Beetroot (beets) is related closely to Swiss chard and shares its distinctive bright red coloration. This is not only manifest in the leaves and stems of the plant but also in the roots themselves, and when they are cut or bruised they exude a wonderfully deep red juice. When it is cooked, the flesh is still a very deep colour, even though it loses a lot of colour in the water if it is boiled (baking preserves it). Not everyone likes this coloration, because it has a tendency to stain not only other food, but lips and clothes as well.

However, although you never see them in greengrocers, there are also white and golden varieties, which are equally delicious but do not cause the staining. There are also a few fancy ones in which the roots are made up of concentric rings

BELOW **Beetroot growing in a block in a raised bed. This method enables you to control the growing medium and grow crops unsuited to your soil.**

of white and red flesh. The general shape is round or near round, but cylindrical or even tapered varieties are available.

The green or reddish-green leaves can also be eaten when they are young, either in salads or cooked.

Unlike parsnips and carrots, the bulk of the vegetable's swollen root sits on top of the ground so that you can watch its progress and easily determine when it is ready to harvest.

Many of the older varieties have a tendency to bolt, particularly if they are sown early, but there are now ample alternatives that have had this characteristic bred out of them. Another aspect of choosing varieties is related to germination. Most seed is, in fact, made up of a cluster of seeds, which means that when they germinate they produce several seedlings close together. However, if you find that thinning these is fiddly, look out for monogerm varieties, which usually have the word "mono" somewhere in their name.

Cultivation

Sowing time early spring and successionally to early summer
Sowing distance thinly or in stations at 8cm/3in intervals
Sowing depth 1cm/½in
Distance between sown rows 20cm/8in
Thinning distance 8cm/3in
Harvesting early summer onwards

Cultivation

Beetroot (beets) needs an open, sunny position. They will grow in heavy soils, but do best in light ones. The soil should be fertile but not freshly manured. Use a plot that was manured for the previous crop or one into which manure was dug during the

HARVESTING

Harvest beetroot by pulling it by hand from the ground. In heavier soils a fork may be needed to loosen the roots.

PREPARING FOR COOKING

Remove the leaves by twisting them off, 3–5cm/1–2in from the root. This prevents the beetroot (beets) losing their colour by "bleeding" when they are cooked.

previous autumn. Sow directly into the open soil into shallow drills 1cm/½in deep and set 20cm/8in apart. The seed should be station sown at 8cm/3in intervals or sown thinly and thinned to that distance when they have germinated. Beetroot (beet) seed is slow to germinate but it can be speeded up by soaking for an hour in warm water before sowing. Seed can be sown in early spring, once the soil has warmed up to 7°C/45°F, and successively sown at two-week intervals until early summer. An earlier sowing can be made under cloches.

Keep beetroot (beet) weed free but avoid damaging them with a hoe. Keep them supplied with constant moisture. Avoid alternating dry and wet periods, or they may split.

Harvesting

Pull the young beetroot (beets) from the ground while they are still quite small. This will be about seven weeks after sowing. Continue to pull as required. You may need to use a fork to help ease later crops or those in heavy soils from the ground. If possible, do not break the thin root attached to the bottom of the globe, because this will "bleed", causing the beetroot to lose a lot of its colour. For a similar reason do not cut off the leaves; instead, twist them off, leaving about 5cm/2in on the beet.

Storage

Beetroot (beets) can be left in the ground until they are required, except in cold districts, where they can be lifted, cleaned and placed in trays of just-moist sand or peat (peat moss). Store these trays in a cool, frost-free shed or garage.

Pests and diseases

On the whole, beetroot (beets) are reasonably trouble free in terms of possible pests and diseases. Birds may eat the young seedlings when they first appear, so keep these off with netting of some sort. If any diseases occur, burn or destroy the affected plants and re-sow them elsewhere.

ABOVE **Even a small garden such as this can accommodate a selection of crops, including onions and beetroot (beets).**

Varieties
'Action' miniature
'Albina Vereduna' white flesh
'Boltardy' round
'Burpee's Golden' gold flesh
'Cheltenham Green Top' cylindrical
'Cheltenham Mono' monogerm
'Chioggia Pink' pink and white stripes
'Cylindra' cylindrical
'Detroit-Little Ball' miniature
'Dorée' golden
'Forono' cylindrical
'Moneta' monogerm
'Monodet' monogerm
'Monogram' monogerm
'Monopoly' monogerm
'Red Ace' cylindrical
'Tardel' miniature

purple beetroot (beets)

white beetroot (beets)

golden beetroot (beets)

Swedes (Rutabagas or Yellow Turnips)

Brassica napus

Swedes are one of those vegetables that never seem to get into ready-prepared, convenience dishes and yet are still popular with cooks who prepare their own food. They belong, perhaps, to what one might call the category of "wholesome food" (such as stews) rather than high cuisine, but they are increasingly used in a wide range of dishes, including delicate soups. Swedes are convenience food in their own right – it takes only a matter of seconds to pull one from the ground, peel, chop and put it to cook.

Swedes (rutabagas or yellow turnips) are not very old as vegetables go, although no one is certain about their origins. It seems likely that they appeared in Europe as a random cross between turnips and cabbages sometime in the Middle Ages. They did not find their way to Britain until the latter part of the 18th century, and it is thought that they were introduced from Sweden, hence the name. The American name "rutabaga" also has Swedish origins, being derived from *rotbagga*, which is Swedish for "ram's foot", an apt visual description of small or immature swedes.

Cultivation
Sowing time late spring to early summer
Sowing distance thinly
Sowing depth 1cm/½in
Distance between sown rows 38cm/15in
Thinning distance 23cm/9in
Harvesting autumn onwards

Although they are usually considered a rootcrop, swedes (rutabagas or yellow turnips) actually belong to the cabbage family and, as such, suffer from similar pests and diseases. For this reason, they should be included with the cabbages when you are planning a rotational system. The swollen root of the swede is mainly above ground, with just a small amount being buried. In the better garden varieties, the top of the globe is usually purple, while the lower section, which is hidden from the light, is white. The flesh is a creamy-yellow, usually deepening during cooking. The appearance of the foliage clearly shows its close alliance to the cabbage.

Many gardeners used to sow a later crop of swedes (rutabagas or yellow turnips) around midsummer in order to provide "tops", or the leaves, which can be used as greens during spring. These can be grown closer together than suggested above for conventional use.

Cultivation

An open site is required. Like most root crops, swedes (rutabagas or yellow turnips) prefer a light soil, although they can be grown on heavier ground. As with most brassicas, the soil should not be too acid. Lime if necessary to bring it to about pH6.5. The ground should not be freshly manured, but it is important that it contains as much organic material as possible because the soil should be moisture retentive. Add manure during autumn digging. Sow thinly in late spring or early summer into drills that are 38cm/15in apart and 1cm/½in deep. Thin the swedes

LEFT **This is a typical swede, with lots of spreading leaves. This plant should stand in the ground throughout the winter.**

ABOVE **These healthy looking swedes have just been harvested. The spreading stems can be clearly seen. This variety is 'Acme'.**

RIGHT **Swedes are generally round, but can vary in shape depending on the growing conditions. This variety, 'Marian', has become elongated.**

to 23cm/9in apart, preferably doing this in stages. Make sure that the soil is kept moist throughout summer, otherwise any check in the growth may result in woody or split globes. Keep the weeds down.

Harvesting

Swedes (rutabagas or yellow turnips) can be harvested from autumn onwards, throughout the winter, once they are large enough to use. Lift the globes as they are required. In most soils they can simply be pulled from the soil, but in heavier ones they may need loosening with a fork first.

Storage

Swedes (rutabagas or yellow turnips) are completely hardy and can be left in the soil as long as necessary. Some varieties become woody if they are left in the ground beyond the turn of the year, however, so these should be lifted and stored in trays of just-moist sand or peat (peat moss) and placed in a cool, frost-free shed or garage.

Pests and diseases

Being brassicas, swedes are prone to the same diseases as the rest of the cabbage family. Flea beetles are a particular scourge and the leaves should be dusted with derris as soon as they are spotted. Mildew can also be a problem, but there are now varieties that are resistant. Club root is another problem to look out for.

Varieties	
'Best of All'	'Marian'
'Brora'	'Ruby'
'Devon Champion'	'Western Perfection'

purple-topped swedes (rutabagas or yellow turnips)

Turnips
Brassica napa Rapifera Group

Like swedes (rutabagas or yellow turnips), turnips are members of the cabbage family. The origins of the turnip go back so far that they are obscure, but the wild plant from which it is derived is still commonly found throughout Europe and Asia and is thought to have been cultivated as far back as prehistoric times. The long history has meant that many forms have appeared in cultivation, particularly in China and Japan. The popularity of the turnip has waned in the West, and with it a number of different forms, although there are still some 30 varieties from which to choose.

The Western form of the turnip is round, sometimes an almost perfect globe, sometimes slightly flattened. It has one thickish root or several roots emerging from the base. The skins are a creamy-white, and the top of the globe can be green, purple, white or creamy-yellow. The flesh is white or yellowish. The globe is partly sunk into the ground, but most of it is above ground. In Asia long-rooted varieties are also grown, and seed of this form is sometimes available in the West. It is also possible sometimes to find old European varieties with long roots.

The fleshy ball is cooked and eaten, but many gardeners also enjoy the young

BELOW **A well-shaped, purple-topped turnip. It is advisable to keep turnips moist so that they will grow quickly.**

leaves, which are cooked as spring greens. Summer turnips are more succulent and lend themselves to a range of dishes. Those that are overwintered are generally not quite as tender, but they are useful in casseroles, stews and soups. In Japan they are often eaten raw.

Cultivation

Because turnips are a member of the brassica family, they should be included with cabbages in the rotational sequence. They need an open, sunny situation and, preferably, a light soil, although they can be grown in heavier ground. There must be plenty of organic material in the soil so that it does not dry out. The manure should either be left from a previous crop or be dug in during the previous autumn.

Cultivation

Summer
Sowing time late winter (under cloches) to early spring
Sowing distance thinly
Sowing depth 1cm/½in
Distance between sown rows 23cm/9in
Thinning distance 13cm/5in
Harvesting summer

Autumn and winter
Sowing time mid- to late summer
Sowing distance thinly
Sowing depth 1cm/½in
Distance between sown rows 30cm/12in
Thinning distance 20cm/8in
Harvesting autumn and winter

Greens
Sowing time late summer
Sowing distance thinly
Sowing depth 1cm/½in
Distance between sown rows 8–10cm/3–4in
Thinning distance none
Harvesting spring and early summer

Sow early varieties of turnip under cloches in late winter for early crops or in open ground from early spring onwards. Sow seed 1cm/½in deep in drills 23cm/9in apart. When the seedlings are big enough to handle, thin them to about 13cm/5in apart. Continue to sow at two- to three-week intervals for a continuous

HARVESTING

Turnips can be harvested by simply pulling them from the ground.

ABOVE These turnips – a variety known as 'Tokyo Cross' – have just been harvested and will grace any dining table.

supply of small, tender turnips throughout the summer. For varieties to be harvested from the autumn and winter, sow in midsummer. They should be at the same depth, but rows should be about 30cm/ 12in apart. Thin the seedlings to 20cm/8in.

If you want to grow turnips just as "greens", sow thinly in late summer and there should be no need to thin. Rows can be as close as 8–10cm/3–4in.

The secret of growing good turnips is to keep them moist so that they can grow quickly. Keep them weeded.

Varieties	
'Golden Ball'	'Milan White
'Green Top Stone'	Forcing'
'Hakutaka'	'Orange Perfection'
'Imperial Green	'Presto'
Globe'	'Purple Top Milan'
'Jersey Navet'	'Red Milan'
'Manchester Market'	'Snowball'
'Market Express'	'Stanis'
'Milan Early	'Stone'
White Top'	'Tokyo Cross'
'Milan Purple	'Tyfon'
Top Forcing'	'Veitch's Red Globe'

Harvesting

Harvest the early and summer varieties as soon as they are the size of golf balls. They can be eaten when they are slightly larger, but they are at their best at this size. Larger and older turnips become woody, so rather than sowing one long row, it is better to sow short rows at different times to provide a steady supply of young turnips. Varieties sown in midsummer can be harvested from autumn onwards as they are required. The "greens" can be harvested as young leaves from spring into summer.

Storage

Turnips can be left in the ground until they are required. In very cold areas or if they are likely to be frozen in the ground and impossible to extract, they can be lifted, the tops removed and the globes stored in trays of just-moist sand or peat (peat moss), and kept in a frost-free place.

Pests and diseases

Turnips suffer from the same problems as cabbages. Flea beetle, which is likely

ABOVE The distance between the plants in this row of red-topped turnips is just right for growing them successfully.

to be the worst pest, should be treated with derris dust.

Diseases can include violet root rot and club root. Destroy any affected plants.

green-topped turnips

Kohl Rabi

Brassica oleracea Gongylodes Group

Although it is not strictly a root vegetable, kohl rabi is placed in this group because of its similarity to the turnip. In reality, it is a short-stemmed cabbage, but the stem has swollen into a round ball. The fact that it is a stem can be seen from the cabbage-like leaves that sprout out from all around the swelling, unlike those of a turnip, which grow on top. The skin is either green or purple, depending on variety, and the flesh is white. Because it is a stem, kohl rabi sits on or just above the ground, with a taproot descending into the soil.

This curious vegetable is a relative new-comer to gardens, and it is thought to have originated in Europe as late as the 15th or 16th century, although it may have developed earlier – Pliny describes a similar type of vegetable being grown by the Romans in the 1st century AD. No matter when it originated, kohl rabi is not as popular today as it should be. Even after four centuries it is still considered something of a rarity in France and Britain, although it is more widely grown in Germany and Austria – as is testified by varieties such as 'Purple Vienna' and 'White Vienna' – as well as in Eastern Europe.

Kohl rabi has a fresh, mild taste, which is somewhat similar to that of turnips, and it is useful in a wide range of dishes,

including soups, as well as being eaten as a vegetable in its own right. It can also be eaten raw – in salads, for example. From the gardener's point of view it has the advantage over the turnip in that it can be grown in drier conditions yet still retain its succulence. Most varieties should be harvested while they are still quite small – about the size of a tennis ball – but some varieties, such as 'Gigante', which comes from the Czech Republic, usually grow to 4.5kg/10lb or more but remain succulent. Unfortunately, 'Gigante' is not an easy variety to get hold of, but it is definitely worth growing if you come across any seed. Purple-skinned varieties of kohl rabi are slightly hardier than white-skinned forms.

ABOVE **The leaves of these healthy looking kohl rabi are in perfect condition. The kohl rabi have been planted in a block.**

Cultivation

Kohl rabi needs an open, sunny situation, preferably with light soil, but they will grow on heavier ground. The soil should be well manured, ideally from an earlier crop or during the previous autumn. The seed should be sown thinly in drills, about 1cm/½in deep and 30cm/12in apart. Sowing can start under cloches in late winter for an early crop or early spring in the open ground. Continue to sow at three-week intervals until late summer for a continuous crop of tender roots. Thin to about 15cm/6in for earlier crops and to 20cm/8in for later ones. Watering is not as crucial as for turnips, but they are less likely to split if the moisture supply to the roots is constant. Keep weeded, but avoid damaging the roots with the hoe.

Harvesting

The stems are best harvested when they are about the size of tennis balls. Most varieties get rather woody after that. Later crops can be left in the ground until early winter and

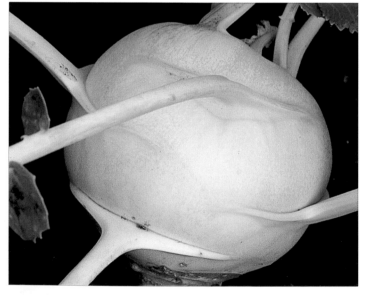

LEFT **This is a perfect specimen of kohl rabi, which is ready for harvesting. Use in soups, for example, or eat as a vegetable in its own right.**

Cultivation

Sowing time late winter (under cloches) and early spring to late summer
Sowing distance thinly
Sowing depth 1cm/½in
Distance between sown rows 30cm/12in
Thinning distance 15–20cm/6–8in
Harvesting summer onwards

possibly even later in milder areas. They are very easy to harvest as they can be simply pulled from the ground. When harvesting, shorten the root and cut back the leaves, leaving short stems before taking them into the kitchen for preparation.

Storage

There is no need to store kohl rabi because they should be pulled from the ground as required. In colder areas the last crop can be pulled, cleaned and stored in trays of just-damp sand or peat (peat moss), but they do not keep as well as other root crops as they tend to shrivel.

Pests and diseases

Kohl rabi suffers from the same kind of pests and diseases as cabbage. Flea beetles can be one of the worst pests, and leaves should be dusted with derris if an infestation occurs.

ABOVE **A purple-skinned kohl rabi, showing the soft bloom that appears on the skin.**

LEFT **Grow kohl rabi quickly, with plenty of moisture. This one was grown in conditions that were too dry.**

white-skinned kohl rabi

Varieties

'Adriana'	'Purple Vienna'
'Gigante'	'Quickstar'
'Green Early Ball'	'Rapidstar'
'Kolpak'	'Roblau'
'Kongo'	'Rowel'
'Lanro'	'Trero'
'Purple Danube'	'White Danube'
'Purple Early Ball'	'White Vienna'

Salsify and Scorzonera

Tragopogon porrifolius and Scorzonera hispanica

Although salsify and scorzonera are different plants, they are closely related, not only botanically but also in the manner in which they are grown and used. Neither is in the mainstream of vegetables, which is surprising because both are delicious. Salsify is, in fact, also known as vegetable oyster or oyster plant because of its taste. The roots are, however, not among the easiest to prepare – they are relatively narrow with plenty of smaller roots, which makes peeling difficult. In addition, they discolour very quickly once they have been peeled. In the kitchen, despite the fine taste, they are not very versatile since they are usually used as vegetables in their own right rather than as part of other dishes.

Salsify originated from the countries around the Mediterranean, although garden escapees have naturalized over a large part of Europe and North America. Scorzonera is not quite as rampant and is still restricted to Europe, from the warm Mediterranean countries to the arctic wastes. As with most vegetables their history is rather uncertain, but salsify is thought to have been first cultivated in Italy in the 16th century, while scorzonera was grown in Spain and Italy even earlier.

Both vegetables have long, narrow tap-roots, which are covered in thinner side roots. Salsify has a yellowish skin, rather like that of a parsnip, and scorzonera has a dark brown or black skin. They are grown mainly for the roots, but the young shoots and flower-buds can also be eaten. Salsify is also grown as an ornamental plant for its attractive purple flowers, although the leaves can be rather untidy. The flowers produce copious amounts of seed, which soon drifts away and germinates. Scorzonera has inconspicuous yellow flowers.

These vegetables are usually sold by their name rather than under the name of a cultivar, since few of the latter have been bred. However, one variety of salsify is well known – 'Sandwich Island'.

ABOVE **A basket of salsify just after the crop has been harvested, showing the small side roots that make the roots "hairy" and difficult to clean.**

Cultivation

Choose a site that is sunny and open. As with most root crops, both vegetables like a light soil, although they will grow in heavier conditions. The soil should be deeply dug and have humus added well in advance of sowing because they do not like freshly manured ground. To be sure of having a sufficiently large crop, both must be sown as early as possible to give a long growing season, although scorzonera should not be sown too early or it will run to seed. Seed should be sown by mid-spring, 1cm/½in deep in drills set 25cm/10in apart. Use fresh seed rather than any left from a previous season. Thin the seedlings to 15cm/6in apart. Although they can be grown closer together, they are more difficult to dig up individually.

Neither vegetable needs a great deal of attention, apart from being kept weeded. On the whole, they will not require water-ing, although if there is a prolonged drought, give them a good soaking once a week.

Harvesting

Like parsnips, salsify and scorzonera taste best after they have experienced a frost. This is not to say that you cannot harvest earlier, and they are usually ready from mid-autumn onwards. Dig the roots

LEFT **This block of salsify shows clearly how untidy and unattractive the foliage is. The resulting crop, however, is its own reward.**

Cultivation

Sowing time early to mid-spring
Sowing distance thinly
Sowing depth 1cm/½in
Distance between sown rows 25cm/10in
Thinning distance 15cm/6in
Harvesting autumn and winter

ABOVE **Scorzonera leaves are wider and more glossy than those of salsify, which are quite untidy in appearance.**

RIGHT **Salsify is worth growing for its flowers alone.**

up with a fork as required, taking care not to bruise or damage them. Salsify should be harvested and used during the first winter because it is a biennial. Scorzonera, however, is a perennial and can be left in the ground and harvested in the following autumn and winter, which gives the roots the chance to get larger.

Storage

Both plants are very hardy and can be left in the ground until needed, although it can be a good idea to lift a few and store them in trays of just moist sand if a hard frost is forecast, because it may then be difficult to get them out of the ground.

Pests and diseases

Neither salsify nor scorzonera tends to suffer from pests or diseases.

Varieties

Salsify
Most are listed simply as
salsify or vegetable oyster.
'Mammoth'
'Sandwich Island'
Scorzonera
Most are listed simply as scorzonera.
'Duplex'
'Lange Jan'
'Maxima'
'Russian Giant'

salsify

scorzonera

Potatoes
Solanum tuberosum

The potato is one of the most important food crops in the world. The family to which it belongs, Solanaceae, is found worldwide, although the potato itself originates from a fairly restricted area in the Andes, spreading up into Mexico. There are many species involved in the botanical development of the potato, which is very complicated, and the history of the potato in cultivation is almost as complicated as its botanical history.

The potato has been grown as a vegetable in the Andes for thousands of years, and the Incas were discovered to be eating it by the conquering Spanish in the late 16th century. Taken to Italy, it eventually spread to the rest of Europe. The original cultivars were not particularly hardy, and it took a long time for the potato to catch on in northern Europe and two centuries before it was widespread in Britain.

The tubers – that is, the swellings on the roots – are eaten. All other parts, including the leaves and the fruit, are poisonous. If the potatoes themselves are exposed to light for any length of time, they turn green, and this, too, is poisonous unless cooked.

Potatoes are grown from "seed potatoes". These are not seeds in the conventional sense, but potato tubers that have been selected for growing. Once they have

been planted, the seed potatoes start to sprout, producing roots and leaves. As the roots grow, new tubers are formed on them, and these are harvested when they are large enough.

Because potatoes are so widely distributed, there are hundreds of varieties from which to choose. Many are suited to particular climates, and different types will be found in different countries. The varieties differ in a number of respects. The first main difference is the timing of the crop, and there are two main groups, earlies and maincrop, which are further subdivided into first earlies and so on. The next main difference is use. Some are better for baking or roasting; others are better for boiling or frying; others are suitable for salads.

ABOVE **Potatoes have attractive flowers. In early crops, the opening of the flowers is an indication that the tubers are ready.**

Finally, and in some respects the most important criterion, is flavour. Most varieties taste quite different from each other, and many gardeners have their own favourites, although this does not stop them from experimenting with different ones.

Given these characteristics, it might be supposed that gardeners would grow several cultivars. However, potatoes can

LEFT **This row of potatoes shows the earth drawn up around the stems.**

BELOW **A crop of newly dug salad potatoes, "drying" in the sun.**

Cultivation

First earlies
Planting time early spring
Planting distance 30cm/12in
Planting depth 10–15cm/4–6in
Distance between rows 45cm/18in
Harvesting early summer

Second earlies
Planting time mid-spring
Planting distance 38cm/15in
Planting depth
10–15cm/4–6in
Distance between rows 60cm/24in
Harvesting summer onwards

Maincrop
Planting time mid- to late spring
Planting distance 38cm/15in
Planting depth 10–15cm/4–6in
Distance between rows 75cm/30in
Harvesting autumn

take up a lot of space in the garden and they are relatively inexpensive to buy. Many gardeners, therefore, prefer to restrict themselves to growing a few earlies, which have an incomparable flavour when taken straight from the ground to the kitchen, and to go to the greengrocer for the rest of the year. The ground on which the earlies were grown can be used for later crops, such as cabbages or leeks.

There are so many varieties that it could take more than one gardening lifetime to get through them all by sowing one or two varieties each year. One way of trying as wide a range as possible is to get together with two other gardeners and to buy bags of, say, three potatoes each and to divide them up between yourselves so that each of you can grow a small number of nine

varieties rather than a large number of three varieties. Keep a note of those you like best and make them your maincrop for the following year.

It is possible to enjoy new potatoes at Christmas too by planting a few in large pots in early autumn and keeping these in the greenhouse.

Cultivation

Potatoes are best grown in an open, sunny position. As earlies are likely to emerge through the ground before the last of the frosts, try to choose a warm, protected spot away from frost pockets. They will grow on most soils, although they prefer slightly

LEFT **A recently harvested uprooting of red-skinned potatoes, all evenly shaped and with good-quality skin.**

ABOVE **This large kitchen plot contains rows of neatly earthed- (hilled-) up potatoes. Frosts can be a problem for the emerging foliage.**

acid conditions. The soil should be fertile but avoid planting potatoes on newly manured grounds.

Earlies should be chitted. This involves standing the seed potatoes on a tray so that the eyes are facing upwards. Place the tray in a cool but frost-free place that is in the light although out of direct sunlight. Short shoots will appear, and this gets the crop off to a good start. Maincrop can be treated in the same way, although it is not essential.

First earlies are planted in early spring followed by second earlies two weeks later. Draw out a row with a hoe about 10cm/4in deep and place potatoes at 30cm/12in intervals. Rows should be 45cm/18in apart.

ABOVE **This harvesting of early potatoes is now ready for transferring to the kitchen. They will make delicious "new potatoes".**

Before planting, place the potatoes in a tray in a light place (but out of direct sunlight) in order to "chit". This means that the potatoes produce shoots.

Hoe out a trench 10cm/4in deep and lay the tubers about 30–40cm/12–15in apart, depending on the type. Cover with soil and earth (hill) up into a low ridge.

When the shoots reach 23–25cm/9–10in long, draw the soil around them along the rows.

Alternatively, the potatoes can be planted in holes dug with a trowel or with a special potato planter. Whichever method you use, cover the potatoes with soil and then draw up more soil to form a low ridge above them. When the shoots reach heights of 23–25cm/9–10in, draw earth up around them along the rows to make certain that all the tubers are well covered; otherwise they turn green. Continue to do this until the foliage touches across the rows.

Second earlies and maincrop are treated in the same way, except that they are planted in the second half of spring and the potatoes are set 38cm/15in apart and in rows 60cm/24in apart for second earlies and 75cm/30in apart for maincrop.

Keep an eye on weather reports, and if frost is forecast cover any shoots with newspaper or horticultural fleece. Keep all potatoes, especially earlies, watered if there is a prolonged dry spell forecast.

An alternative method of growing potatoes is to plant them under a sheet of black polythene (plastic). Place the polythene along the row and anchor it by burying the edges in the soil. Cut slits at the relevant intervals and plant potatoes through them.

FROST PROTECTION

Once the potato shoots have emerged through the soil, it is important to take note of any frost forecasts. The shoots will need protecting from possible frost damage. Cover them over with horticultural fleece or even with newspaper.

HARVESTING

To harvest, dig a fork well under the potatoes and draw it up through the soil, bringing the tubers up with the earth.

Varieties

First earlies
'Arran Pilot' white skin, early
'Epicure' white skin, early
'Foremost' white skin, waxy yellow flesh
'Maris Bard' white skin, waxy texture, very early
'Pentland Javelin' white skin, waxy flesh last of the earlies to crop
'Ulster Chieftain' white skin, floury texture

Second earlies
'Estima' white skin, waxy yellow flesh, good boiler
'Kondor' red skin, yellow flesh, good boiler
'Marfona' white skin, heavy cropper, good for baking
'Maris Peer' white skin, waxy texture, good boiler
'Wilja' white skin, waxy yellow flesh, good salad potato

Maincrop
'Cara' pink skin, white floury flesh, late
'Desiree' pinkish red skin, waxy yellow flesh, good for baking and for fries
'King Edward' pink and white skin, creamy floury texture, good for baking and roasting
'Maris Piper' white skin, floury texture, heavy cropper, good for baking
'Pentland Dell' white skin, floury texture, heavy cropper, good for baking and roasting
'Pink Fir Apple' pink skin, yellow waxy flesh, wonderful salad potato
'Ratte' white skin, yellow waxy flesh, excellent salad potato
'Romano' red skin, firm white flesh, good boiler

maincrop whites

earlies

salad

maincrop reds

salad reds

Harvesting

Early potatoes are harvested in early summer, usually just as their flowers are opening, which should be about 12 weeks after planting. They are usually lifted as they are required. Maincrop are left in the soil until the autumn and are usually all lifted at once and stored. To harvest earlies, dig a fork in well below the potatoes and lever them out of the soil, at the same time pulling on the haulm (stems and leaves). For maincrop, remove the haulm about two weeks before harvesting so that the skins on the potatoes harden. Lift the maincrop on a dry, warm day and leave them lying in the sun for an hour or two to let them dry and to harden the skins.

Storing

Do not leave potatoes in the light for too long. Pack them into hessian (burlap) or paper sacks and store them in a dark, cool but frost-free place. Alternatively, they can be stored in trays as long as no light gets to the tubers. Regularly check all potatoes and remove any that have started to rot.

Pests and diseases

The worst problem that can occur is blight, which is particularly prevalent in wet years. The leaves go yellow and brown and start to curl. Eventually the haulm seems to fall to pieces. The potatoes develop black patches, which eventually turn into a slimy, evil-smelling rot. Do not plant potatoes on

ground that was affected the year before (either from potato or tomato blight). Earth (hill) them up well to keep the spores from the tubers. If necessary, spray with the appropriate copper-based fungicide, preferably in wet years before blight appears. Look out for resistant varieties.

Another common disease is potato scab, which disfigures the surface of the tubers. To avoid it occurring, do not grow potatoes on ground that has been recently limed or manured. Other diseases include spraing, violet root rot and blackleg.

The main pests are slugs and wire-worms, both of which eat holes in the tubers. Other pests can include cutworms and potato cyst eelworms.

Jerusalem Artichokes
Helianthus tuberosus

Surprisingly, these potato-like tubers are grown on plants that are sunflowers. Unlike the dinner-plate-sized flowers of its relative, however, the flowers of the Jerusalem artichoke are small, but borne on equally tall stems. The knobbly tubers are found below ground, and they can used as a vegetable in their own right and cooked in the same way as potatoes or parsnips – roasting is a particularly good way of cooking them. They have a lovely distinct flavour but also combine well in other dishes, especially soups, and can be eaten raw. The tubers should be about the size of a chicken's egg; larger ones can be cut into pieces.

ABOVE **Here, an uprooted Jerusalem artichoke plant clearly shows the tubers that are now ready for harvesting.**

Jerusalem artichokes have no connection with Jerusalem nor with globe artichokes. They originated in North America and were brought to Europe in the 16th century, eventually finding their way to Britain via Holland in the early 17th century. The name Jerusalem could be a corruption of the Italian word for sunflower, *girasole*, or it may be derived from the name of the town in Holland, Terneuzen, from where they were sent to Britain.

This is a very easy vegetable to grow. It is not particular about the soil and it is troubled by few pests and diseases. The only real problem is getting rid of it if you decide to stop growing it at any stage. A single piece of one of the many tubers left in the ground will resprout to produce a new plant, and it is, unfortunately, easy to miss one or more pieces. The regrowth normally appears in the row, however, and it will not spread throughout the garden unless you are careless enough to distribute the tubers about.

Although Jerusalem artichokes are grown primarily as a vegetable, they can also be grown to provide a temporary windbreak. They grow rapidly, sometimes to 3m/10ft, and make a dense hedge of wiry stems that needs no support except in exposed sites.

The mature plants make excellent windbreaks within the kitchen garden, as well as creating visual screens that can be used to divide up the garden.

Cultivation

Unlike most vegetables, Jerusalem artichokes are tolerant of light shade. They are also tolerant of a range of soils, even growing in poor ones, although best results will be obtained from ground that has been manured during the previous autumn. Do not overfeed because this may result in lush vegetation at the expense of tubers.

Try to purchase named varieties but, if you cannot find them, tubers from the greengrocer can be used. The planting time is not critical – any time in spring will do. Plant the tubers 10–13cm/4–5in deep in holes made with a trowel. They should be about 38cm/15in apart and the rows should be 90cm/3ft apart.

They need little attention apart from being kept weed free. If they are likely to be rocked by the wind, draw earth up around the stems to help stabilize them so that the tubers are not disturbed. In very windy sites, individual stems may need to be supported with canes. The stems can be cut off in summer at about 1.8m/6ft to lessen the chance of wind damage – this is necessary not so much because the

LEFT **A basket of recently harvested Jerusalem artichokes. These are perfect easy-to-peel specimens that are not too knobbly.**

RIGHT **The top growth of Jerusalem artichokes shows its relationship with the sunflower. Unfortunately, all this lush growth is of no use except for making compost.**

plants will be flattened but because the tubers will be disturbed by the movement of the plants and not develop properly.

Harvesting

The tubers can be lifted once the leaves start to wither in autumn. The skins should be pale brown, without any soft patches.

Cut off the stems, then lift the tubers with a fork, digging right under them. Sift through the soil to check that all the pieces are removed. Any piece of tuber remaining in the soil will grow again in the following year. This is all right if you plan to plant in the same place next year, but a nuisance if you do not. They can be quite difficult to eradicate, especially in heavy soils where it is easy to miss tubers, so harvest carefully.

Storing

Jerusalem artichokes are frost hardy and are best stored in the ground and dug only as they are required. A few can be dug if frost threatens to freeze the soil, making digging impossible, and stored in trays of just-moist sand or peat (peat moss) in a frost-free shed or garage.

Pests and diseases

Jerusalem artichokes do not attract pests and diseases.

Jerusalem artichokes

Cultivation
Sowing time spring
Sowing distance 38cm/15in
Sowing depth 10–13cm/4–5in
Distance between sown rows 90cm/3ft
Harvesting summer onwards

Varieties
Often listed simply as Jerusalem artichokes.
'Boston Red'
'Dwarf Sunray'
'Fuseau'

Radishes

Raphanus sativus

Radishes are one of the easiest and quickest of all crops to grow. The rapidity with which they appear through the soil makes them suitable for children to grow, because little patience is required, and, indeed, many gardeners' first experience of growing vegetables was with this humble plant. However, the wide range of types and varieties that are available make this a vegetable that is of as much interest to the mature gardener as to the embryonic one.

The radish has a long history as far as cultivation is concerned, having been known in Ancient Egypt. Its origins are obscure, but it probably derived from native plants found growing in Mediterranean countries. At first, varieties had long, tapering roots, originally black, later white, and these larger rooted forms are still

cultivated in Europe. By the 18th century, however, the more familiar round ones with red skins began to appear.

Today the small, red-skinned radishes are the most frequently grown, and these are mainly used in salads or as a decorative garnish. In China and Japan, where the large varieties are still common, they are eaten both raw and cooked, and the large-rooted types are becoming more widely grown in the West, especially new varieties imported from China. These larger varieties

ABOVE **These round radishes are suffering from slug damage (top) and from cracking due to irregular watering (middle).**

have the advantage that they can be left in the ground for longer and so make a valuable contribution to the selection of winter crops.

One of the advantages of the short life-cycle of the radish is that it can be grown among slower growing crops, thus making the best use of the available ground. Radishes make good markers if they are sown along with a vegetable that is slow to germinate, such as parsnips. Because

BELOW **These neat rows of radishes have been planted in abundance. You will have to consume large quantities to grow so many at once.**

HARVESTING

Radishes are harvested simply by pulling them from the ground by hand. They should be harvested when they are large enough to eat.

radishes appear quickly they will indicate the position of the row so that the parsnip seeds are not accidentally disturbed by hoeing or weeding.

Cultivation

Ordinary summer radishes do not need either a deep or particularly rich soil. They prefer one that does not dry out or they will quickly run to seed. Slow-growing radishes also tend to be woody and over-hot to the taste. They should be grown in an open, sunny position.

Sowing can start under cloches in late winter or in early spring in the open soil. Sow in shallow drills about 1cm/½in deep, set about 15cm/6in apart. Water the soil along the row if it is dry at the time of sowing. Sow thinly so that little thinning is required, then thin to about 2.5cm/1in. Do not sow too much at once because radishes are rapidly past their best, and it is better to

Varieties

Summer	'Saxa' globe
'Cherry Belle' globe	'Scarlet Globe' globe
'Crystal Ball' globe	'Sparkler 3' globe
'Flamboyant Sabina'	**Winter**
cylindrical	'Black Spanish Long'
'French Breakfast'	'Black Spanish
cylindrical	Round'
'Juliette' globe	'China Rose'
'Long White Icicle'	'Mino Early'
tapering	'Minowase'
'Prinz Rotin' globe	'Violet de Gournay'

sow short rows every two weeks to obtain a succession of crops than one long one in which many of the roots will be wasted. Do not let them dry out.

Sow the larger winter radishes at about midsummer. Do not sow too early or they may run to seed. These should be sown in drills set 25cm/10in apart. When they are large enough to handle, thin to about 13cm/5in apart.

Harvesting

Summer radishes should be pulled when they are large enough to eat. Discard any that have become large or old because these will be too woody as well as too hot to eat. Winter radishes can be dug up from autumn onwards.

Storage

Summer radishes quickly shrivel once they are out of the ground and should be used as soon as possible after harvesting. Long-rooted winter varieties can be left in the ground until they are required. In very cold areas or if severe frosts are threatened, which would make digging them from the ground impossible, dig the roots and store them under cover in trays of just-moist peat (peat moss) or sand.

Pests and diseases

Although they may not look like it, radishes are related to cabbages and so suffer from the same pests and diseases. Flea beetle is likely to be the worst problem, and should they appear, young plants should be dusted with derris. Slugs are also partial to radishes and can leave unsightly holes in the roots. If anything worse than this happens, scrap the plants and re-sow elsewhere in the garden.

ABOVE **A bunch of recently harvested cylindrical radishes. They should not be allowed to grow too large, or they become woody and very hot.**

radishes

PEAS AND BEANS

Peas
Pisum sativum

Of all vegetables, peas are perhaps the best reason for growing one's own: it is impossible to buy peas that taste anything like those that are picked straight from the garden. However, the difficulty is that if you want to grow a succession of crops to give you peas throughout the summer, you will have to devote quite a large area to them. This is not the problem it once was, however, because the majority of peas are now much shorter, and even if you have space to grow only a few in a large bucket, the effort is worth it for the taste alone.

Peas are one of the oldest vegetables cultivated by man. They have been found in settlements from the Late Stone Age onwards – that is, nearly 8000 years ago. One of the advantages of peas has always been that not only can they be eaten fresh, either raw or cooked, but they can also be dried and stored for later use.

The Romans, in particular, spread the cultivation of peas, probably introducing them to Britain. Surprisingly, they seem to have vanished from cultivation in Britain and were reintroduced from mainland Europe only in the 16th century. The wild pea, from which the cultivated form was developed, is still found growing in Turkey, and it is thought that this is where they probably originated, especially as some of the earliest archaeological finds come from that area.

Until about 50 years ago, peas grew to 1.8m/6ft or more and had to be supported with pea-sticks. Modern varieties are generally quite short, however, and can be easily supported with low wire netting or even a couple of strings stretched horizontally. Some varieties need no support at all.

Although the peas themselves are generally regarded as the "vegetable", from surprisingly early – certainly before the end of the 16th century in Britain – there have been forms with edible pods. There are various types of pea. First earlies are the earliest of the year. Those that are overwintered have smooth skins, but there are less hardy varieties, which are planted in early spring, and these have wrinkled skins. Although they are less hardy, they taste sweeter. Second earlies and maincrop all have wrinkled skins.

Mangetout (snow) peas, also known as sugar peas, can be eaten whole when the peas are still immature. Snap peas also have edible pods but can be eaten when they are more mature. Asparagus peas have winged pods and an asparagus-like taste. Petit pois are small, sweet-tasting peas.

ABOVE **Pea-sticks can be used to support tall varieties of peas.**

Cultivation
Peas like an open, sunny site. The soil should be fertile, with manure or compost incorporated during the previous autumn. First earlies can be sown in late autumn and then overwintered; remember to cover the plants with cloches in colder areas. Alternatively, they can be sown in the late winter or early

SOWING

Peas can be sown in a double row along a shallow trench, in an open, sunny position.

PROTECTING AGAINST BIRDS

Covering the plant with a wire netting guard will keep the birds away.

Cultivation

Earlies
Sowing time late autumn, late winter
or early spring
Sowing distance 5cm/2in
Sowing depth 5cm/2in
Distance between sown rows 60–90cm/2–3ft
Thinning distance no need to thin
Harvesting early summer

Second earlies
Sowing time early spring
Sowing distance 5cm/2in
Sowing depth 5cm/2in
Distance between sown rows 60–90cm/2–3ft
Thinning distance no need to thin
Harvesting early summer

Maincrop
Sowing time early spring to early summer
Sowing distance 5cm/2in
Sowing depth 5cm/2in
Distance between sown rows 60–90cm/2–3ft
Thinning distance no need to thin
Harvesting summer to early autumn

spring. They can also be grown under cloches if necessary. Crops can then be sown at intervals until the early summer.

The easiest way to sow peas is to pull out a flat-bottomed trench with a hoe, about 15–20cm/6–8in wide and 5cm/2in deep. The peas are then sown in pairs, one on each side of the trench with the seeds at 5cm/2in intervals. Alternatively, they can be sown in a single drill at the same intervals. The distance between rows varies between 60–90cm (2–3ft), depending on the height of the peas. Add supports when the peas reach 5–8cm/2–3in high and the tendrils start to form. Use plastic pea netting, which is sold specially for the purpose, wire netting or pea-sticks. Once the flowers start to appear, keep the peas watered during dry weather.

Harvesting
Pick the pods as soon as the peas have swollen and are large enough to eat. Mangetout (snow) peas and similar types should be picked before the pods get tough.

ABOVE **Wire netting can be used to support shorter varieties of peas.**

Keep picking the peas as they mature. The peas of many modern varieties, which have been created for agricultural needs, mature at the same time, and this can be a problem for the gardener.

Storage
Peas are best picked straight from the plant, although they can be frozen, which is one way of coping with a glut so that they are available through the whole year. Although it is not common now, they can also be kept by drying.

Pests and diseases
Unfortunately, peas are prone to quite a number of pests and diseases. At an early stage both mice and birds can eat the seed. Birds will also strip the emerging seedlings, and it may be necessary to protect them with wire netting. Aphids and pea thrips can also be a problem.

Mildew is something that affects crops most years, especially later in the season. It can normally be ignored, but you may prefer to use varieties that are less prone to mildew.

Varieties

Round
'Bountiful' early, tall
'Douce Provence' early, short
'Feltham First' early, short
'Meteor' early, short
'Pilot' early, medium

Wrinkled
'Alderman' maincrop, tall
'Banff' early, short
'Early Onward' early, tall
'Hurst Beagle' early, short
'Hurst Greenshaft'
maincrop, short
'Little Marvel' maincrop, short
'Miracle' maincrop, tall

'Onward' maincrop, short
'Top Pod' maincrop, medium

Petit pois
'Darfon' maincrop, short
'Minnow' maincrop, short

Mangetout
'Herault' early, tall
'Honey Pod' early, short
'Nofila' early, short
'Norli' early, short
'Oregon Sugar Pod' maincrop, medium
'Sugar Short Sweet Green' maincrop, medium

Asparagus pea
Usually listed by its name rather than by variety.

mangetout (snow) peas

round peas

round peas

Runner Beans
Phaseolus coccineus

Although many gardeners have given up growing peas because they feel they take up too much space, very few seem to have given up runner beans for the same reason. Possibly it is because they are seen as better value for money and space because they continue to crop over a long period and it is possible to freeze any excess for later use. As with peas, fresh runner beans are far better than those you buy in the shops, so the effort is certainly worthwhile.

Runner beans originated in Mexico, where they have been grown for more than 2,000 years, long before the Spanish conquistadors arrived. They were introduced to Europe in the 16th century but were at first grown more for their decorative qualities than for their culinary ones. Even today their presence in a kitchen garden is notably ornamental, although the beans are usually eaten as well as admired.

Runner beans usually grow up to about 1.8m/6ft, although in good soil they will grow to 2.4m/8ft or more. There is, however, little to be gained from growing them so tall because it is difficult to harvest the topmost beans. Dwarf varieties are available for those who want them, but they have never become very popular, partly because yields are lower and partly because all the beans tend to mature at the same time. The pods are long and rather coarse in texture, much coarser than the equivalent French (green) beans. This coarseness

also applies to the texture, and it is important to pick the pods young – once they age they become very stringy. Some varieties are less stringy than others.

The pods are usually eaten along with the young beans, but they can be allowed to mature and the fully grown beans dried and eaten later in the year.

The general colour of the flowers is red, hence the old name of scarlet runner beans, but there are now other colours, including white and mauve. These are very useful in decorative schemes, and they still produce a good crop of beans.

Cultivation

Beans do best in an open, sunny position; in more exposed areas they should be protected from winds, partly to prevent them from blowing over and partly because pollination is more difficult in such conditions. They will grow in quite poor soil but do best in a soil that has been well manured during the previous autumn. The traditional method is to dig a deep trench and bury plenty of compost and manure, even old newspaper. The idea is not so much to provide nutrients, although this is obviously important, but to create an area around the roots that retains plenty of moisture.

Beans must not appear above ground before the last frost has passed, so early summer is usually the earliest one can begin planting. To get them off to a good start, sow beans individually in pots or modules and plant out when the weather is right. Alternatively, sow directly into the

ABOVE **This is a good crop of runner beans which is accompanied by the flowers to produce more.**

soil. If you are able to make an early start, it is often a good idea to sow again some three weeks later so that there is a continuous crop until the first frosts of winter.

Before sowing or planting you will need to construct some form of support up which the beans will climb. This can be in the form of a single or double row (double is usually preferable) of poles, canes or strings for them to climb up, or it can be a wigwam or tepee – that is, a circle of poles or canes, pulled together at the top with string to form a cone. The distance between the poles or strings should be about 25cm/10in, for although they will grow closer together, it is easier to pick the beans if the plants are not too close.

Plant or sow one bean at each pole. Many gardeners sow two or three beans at each position – "one for the crow, one for the slug and one for the kitchen" – and remove the weaker seedlings, leaving just one. The beans are self-clinging but may need help to go up the right pole or string, as they often seem to prefer their neighbour's. Make sure that the soil is always moist, especially in dry periods.

HARVESTING

Harvest the beans when they are large enough, but avoid the older, tougher beans.

Cultivation

Runner beans
Sowing time late spring (under glass)
to early summer
Sowing or planting distance 25cm/10in
Sowing depth 5cm/2in
Distance between sown rows 90cm/3ft
Thinning distance no need to thin
Harvesting late summer until first frosts

Dwarf runner beans
Sowing time late spring (under glass)
to early summer
Sowing or planting distance 15cm/6in
Sowing depth 5cm/2in
Distance between sown rows 45cm/18in
Thinning distance no need to thin
Harvesting late summer until first frosts

RIGHT **A wigwam or tepee of runner beans supported by long bamboo canes.**

Sow or plant dwarf varieties at 15cm/6in intervals in a single row with 45cm/18in between rows. Pinch out any long shoots that develop. After harvesting, cut down the beans but leave the roots to rot in the ground; they contain stores of valuable nitrogen.

Harvesting
Pick the pods as soon as the beans begin to swell, which is usually when the beans are about 15cm/6in long. Some varieties, especially those developed for exhibition, can be considerably longer than this. A larger crop can be encouraged by picking regularly, putting any excess in the freezer. It is also important to pick regularly because old beans become stringy and inedible.

Storage
Beans do not keep well and should be eaten as they are harvested. The only storage method used today is freezing, although in the past they were often preserved in salt.

Pests and diseases
Slugs and snails are always a problem when the plants first emerge, and they can easily kill the entire planting. Runner beans are otherwise generally problem free, apart from possible attacks of blackfly.

Powdery mildew and chocolate spot may also occur.

Varieties

Runner beans
'Achievement' long pods
'Butler' stringless,
medium-length pods
'Czar' white seeds, long pods
'Desirée' stringless, long pods
'Enorma' long pods
'Ivanhoe' stringless,
lilac seeds, long pods
'Kelvedon Wonder' early, short pods
'Lady Di' long pods
'Painted Lady' medium-length pods
'Polestar' early, stringless,
medium-length pods
'Prizewinner' medium-length pods
'Red Knight' stringless
'Red Rum' early, short pods
'Royal Standard' stringless, long pods
'Scarlet Emperor' early, long pods
'Streamline' long pods
'White Emergo' white seeds, long pods

Dwarf runner beans
'Gulliver'
'Hammond's Dwarf Scarlet'
'Pickwick'

runner beans

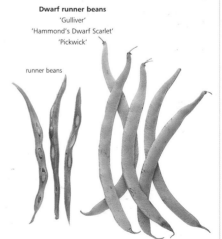

French (Green) Beans

Phaseolus vulgaris

French (green) beans are among the oldest type of cultivated bean. They originated in Central and South America, where evidence suggests that they were being grown at least 8,000 years ago. They did not reach Europe until the 16th century, when they were introduced by the returning Spanish. The English name "French beans" presumably derives from the fact that the beans were introduced into Britain from France.

There are several distinct forms of French (green) beans, the most obvious distinction being between the dwarf and climbing varieties. Recently, climbing varieties have become a popular alternative to runner beans and this makes them seem to be a modern development, but, in fact, they are the older of the two types, dwarf beans not having been widely grown until the 18th century.

French (green) beans are either eaten whole, while the seeds are still immature, or grown on and the seeds dried and used as haricot (navy) beans. Some varieties are better for drying than others. Pods vary: they can be green, purple or yellow, and they can be round or flat. The flat varieties tend to be more succulent, and the flat ones often become rather stringy when they become old.

Like runner beans, French (green) beans are frost tender and need to be sown or planted out after the last frosts. They also need warm soil in which to germinate and thrive. They are, however, quicker to mature than runner beans and so provide a valuable early crop. They also have a quite different flavour and so bring welcome variety to the kitchen.

Dwarf varieties are still the most popular, especially as they do not take up much room and are useful in small gardens. In addition, the yield is high and the season for each sowing is relatively long. The climbers or pole varieties are a useful alternative to runner beans because of their different taste and earlier harvest and also because they do not become so stringy. The variety of coloured pods makes them valuable in the ornamental kitchen garden.

Cultivation

French (green) beans, both dwarf and climbing, need a sunny, open site. The soil should be fertile but free-draining, preferably manured during the previous autumn. An early start can be made by sowing the beans in pots or modules under glass in late spring and planting out after the threat of frost has passed. Alternatively, they can be sown directly into the soil and covered with cloches. Most gardeners, however, tend to wait until early summer and sow directly into the soil, when the conditions should be perfect. Sow in a single or double row, spacing the beans about 8cm/3in apart in rows set 45cm/18in apart. They should be planted about 4cm/1½in deep. Climbing or pole varieties should be treated in the same way as runner beans. Keep watered in dry weather.

Harvesting

Harvesting can usually begin seven or eight weeks after sowing. Pick while the seeds are still immature and go on picking for as long as the beans cook and eat well. Leave those that you want to treat as haricot (navy) beans until the pods have swollen and turned yellow. Cut the whole plants and hang them up in a dry place to complete the drying. Shell and store.

Storage

French (green) beans are best used fresh from the plant, but they can be frozen, which is a good way of dealing with a glut. Haricot (navy) beans should be dried and stored in airtight jars.

Pests and diseases

On the whole French (green) beans are not prone to many problems. Slugs and snails are the most likely nuisance, especially when the plants are first emerging, but they can also eat the pods as well. Blackfly and fungal diseases may also be a problem.

Cultivation		
Dwarf beans		
Sowing time late spring (under glass) to early summer		
Sowing or planting distance 8cm/3in		
Sowing depth 4cm/1½in		
Distance between sown rows 45cm/18in		
Thinning distance no need to thin		
Harvesting late summer until first frosts		
Climbing beans		
Sowing time late spring (under glass) to early summer		
Sowing or planting distance 15–25cm/6–10in		
Sowing depth 4cm/1½in		
Distance between sown rows 90cm/3ft		
Thinning distance no need to thin		
Harvesting late summer until first frosts		

SOWING

Sow the beans in a single or double trench, once the threat of frosts has passed.

HARVESTING

Do not to pull too hard when harvesting French (green) beans because the plants may be pulled from the ground.

ABOVE **These climbing French (green) beans are being supported by a bamboo cane.**

ABOVE **These striking purple French (green) beans are now ready for harvesting. It seems a shame to pick such a decorative crop.**

Varieties

Dwarf beans
'Annabel' green, slim pods, stringless
'Canadian Wonder' green, flat pods
'Daisy' green, long pods, stringless
'Delinel' green, slim pods, stringless
'Golddukat' yellow waxpod, pencil pods
'Golden Sands' yellow waxpod, stringless
'Masai' green, very slim pods
'Mont d'Or' yellow waxpod
'Purple Queen' purple, round pods, stringless

'Purple Tepee' purple, round pods, stringless
'Radar' round pods, stringless
'Royalty' purple, stringless
'Sprite' green, round pods, stringless
'Tendergreen' green, pencil pods, stringless
'The Prince' green, flat pods, early
Haricot (navy) beans
'Brown Dutch'
'Chevrier Vert'
'Comtessa de Chambord'
Climbing beans
'Blue Lake' green, round pods, stringless, white seeded

'Hunter' flat pods, stringless
'Kentucky Blue' round pods
'Largo' round pods, stringless
'Mont d'Or' golden, slightly flat pods, near-black beans
'Veitch's Climbing' green, flat pods

yellow-coloured French (green) beans

climbing French (green) beans

purple-coloured French (green) beans

French (green) beans

Broad (Fava) Beans

Vicia faba

Unlike other forms of bean, broad (fava) beans can be an acquired taste; not every-body likes them. However, when they are cooked straight from the plant, home-grown beans have a flavour that is never found in bought ones, so if you have not enjoyed them in the past, grow some and try them again – you may be pleasantly surprised. These beans also have the advantage of being one of the first vegetables of the year to mature. While the other two main forms of garden bean come from the Americas, the broad (fava) bean is native to the Old World, probably originating in the Near East. Like the pea, it has been grown since Neolithic times, and, also like the pea, it can be eaten fresh or it can be dried and stored, which is a valuable attribute that has been appreciated right up to the advent of the freezer.

ABOVE **A row of healthy young beans at an early stage of their growth.**

Broad (fava) beans are categorized in various ways. Sometimes it is by length of pod. The long-pods have up to eight kidney-shaped beans in each pod, whereas the Windsors, the short-podded form, have only half that number of seeds, each of which is rounded. They can also be categorized by the colour of the seeds, which can be green, white (pale green, really) or mahogany-red; green seeds are better for freezing. They are also categorized as dwarf or tall forms, the former being better for the small garden. Finally, they can be divided into those that can be overwintered and those that are best sown in spring; this generally corresponds to the divisions between long-pods and Windsors, as the long-pods tend to be hardier.

PINCHING OUT

Pinching out the tops of the beans is a good practice because it discourages blackfly. The tops can then be boiled and eaten.

Cultivation

These beans need an open, sunny site, which is protected from strong winds, especially if you are growing overwintering types. A reasonably fertile soil is required, and this is best achieved by incorporating manure or compost during the autumn dig. Over-wintering varieties can be sown in late autumn. Other types should be sown in late winter or early spring. Although new varieties have extended the sowing season until early summer, most varieties need to be sown before the end of spring.

Sow in double rows in a shallow trench, 23cm/9in wide and 4cm/1½in deep. Alternatively, sow each seed individually with a dibber. In both cases, the seeds should be about 23cm/9in apart, and the rows should be 60cm/24in apart. Seeds can also be raised in pots or modules in late winter under glass and planted out in spring.

Taller varieties will need to be supported with string tied to canes that are set at intervals along each side of the double row. When the beans are in full flower, pinch out the tender top by 8cm/3in to reduce the chance of blackfly infestation and to make the pods fill out. Water during dry periods.

Harvesting

Pick the pods when the beans inside them have swollen. Some can be picked at an earlier stage for cooking whole. Do not allow the beans to become too old – that is, when they are leathery and pliable – or they will be tough and too floury. Some people like to cook and eat the young tops when they are removed.

Storage

These beans are undoubtedly best when picked straight from the plant, but any excess can be frozen for future use. They can also be dried.

Pests and diseases

The most serious problem is blackfly, but this can often be avoided by removing the tips of the plant (see left). On the whole, these beans are reasonably trouble free, although chocolate spot can be a problem. This can usually be ignored, but burn or destroy the affected plants when they are finished with rather than put them on the compost heap.

STAKING

Taller varieties of broad (fava) beans will need supporting with string tied to canes that are set at intervals along the rows.

Varieties

'Aquadulce Claudia' long-pod, white seeds
'Bunyards Exhibition' long-pod, white seeds
'Express' pale green seeds
'Hylon' long-pod, white seeds
'Imperial Green Longpod' long-pod, green seeds
'Jade' long-pod, green
'Jubilee Hysor' white seeds

'Jumbo' large green seeds
'Masterpiece Green Longpod' long-pod, green seeds
'Meteor Vroma' green seeds
'Red Epicure' red seeds
'Relon' long-pod, green seeds
'The Sutton' dwarf, pale green seeds
'White Windsor' white seeds

broad (fava) beans

ABOVE **This row of broad (fava) beans is being supported with canes and string.**

Cultivation

Sowing time late autumn, late winter to late spring
Sowing or planting distance 23cm/9in
Sowing depth 4cm/1½in
Distance between sown rows 60cm/24in
Thinning distance no need to thin
Harvesting early to late summer

MARROWS & SQUASH CROPS

Marrows and Courgettes (Zucchini)
Cucurbita pepo

Although marrows (zucchini), pumpkins and squashes are essentially the same plant, they are dealt with separately because they are usually considered differently in the garden and kitchen. First, it is important to consider the difference between marrows and courgettes (zucchini). In fact, there is no real difference: courgettes are an immature form of marrow, and, if left to grow, will turn into marrows. However, some varieties are best grown as one or the other.

ABOVE **A female flower on a developing courgette (zucchini). The male flowers are often picked before they are open and used in cooking.**

The history of the marrow (zucchini) is not really known, and although they came to Europe from North America, there are no longer any native species that correspond to the plants we grow today. The marrow reached Europe in the 16th century and has been grown ever since. The idea of eating immature marrows as courgettes (zucchini) is a relatively recent development.

There are two types of marrows (zucchini): trailing and bush. The trailing forms throw out long stems that cover a great deal of space, and can be trained over a trellis or archway. The fruits appear at intervals along the stems. Bush varieties are much more compact, and the fruits grow from the central cluster of stems. They take up less space and are far better plants for small gardens. Courgettes (zucchini) are usually only grown as bushes; marrows are grown as either type.

In recent years courgettes (zucchini) have become much more popular than marrows (zucchini), partly because many people find that marrows are watery and bland and partly because, as families have become smaller, a whole marrow is difficult to dispose of in one sitting. However, marrows still have their devotees, and there are some very tasty ways of cooking them.

Courgettes (zucchini), on the other hand, are not only a more convenient size but, being immature, they do not dissolve into pulp quite so readily when they are cooked. They also have a more positive flavour. Nearly everybody who grows courgettes accidentally leaves at least one on the plant, which develops into a marrow (zucchini), so there is every opportunity of trying both. The flowers can also be eaten, either raw or cooked.

Marrows (zucchini) were traditionally grown on compost heaps. The heaps or bins were made up during winter and spring, topped with earth and left until the following autumn before being spread. The high concentration of rich, fibrous material meant that moisture and nutrients were in abundant supply, creating the ideal conditions for these plants during the summer growing season. They can, of course, be grown in ordinary vegetable plots, but using the compost heap does save space, which can be used for other crops.

Cultivation

Marrows and courgettes (zucchini) like an open, sunny situation and a rich, moisture-retentive soil. As noted above, they can be grown on the compost heap or in a bed that has been heavily manured during the previous autumn. They are frost tender, so plants should not be put outside before the last frosts have passed, unless they are protected with cloches.

Plants can be raised under glass by sowing the flat seed edgeways in individual pots or in modules in late spring or sown directly in the

LEFT **Do not plant courgettes (zucchini) too close together; leave space to harvest the fruit.**

PLANTING OUT

This marrow (zucchini) is being planted in its fibre pot. It has been grown like this to prevent disturbing the roots.

soil in early summer. Germination is speeded up by soaking the seed in water overnight. Keep seed that has been planted in the open warm by covering the soil with a jamjar or cloche until the seed has germinated. Sow two seeds at each position and remove the weaker if both germinate. Even if you sow in the open, sow a few in pots as insurance against sudden cold weather or the ravages of slugs.

Bush types can be left to develop by themselves but trailing varieties may need to be trimmed back if they get too vigorous. They can be left to trail outwards, like the spokes of a wheel, if there is enough space or they can be trained round in a circle, if

HARVESTING

Harvest a marrow (zucchini) by cutting it off at the base with a sharp knife.

Cultivation
Bush
Sowing time late spring (under glass) to early summer
Sowing or planting distance 90cm/3ft
Sowing depth 4cm/1½in
Distance between sown rows 90cm/3ft
Thinning distance no need to thin
Harvesting midsummer onwards
Trailing
Sowing time late spring (under glass) to early summer
Sowing or planting distance 1.2–1.8m/4–6ft
Sowing depth 4cm/1½in
Distance between sown rows 1.8m/6ft
Thinning distance no need to thin
Harvesting midsummer onwards

the stems are pegged down as they grow. If they are grown up a trellis or some other support, the shoots must be tied in regularly. Towards the end of summer remove the tips of each shoot. Keep well watered.

Harvesting

Courgettes (zucchini) are best harvested while they are still young – that is, when they are about 10cm/4in long – but in practice they can be harvested at any time, and circumstances usually dictate that they

are picked at any stage between being a courgette and a small marrow (zucchini). If they are left on the plant, courgettes will eventually develop into full marrows and can be cut at any time until the first frosts. Whatever the size of the crop, cut through the stem 2cm/¾in or more away from the fruit.

Storage

Courgettes (zucchini) are difficult to store for more than a few days and are best eaten fresh from the plant. They can be frozen, although they become less firm. Marrows (zucchini), in contrast, will last for several weeks after picking, especially if they have been left to mature and ripen. Pick marrows at the end of the season, before the first frosts, and then store them in a frost-free place for several weeks, on trays or hanging in net bags.

Pests and diseases

Although generally trouble free, slugs are the most severe problem, eating right through the stem if not checked.

Cucumber mosaic virus is the most common disease, causing mottled leaves and distorted fruit. The plant should be burned or destroyed. In some years powdery mildew is also a problem; rightly or wrongly gardeners tend to ignore it.

Varieties		
Bush	**Trailing**	**Courgettes (Zucchini)**
'All Green Bush'	'Long Green Trailing'	'Ambassador'
'Badger Cross'	'Long White Trailing'	'Burpee Golden Zucchini'
'Green Bush'	'Table Dainty'	'Bush Champion'
'Long Green Bush'	'Tender and True'	'Defender'
'Long White Bush'		'Early Gem'
'Minipak'		'Gold Rush'
		'Greyzini'
		'Tondo di Nizza'
		'Zucchini'

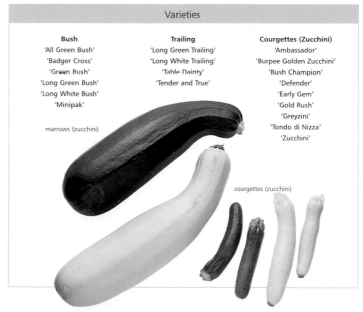

marrows (zucchini)

courgettes (zucchini)

Pumpkins
Cucurbita maxima

The pumpkin is a curious vegetable. In some arable areas it is treated seriously and grown for the kitchen; in other areas it is planted for fun, to see who can grow the biggest, or it is grown to be carved and hollowed out for a Hallowe'en lantern or mask. Whether for decorative or culinary use, pumpkins are definitely worth growing if you have the space.

Originally from South America, where they have been part of the staple diet for centuries, pumpkins are extremely popular in North America, and it is from there that their recent revival in Britain has come. They are, in fact, winter squashes but are frequently separated from the other members of the family simply on grounds of their size and uses. The distinctive name of pumpkin is usually given to the large, round winter squashes.

Some people consider pumpkins rather too large for consumption, but not all pumpkins need be big. The smaller ones, no more than 30cm/12in across, have usually been bred for taste rather than appearance and there is plenty of flesh on them for most purposes. Similarly, not all are the golden colour of Hallowe'en and show-bench pumpkins. 'Crown Prince' for example, has a bluish-grey skin and is only 30cm/12in

ABOVE **The skins of pumpkins should be hardened in the sunshine.**

LEFT **A healthy crop of pumpkins.**

across. The dense flesh, a deep old-gold colour, tastes delicious when cooked, and 'Crown Prince' will store much better than its big brash cousins.

Although pumpkins take time and patience, they are good plants with which to encourage young gardeners. The prospect of growing a huge vegetable that will weigh several hundred pounds – so heavy that even their parents can't lift it – seems to appeal to children, although what the cook does with so much pumpkin flesh defies thought – there is a limit to the amount of pumpkin soup and pies one can consume.

Cultivation

Pumpkins need a sunny site that is open and yet protected from strong winds, which can soon tear the large leaves to shreds. The soil should be rich in well-rotted organic material, not only to feed the pumpkins but also to hold plenty of moisture in the soil. At

each site, dig a pit 45cm/18in deep and 60cm/24in square and half-fill it with manure before replacing the top soil. In late spring start the pumpkins off in the greenhouse in modules or fibre pots. They do not need such a high temperature as cucumbers – a gentle heat of 15–18°C/59–64°F will be adequate. You can speed up germination by soaking the seed in water overnight.

PLANTING

Pumpkins are rich feeders and appreciate moisture near their roots, so add plenty of organic material to the soil when planting.

HARVESTING

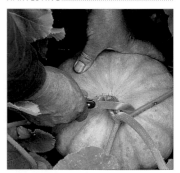

Harvest pumpkins when they have reached their mature colour by cutting through the stem at the top with a sharp knife.

Cultivation

Sowing time late spring under glass
Sowing or planting distance 1.8m/6ft
Sowing depth 4cm/1½in
Distance between sown rows 1.8m/6ft
Thinning distance no need to thin
Harvesting autumn

RIGHT **This is a large bed of pumpkins and squashes. Such close planting makes harvesting difficult, unless they are all harvested at once.**

When the threat of frost is passed, plant in the prepared ground at distances of 1.8m/6ft or further apart for more vigorous varieties. Keep the plant within bounds by training the stems in a spiral around the plant, pinning them down with wire pegs. If you want to grow giant specimens, reduce the number of young fruit to between one and three. Water regularly and apply a high-potash liquid feed at least once every two weeks and more frequently for giant fruit. Towards the end of summer, pinch out the tips of the shoots. Stop watering and feeding once the fruit is mature.

Harvesting

Harvest the pumpkins when they have reached their mature colour: deep orange or blue-grey. A good indicator that they are ready is that the stems begin to split. Cut them with a stem of about 5cm/2in. Make sure that they are all picked before the first frosts. Place them in a sunny position for about a week so that the skins fully harden.

Storage

Orange-skinned pumpkins will store for several weeks in a frost-free position. Blue-grey ones will last much longer, sometimes up to several months.

Pests and diseases

On the whole, pumpkins are trouble free. Slugs are probably the most severe problem and will eat right through the stem if not checked.

Cucumber mosaic virus is the most troublesome disease. The leaves become mottled and the fruit distorted. Destroy the entire plant.

Varieties

'Atlantic Giant' very large, orange skin
'Crown Prince' medium-sized, grey-blue skin, stores well
'Hundred Weight' large variety, yellow skin, stores well
'Jack Be Little' very small, orange skin, stores well
'Jackpot' medium- to large-sized, mottled orange and green skin

'Janne Gros de Paris' large, rough pink skin, stores well
'Mammoth' large, orange skin
'Small Sugar' small- to medium-sized, orange skin
'Spellbound' medium-sized, orange skin, stores well
'Spirit' medium-sized, orange skin
'Tom Fox' medium-sized, orange skin

pumpkins

Squashes
Cucurbita maxima

When it comes to definitions, squashes can be a confusing group of plants. In the broadest sense of the word, squashes include marrows (zucchini) and pumpkins as well as what are known as winter and summer squashes, because they all belong to the same botanical grouping and because their cultivation is broadly the same. However, many gardeners distinguish among squashes, marrows and pumpkins, because not only do they look different but they are grown and used in slightly different ways.

ABOVE **Harvest squashes by cutting through the stem with a sharp knife.**

There are two types of squash: summer squashes and winter squashes. The main difference is that winter squashes will store for long periods in winter, whereas summer squashes are for more immediate use, although they will keep for a few weeks. Marrows (zucchini) are types of summer squash; many pumpkins are types of winter squash. Pumpkins and squashes tend to merge together, and it is sometimes difficult to know if a specific variety is one or the other. In reality, it does not matter: it is only a name, and the growing and the eating are the same.

Squashes are a diverse group of plants, and many of them exhibit weird shapes – some have crooked necks or look like a Turkish turban or even a flying saucer – while others have ribbed or warty surfaces. The flesh ranges in colour from almost white to deep orange. The taste also varies, but, like marrows (zucchini), the flavour is not particularly intense. Although they undoubtedly do have culinary value, they are often grown for their appearance, the wide range of shapes and colours making them not only attractive but also intriguing.

Originally from South America, squashes were introduced to Europe by returning conquistadors and explorers in the 16th century. The majority of the vast range of varieties have been developed in South and North America, and it is only recently that they have regained popularity in Britain.

Cultivation

The cultivation for both summer and winter squashes is basically the same, it is only in their storage that there is any real difference. They need an open, sunny site that is protected from strong winds. Squashes like a soil that is rich in organic matter, both to provide them with nutrients and to hold an ample supply of moisture. Dig in plenty of manure or compost in the autumn.

Sow squashes under glass in a medium temperature of about 18°C/64°F. Because they do not like root disturbance, grow them individually in modules or fibre pots. Once the frosts have passed, they can be planted out, setting them at least 1.8m/6ft apart. Alternatively, they can be sown where they are to grow. Sow two seeds at each station, removing the weaker seedling once they have germinated. Sowing should be in early summer, after the frosts have passed. As the stems grow, they can be trained around in a spiral to save space and pinned down with wire pegs. Many types of squash can be grown as climbing plants and trained up a trellis or netting. Keep the plants well watered, and feed with a high-potash liquid fertilizer about once every ten days.

Harvesting

Squashes are ready to harvest when the stems begin to split. Cut the summer squashes when they are large enough to eat and while the skin is still soft (your finger-nail should easily sink into the skin). Cut

LEFT **If necessary, reduce the size of squash plants by cutting off the trailing stems, two leaves above a fruit.**

Cultivation

Summer
Sowing time late spring (under glass)
to early summer
Sowing or planting distance 1.8m/6ft
Sowing depth 4cm/1½in
Distance between sown rows 1.8m/6ft
Thinning distance no need to thin
Harvesting late summer and autumn
Winter
Sowing time late spring (under glass)
to early summer
Sowing or planting distance 1.8m/6ft
Sowing depth 4cm/1½in
Distance between sown rows 1.8m/6ft
Thinning distance no need to thin
Harvesting autumn

them with a short length of stem attached. Winter squashes can be cut in the same way if they are to be used straightaway; for winter storage leave them on the plants for as long as possible, but harvest before the first frosts. If possible, leave in the sun for a few days before storing to harden the skin.

Storage

Summer squashes can be stored for a short while – two weeks or so, but generally not much longer. They are best used straight from the plant. If the skins of the winter squashes have been hardened, they will keep for several weeks in a frost-free place. They can be stored in nets or in trays, each squash placed so that it is not touching its neighbour.

PROVIDING SUPPORT

Support growing squashes on straw to prevent them from being damaged.

Pests and diseases

On the whole, squashes are usually trouble free. Slugs are once again the most severe problem and they will quickly eat straight through the stem if they are not checked in time.

Cucumber mosaic virus is the most troublesome of the potential diseases. The leaves become mottled and the fruit

ABOVE **A terracotta saucer can be used to protect squashes instead of a layer of straw.**

distorted. The whole plant should be destroyed if it is affected. In some years powdery mildew can also be a possible problem; rightly or wrongly, most gardeners find that its occurrence can usually be safely ignored.

Varieties

Summer
'Custard White' round, white skin, scalloped edges
'Dawn' yellow skin, crooked neck
'Little Gem' round, dark green skin, pale flesh
'Orangetti' cylindrical, orange skin,
spaghetti-like flesh
'Scallopini' discus-shaped, green skin,
scalloped edges
'Table Ace' small and acorn-shaped,
dark green skin, orange flesh
'Vegetable Spaghetti' cylindrical,
sphagetti-like flesh
Winter
'Butternut' cylindrical, cream skin, orange flesh
'Cobnut' cylindrical, cream skin, cream flesh
'Cream of the Crop' ribbed oval
fruit, cream skin, cream flesh
'Early Acorn' oval-shaped,
dark green skin, orange flesh
'Golden Hubbard' oval, yellow knobbly skin
'Green Hubbard' oval, green knobbly skin

'Sweet Dumpling' ribbed and rounded fruit,
cream and dark green skin, orange flesh
'Turk's Turban' turban shaped, green,
cream and orange skin

winter
squashes

Cucumbers
Cucumis sativus

One of the quickest ways to prepare a meal is to pop into the garden, grab a lettuce, some tomatoes and a cucumber. Add some fresh, crusty bread – and there you are. Most gardeners grow lettuces and tomatoes, but fewer grow cucumbers, perhaps because they think they require a greenhouse or they are difficult to grow. They need not be either. Outdoor cucumbers can be grown as easily as courgettes (zucchini), which few gardeners find a problem.

Cucumbers have been used as a vegetable for the best part of 5,000 years. They were first grown and eaten in India, where they were developed from a native species, and from there they spread north-east into China and north-west into Greece and Rome.

There are several colours and shapes. In the West we are more used to long cucumbers with green skins, but they can also be oval or even round, and colours can range from white to yellow.

As far as the gardener is concerned, there are two types of cucumber: the climbing varieties with long fruit that are grown under glass and the ridge varieties that are much shorter and are grown in the open. The advantage of greenhouse varieties is that they can be started earlier and are not as dependent on the weather. Ridge varieties, on the other hand, need less looking after and are less prone to attack by pests and diseases, which thrive in the warmth of the greenhouse. From the culinary point of view, the greenhouse forms are often preferred, mainly because outdoor cucumbers have tough, often prickly, skins and do not look quite as elegant as their indoor cousins. Until recently, many outdoor varieties tended to taste bitter, but this is now no longer generally the case.

Gherkins are a form of ridge cucumber, which are used for pickling. Any immature ridge cucumber can be used, but some varieties have been specially bred for the purpose. Like courgettes and marrows (zucchini), there is no difference in cultivation technique other than the time of picking.

Cultivation

Greenhouse cucumbers need a high temperature in which to germinate and a high temperature in which to grow. Using seed of all-female varieties – they are less likely to be bitter – sow two seeds, edgeways, in pots or modules and place in a propagator at 24°C/75°F. When they germinate, remove the weaker seedling and reduce the temperature to 21°C/70°F. Plant the young plants with as little

ABOVE **Ridge or outdoor cucumbers growing in the open need a sunny spot that is sheltered from the wind.**

root disturbance as possible into growing bags, two per bag depending on the size. Use square-meshed netting or a system of poles and horizontal wires as supports, and tie in the shoots as they grow. Pinch out the tip of the shoot when it reaches the roof. Tie the laterals to horizontal wires and pinch out the tips two leaves beyond the first fruit to form. Water to keep the soil constantly moist and throw some water on the floor of the greenhouse to keep the atmosphere humid. Keep the house shaded. Once the fruit start to develop, feed them with a high-potash liquid feed once every two weeks.

Ridge or outdoor cucumbers need a sunny spot sheltered from the wind. Add plenty of well-rotted manure to the soil before sowing. Sow ridge cucumbers either inside in pots or outdoors where they are to grow. If sown directly, cover them with a glass jamjar or cloche to raise the temperature. Do not sow until after the threat of frost has passed and the soil has warmed up. Sow, leaving about 75cm/30in in each direction between plants. If the seed is germinated in pots, ensure that the roots are not disturbed when they are transplanted. Fibre pots can help with this,

LEFT **A ridge or outdoor cucumber, with its attractive yellow flowers and tough, prickly skin clearly on display.**

Cultivation

Greenhouse
Sowing time late winter onwards
Sowing or planting distance 60cm/24in
Sowing depth 2.5cm/1in
Thinning distance no need to thin
Harvesting midsummer onwards
Ridge
Sowing time late spring (under glass)
to early summer
Sowing or planting distance 75cm/30in
Sowing depth 2.5cm/1in
Distance between sown rows 75cm/30in
Thinning distance no need to thin
Harvesting midsummer onwards

ABOVE **This ridge or outdoor cucumber has been trained up a cane tripod. The large leaves and fruits have a pleasing architectural quality.**

ABOVE **Climbing varieties of cucumber are grown under glass. They have smooth skins and are longer than ridge varieties.**

ridge cucumber

greenhouse cucumber

Varieties	
Ridge	'Pepinex'
'Burpless Tasty Green'	'Petita'
'Bush Champion'	'Telegraph'
'Crystal Apple'	'Telegraph
'Long Green Ridge'	Improved'
'Masterpiece'	**Gherkins**
Greenhouse	'Bestal'
'Birgit'	'Venlo
'Fenumex'	Pickling'

because the cucumbers can be planted without removing them from the pots. Pinch out the tip of the main shoot after six leaves have formed so that the plant bushes out. Water freely. Once the fruit start to develop, feed with a high-potash liquid feed once every two weeks.

Harvesting

Cut the fruit with a short length of stalk as soon as they are large enough to eat. Pick frequently and more fruit will develop. Harvest gherkins when they are 5–8cm/ 2–3in long.

Storage

Keep for no more more than a few days; they are best eaten fresh.

Pests and diseases

Slugs and snails can quickly eat through a stem, killing the plant; remove by your preferred method. In the greenhouse, red spider mite and whitefly may be a problem.

SHOOT CROPS

Asparagus
Asparagus officinalis

Asparagus was once the food of the wealthy – if you didn't have your own garden, you couldn't grow it. Nowadays it is much more widely available, but shoots cut straight from the garden and cooked immediately still taste best. Asparagus is not only good to eat, but the decorative foliage has a wonderful filmy quality about it. A great uncle of mine grew asparagus all his long life, not to eat it, but so that he could use the cut foliage with his sweet peas. In a potager or decorative kitchen garden, the great plumes of finely cut foliage make a fine display.

ABOVE **Harvest asparagus by cutting the stems below the ground.**

The tender shoot of asparagus is the part of the plant that is eaten. The shoot emerges from below ground in late spring and early summer. Once it gets above approximately 15–20cm/6–8in long it becomes tough-skinned and rather chewy and is then best left, the remaining shoots developing into tall foliage stems with inconspicuous flowers and, eventually, orange-red berries.

Asparagus grows wild throughout Europe and has been eaten and possibly cultivated from at least the time of the Ancient Greeks. It has long been grown in gardens, but the main disadvantage is that it takes up quite a lot of space. If you have a small garden but want to grow asparagus, try planting one or two crowns in the flower borders, picking the spikes in early summer and then leaving them in the border as a decorative foliage plant.

One of the attractive features of creating an asparagus bed is that it lasts for at least 20 years, and apart from a little maintenance, not much effort is required to produce a wonderful feast each year. Asparagus plants are either male or female. Male plants have the advantage of being more productive and not producing seed (which readily self-sows). Asparagus can be raised from seed, but the results can be disappointing if you use your own collected seed; it is better to buy named varieties on which you can rely. An increasing number of F1 hybrids is available, and these produce very good all-male plants.

Cultivation

Asparagus needs an open, sunny site, and it likes a light, preferably sandy soil, although it can be grown in any soil as long as it is free-draining and reasonably fertile. In heavy soils it can be grown by raising the level of the soil or by making a raised bed. In the autumn before planting, dig the bed, removing all traces of perennial weeds and incorporating plenty of well-rotted manure or compost. In the spring dig out a trench 20cm/8in deep with an 8cm/3in ridge running down the centre. If more than one row is required, set the trenches 90cm/3ft apart. Set each asparagus crown on the ridge, spreading out its roots around it.

Each crown should be 45cm/18in apart. Cover them with soil to a depth of 8–10cm/3–4in.

If you are growing from seed, soak them overnight in water and sow in a drill 1cm/½in deep. Do this in spring. Thin to 15cm/6in and transplant the following spring in the same manner as for bought crowns above. As the plants grow, draw in more earth from the side of the trench until it is filled.

Do not cut any spears in the first year and only one or two from each plant during the next year. Each spring, cover the trench with a layer of manure or compost, leaving it slightly heaped up so that over the years the row becomes earthed (hilled) up in the

APPLYING A SPRING MULCH

In the spring, before growth starts, apply a deep mulch of manure over the rows of asparagus.

CUTTING DOWN IN AUTUMN

In the autumn, as the asparagus fronds are turning brown, cut them down to the ground.

same way you treat potatoes. Keep the ground weeded. Cut down the ferns as they begin to turn yellow and, if possible, before the berries begin to ripen; alternatively, pick all the berries. If they are left on the plants the birds will eat them and before long asparagus will be appearing all over the garden. For the same reason, avoid putting berried stems on the compost heap.

Cultivation

Sowing
Sowing time spring
Sowing depth 1cm/½in
Distance between sown rows 30cm/12in
Thinning distance 15cm/6in
Transplanting following spring
Planting
Planting time early spring
Planting distance 45cm/18in
Planting depth initially 8–10cm/3–4in
Distance between sown rows 90cm/3ft
Harvesting in late spring for six weeks
(third year onwards)

Harvesting

In late spring, when the shoots that have emerged are 10–15cm/4–6in long, cut them by inserting a knife 5cm/2in below the surface of the soil. Only cut through the stem, do not thrash around below the soil level or you may damage spears that have not yet emerged. Make a slanting cut. After the third year cutting can take place over about six weeks.

Storage

Asparagus is best used fresh from the plant, but it can be stored for a couple of days if it is stood in a jug of cold water in the refrigerator.

Varieties

'Accell'	'Giant Mammoth'
'Boonlim'	'Limbras'
'Cito'	'Lucullus'
'Connover's Colossal'	'Martha
'Franklin'	Washington'

ABOVE **Once the harvesting season is over, the asparagus is left to grow to its full height.**

Pests and diseases

Asparagus is usually pest and disease free. Slugs, as usual, are likely to be the worst problem, making holes in the spears. Asparagus beetle can also be a nuisance.

asparagus

Celery
Apium graveolens

Celery is an important vegetable for the kitchen as it is used, at least in part, in many dishes, including basic recipes such as stocks. Its culinary importance is not reflected in the garden, however. At one time no vegetable garden was complete without celery, but it is seen less often today, which may be partly because it is slightly difficult to grow and partly because it needs a constantly moist soil to do well. Whatever the reason, it is a shame it is not more widely grown, because if you do grow it you will find that you are constantly using it and, as always, will find the flavour so much better than shop-bought stalks.

ABOVE **Green varieties of celery, such as the one shown here, do not need blanching.**

Celery grows wild throughout Europe and Asia, and it is rather surprising to learn that it has entered cultivation only in relatively recent times. Celery was first cultivated in Italy as recently as the 16th century but it did not arrive in Britain until the end of the 17th century.

It is the blanched leaf stalks of celery that are eaten. These can be eaten green but taste sweeter if the light has been excluded, causing the stalks to turn white. This always used to be done by heaping earth up round them, but more often these days the stems are wrapped in cardboard or felt. This type of celery is often referred to as trench celery. Breeding has produced celery with self-blanching stems, although not everybody feels that these are wholly successful and that the old-style blanched stalks taste better. There are also forms with green, pink or red stems. There is a form of celery, known as green or American celery, which does not require blanching.

As well as the stems, some people like to eat the heart, the solid part of the plant, where the stems join the root. Some recipes also call for the leaves to be included, particularly when the celery is a flavouring agent rather than a vegetable in its own right. It can be cooked or eaten raw.

Cultivation

There are two ways of growing celery, depending on what type is being grown. To grow traditional trench celery, in the preceding autumn or winter dig out a trench 45cm/18in wide and 30cm/12in deep and put in an 8cm/3in layer of rotted manure. Backfill the trench, leaving it about 10cm/4in deep. Sow the seeds under glass in modules in early spring and place them in moderate heat of 10–16°C/50–61°F. Do not check the plants by subjecting them to a sudden change of temperature or by allowing them to dry out. Once the frosts are over, harden off the plants and plant them out in the trench at 30cm/12in intervals. When the plants reach about 30cm/12in, tie the stems loosely together just below the leaves and draw up earth over part of the stems. Repeat the process three weeks later, pulling up more soil, and again three weeks after this, until the soil is up to the lower leaves. Alternatively,

BLANCHING CELERY

1 Blanching celery stems will make them taste sweeter. When the stems reach a height of about 30cm/12in, tie them loosely together just below the leaves.

2 A collar of cardboard or waterproof paper is tied around the stems of celery. The stems eventually blanch because of the lack of light.

3 Soil can be used to hold the collar in place. Although soil can also be earthed up around the stems to blanch them, a collar will stop soil from getting into the crown.

Cultivation
Trench
Sowing time early to mid-spring
Planting date early summer
Planting distance 30cm/12in
Distance between sown rows 60cm/24in
Harvesting autumn onwards
Self-blanching
Sowing time early to mid-spring
Planting date early summer
Planting distance in blocks 23cm/9in
Harvesting autumn

Varieties	
Trench	'Golden Self-blanching'
'Giant Pink'	'Ivory Tower'
'Giant Red'	'Lathom's
'Giant White'	Self-blanching'
'Hopkins Fenlander'	'Victoria'
'Martine'	**Green**
'New White Dwarf'	'Greensnap'
Self-blanching	'Imperial'
'Celebrity'	'Tall Utah'

plant on flat ground and wrap cardboard or waterproof paper round the stems when they are 30cm/12in long. When the stems grow taller, wrap a second collar round them. Keep the celery well watered and do not allow the soil to dry out.

Self-blanching celery is started in the same way from seed and then planted out in blocks rather than rows, setting the plants at intervals of 23cm/9in in all directions. The dense foliage helps to blanch the stems. Place straw around the outside of the block to help keep out the light. Green celery can be grown in the same way, although there is no need for the straw.

HARVESTING

Harvest the celery by digging beneath it with a fork and levering it out of the soil. Replace any soil around the next plant if it falls away.

ABOVE **The celery planted here with some cabbages is one of the self-blanching varieties now available – 'Golden Self-blanching'.**

Harvesting

Trench celery can be lifted in autumn by digging it up with a fork. Replace soil around the next plant if it falls away. Continue to dig as required. The flavour is improved by the first frosts, but cover the plants with straw in severe weather so that penetrating frosts do not reach the stems. Self-blanching celery can also be harvested as required from the autumn onwards, but it should be lifted by the time of the first winter frosts.

Storage

Leave trench varieties where they are growing until required. In colder areas, before the weather becomes severe, lift and store in a frost-free place, where they should stay fresh for several weeks. Celery can be frozen, but it becomes mushy when it is defrosted, so it can only be used as flavouring or in cooked dishes.

Pests and diseases

Slugs are one of the worst enemies of celery, and it is important to cull them regularly by your preferred method. Other problems can include celery fly and carrot fly.

Diseases include celery heart rot and celery leaf spot. Boron deficiency, which causes the stems to crack, may also be a problem.

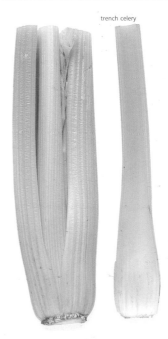

trench celery

Celeriac (Celery Root)
Apium graveolens var. *rapaceum*

Although it is often thought of as a root crop, celeriac (celery root) is considered in this section partly because it fits more neatly beside celery and partly because it is not, in fact, the root but the swollen stem that forms the vegetable. Like cultivated celery, celeriac is derived from the wild celery which is a native plant found in Europe and the Middle East. It was a much later development than celery and is said to have been introduced to Britain from Alexandria in the early 18th century.

Celeriac (celery root) is the swollen area of the plant where the leaf stalks join the root. This produces a hard, round vegetable, often with knobbles and leaf scars over its dirty-looking surface. Although it looks far from appetizing, it is a useful vegetable. It is most frequently used as a flavouring, making an excellent winter substitute for celery, but it is also used as a vegetable in its own right, either cooked or grated raw in a salad.

Celeriac (celery root) is easier to grow than celery because it does not need blanching and is less prone to pests and diseases. However, like celery, it does need a moist soil in order to keep it growing.

Celeriac (celery root) should be given as long a growing season as possible or it will not develop into a large enough size that is worth harvesting and eating. This means that you will have to start off the celeriac plants early under glass.

BELOW **A row of celeriac (celery root), showing perfect spacing between the plants, and leaves trimmed from the tops of the bulbs.**

Earth (hill) up the lower half of the celeriac (celery root) bulb in order to keep it white.

Cultivation
Celeriac (celery root) likes an open, sunny position, but it will tolerate a little light shade. The soil must be rich in organic material, not only to provide nutrients but also to help retain moisture around the roots.

Sow celeriac (celery root) under glass in modules or fibre pots in late winter or early spring. Place them in a propagator at about 15°C/59°F. Maintain an even temperature and keep them watered so that growth is not checked. Towards the end of spring, when the plants are about 8cm/3in tall, harden them off and plant out at 30cm/12in intervals in rows set 30cm/12in apart. Plant them so that the base of the stem is level with the surface of the soil. Remember to keep them watered so that growth is not checked.

Cut off any side shoots that appear and towards late summer remove a few of the lower leaves and earth up around the swollen stem so that it stays white. In cold areas cover the plants with straw to protect from severe frosts.

Harvesting

Dig celeriac (celery root) as needed from autumn onwards. They should be left to develop until they are as large as possible, although they are edible from about 8cm/3in across.

Storage

Unless the weather is particularly severe, celeriac (celery root) can be left in the ground

WATERING

The growth of celeriac (celery root) must not be checked; it must be watered during dry spells.

ABOVE **Remove a few of the lower leaves from the bulb to let the light onto the top. This should be done in late summer.**

until it is required. A covering of straw will help protect it if necessary. In colder areas it can be lifted, cleaned and placed in trays filled with just-moist sand or peat (peat moss) and kept in a frost-free place.

Pests and diseases

On the whole, celeriac (celery root) is relatively trouble free, although slugs can be a problem with young plants. Carrot fly and celery fly may also cause problems.

Cultivation

Sowing time late winter to mid-spring
Planting time late spring to early summer
Planting distance 30cm/12in
Distance between sown rows 30cm/12in
Harvesting autumn onwards

Varieties

'Alabaster'	'Marble Ball'
'Balder'	'Monarch'
'Brilliant'	'Snow White'
'Giant Prague'	'Tellus'

celeriac
(celery root)

Globe Artichokes
Cynara cardunculus Scolymus Group

Globe artichokes were not much grown by the old country gardeners, who tended to concentrate on staple foods rather than "fancy ones". The artichoke was regarded as belonging on the tables of the rich. Today, however, although many people still grow their own vegetables, they are not dependent on doing so and can, therefore, afford to include a few delicacies that are not absolutely necessary to everyday life. Once you have grown and tasted globe artichokes, however, you may join the growing ranks of gardeners who consider them an essential part of their diet.

Unlike most vegetables, the part of globe artichokes that is eaten is the flower-head or, rather, the flower-bud before the flower begins to open. The whole head is boiled or steamed and then various parts consumed. First, the scale-like bracts are removed and the soft fleshy part at the base of each is eaten. As these are removed, the hairy tuft of the flower, the "choke", is revealed. This is usually removed and discarded and then the base of the flower, or the heart, is scooped out and eaten. It can then be served with lots of butter, which, needless to say, gets everywhere.

Globe artichokes were grown by the Ancient Greeks and the Romans, before spreading to the rest of Europe. They are

BELOW **Harvesting an artichoke by cutting the stem just below the head.**

handsome plants, looking a bit like the giant thistle, to which they are related. They are usually grown in the vegetable garden because you need several plants to give a constant supply throughout the summer, but if you decide to have only a couple of plants you could easily grow them in the flower border to save space. They have attractive silvery foliage, and if you leave a few flowers they develop large purple heads, which will usually be covered in bees.

Globe artichokes are usually grown from offsets rather than from seed, which is likely to produce variable results. If you have difficulty in getting offsets, you could initially grow them from seed and select the best plants, then continue to propagate these by division. This can be done by cutting off the young, outer growth from the old plant with a sharp knife in spring. Each

CUTTING BACK

Cut down all stems to ground level when the plant dies back in the autumn. Replace plants after three or, at most, four years.

shoot should be growing strongly and have some roots attached. Plant out immediately. Divisions can also be taken in autumn, when the offset can be potted up and over-wintered in a greenhouse or cold frame.

Cultivation

Globe artichokes need an open, sunny situation. Because they will be in the ground for several years, the soil must be thoroughly prepared. Remove all perennial weeds and incorporate plenty of organic material. In spring plant the offsets at 75cm/30in

COVERING WITH STRAW

Cover the plant with straw during autumn in colder areas.

ABOVE **A bed of globe artichokes with heads that are nearly ready for cutting.**

intervals in rows set 90cm/3ft apart. Trim off about a third of each leaf to reduce water loss while the plant is getting established. Water and keep watered in dry periods.

Seed can be sown in spring about 2.5cm/1in deep in rows 30cm/12in apart. Thin to 15cm/6in apart. Transplant the following spring. In autumn cut down the main stems and draw up soil around the crown. Cover with straw in very cold areas. Replace plants after three or, at most, four years, and aim to replant a third of your plants every year.

Harvesting

Harvest from the second year onwards. Take the flower-heads before they open and while they are still green, cutting about 2.5cm/1in below the head with a sharp knife or secateurs (pruners).

Storage

Globe artichokes should be eaten straight from the plant. They can be frozen but remove the stem and choke first.

Pests and diseases

On the whole globe artichokes are not troubled by many problems. Blackfly can be a nuisance in bad seasons.

globe artichokes

Cultivation

Seed
Sowing time spring
Sowing depth 2.5cm/1in
Distance between sown rows 30cm/12in
Thinning distance 15cm/6in
Transplanting following spring
Offsets
Planting time spring
Planting distance 75cm/30in
Distance between rows 90cm/3ft
Harvesting summer of second year onwards

Varieties

'Green Globe'	'Vert de Laon'
'Purple Globe'	'Violetta di Chioggia'

Rhubarb

Rheum × hybridum

Gardening has many contradictions and rhubarb is one of them. It is a vegetable, but it is mainly used as a fruit – that is, it is eaten with sugar as a dessert. Tomatoes, on the other hand, are, strictly speaking, fruit but are used as a vegetable. Does it matter? These are problems only when you start classifying plants or writing books; in the garden and kitchen it doesn't matter at all.

O riginally rhubarb was grown as a medicinal plant (the root was powdered and used as a laxative), and it was only much later that it was used as a vegetable. It was used in medicine nearly 5,000 years ago in Ancient China, but it was only in the 18th century that it was realized that it also made a good vegetable. Forcing to obtain an early crop was not discovered (accidentally, as all good discoveries seem to be) until early in the following century, less than 200 years ago.

Only the young stalks are eaten, and these must be cooked. The leaves are poisonous, so do not be tempted to experiment with them in an attempt to invent new dishes. The crop is normally harvested from spring to early summer, but it is possible to "force" it, by covering the dormant crown with a box, bucket or, if you can afford it, a decorative terracotta rhubarb forcer. This produces a crop of sweet-tasting stems, several weeks earlier than if the plant is left in the open.

Rhubarb is an easy crop to grow and, once planted, it is not at all demanding. It can be left where it is for 20 years or more, although some gardeners prefer to replace their plants every five years or so in order to keep them vigorous. Rhubarb does take up quite a bit of space, but a couple of plants will keep a small family well supplied. The space may be considered well used because rhubarb plants are also quite decorative, with their huge green leaves and attractive red stems. In summer they throw up large flowering stems, covered with masses of creamy flowers, which can be spectacular.

Cultivation

Rhubarb must have a sunny position, away from shade. The soil should be rich in organic material but it should also be reasonably free draining. Because the site will be in use over a long period of time, take care in its preparation, removing all perennial weeds and digging deeply to incorporate as much well-rotted manure as

Cultivation
Seed
Sowing time spring
Sowing depth 2.5cm/1in
Distance between sown rows 30cm/12in
Thinning distance 23cm/9in
Transplanting following winter
Division
Planting time winter or (if potted) spring
Planting distance 90cm/3ft
Distance between rows 90cm/3ft
Harvesting summer of second year onwards

LEFT **A decorative terracotta rhubarb forcer for producing sweet early rhubarb. Alternatively, a box or bucket can be used.**

possible. In the past new plants were bare rooted and were planted in winter, while they were dormant. This is also a good time to divide an existing plant to start a new one: dig up the old plant and remove an outer section that includes at least one bud. Plants that are purchased in pots can be planted in spring or even summer if they are kept well-watered. They should be spaced 90cm/3ft apart.

Rhubarb can also be grown from seed, but this method takes longer and the quality of the plant cannot be guaranteed in the same way as buying a named cultivar. However, the seed can be sown in 2.5cm/1in drills and thinned to 23cm/9in once they have germinated. Plant out in their final position, in the same way as for dormant crowns, during the following

winter. Water well in dry weather. Apply a mulch of well-rotted, seed-free manure in autumn and again in spring.

To force a rhubarb plant, cover it with a large upturned bucket or other similar container in midwinter. Do not force the same plant for two years running or it will be weakened.

HARVESTING

Harvest by pulling on the sticks of rhubarb so that they come out of their "socket". Cut off the leaves and discard on the compost heap.

Harvesting

Rhubarb is harvested from spring to early summer unless it has been forced, when it can be pulled a few weeks earlier. It is harvested by pulling each stem vertically from close to the base – it will come out of its "socket". Cut off the leaves and discard on the compost heap.

Storage

Rhubarb is best cooked straight from the garden. Otherwise it can be stored by freezing or bottling.

Pests and diseases

There are a few pests and diseases that trouble rhubarb, but you will be unfortunate if you come across them.

Varieties	
'Appleton's Forcing'	'Hawkes Champagne'
'Canada Red'	'Macdonald'
'Champagne'	'The Sutton'
'Early Victoria'	'Timperley Early'
'Glaskin's Perpetual'	'Victoria'

ABOVE **A bed of healthy looking rhubarb is an attractive sight. Remember that rhubarb leaves are poisonous and cannot be eaten.**

rhubarb

Seakale
Crambe maritima

Although seakale is one of the least popular of vegetables, it is not only delicious but is very easy to grow. Perhaps we are all too used to looking abroad for delicacies, which now come with startling ease from all corners of the globe to even the humblest of greengrocers. Seakale has been in cultivation from at least the beginning of the 18th century, but the wild plant was harvested long before that. It is, in fact, native to Britain, where it grows on shingle shores around the coast. Don't rush off and start picking it, however, because, like many leaf and stem plants, it needs blanching before the taste is palatable (also, of course, you should never pick wild plants). The blanched stems are harvested in spring and then cooked and eaten, like asparagus, with lots of butter or with olive oil. The flowering shoots can also be eaten while they are still in bud, much in the manner of broccoli.

Seakale is usually grown from "thongs" or root cuttings, although it can also be grown from seed. There are only a few named varieties – it is a vegetable that varies little from its wild ancestor. Because it is sometimes difficult to obtain plants, it may be easier to grow from seed, discarding any inferior plants and propagating the better forms. 'Lilywhite' is about the only named cultivar, but it is doubtful if all the plants sold under that name are, in fact, true to the original of that name.

Although primarily grown for its blanched stems, seakale is a very attractive plant and is well worth growing in a decorative kitchen garden for its curly, glaucous, purple leaves and the dense mass of honey-scented, white flowers, which appear in early summer. Anyone creating a potager purely for its decorative effect should consider seakale a prime candidate, as should anyone who wants to grow vegetables in the flower border.

Cultivation
Seakale needs an open, sunny position. The soil must be free-draining – sandy or gravelly soil is ideal – and if your soil is very heavy, it may be necessary to create a raised bed. Incorporate manure during the autumn digging. Plants can be grown from bought plants, from root cuttings or "thongs" or from seed. Bought plants should be planted out in spring at 45cm/18in apart in rows the same distance apart.

Take root cuttings or thongs from existing plants in autumn. Cut a few side roots that are about 1cm/½in thick into 15cm/6in lengths. Tie these in a bundle and put them vertically (make certain the top of the root is at the top) in the garden in well-drained soil or in a large pot filled with free-draining compost (soil mix). The top of the roots should be about 5cm/2in below the surface. Towards the end of next spring, once shoots have appeared from the bundle, separate them and plant them out at the same intervals as for bought plants. Alternatively, dig up the plants in autumn and place them in boxes of compost with the buds at the surface. Place in a dark place with the temperature about 10°C/50°F.

Seed should be sown in spring in drills 4cm/1½in deep. Soak the seed in water overnight before sowing. Thin seedlings to 23cm/9in. Transplant the resulting seedlings to their final position the following spring.

Cultivation		
Seed		
Sowing time spring		
Sowing depth 4cm/1½in		
Distance between sown rows 30cm/12in		
Thinning distance 23cm/9in		
Transplanting the following spring		
Plants		
Planting time spring		
Planting distance 45cm/18in		
Distance between rows 45cm/18in		
Harvesting summer of second year onwards		
Thongs		
Cuttings struck autumn		
Transplanting late spring		
Planting distance 45cm/18in		
Distance between rows 45cm/18in		
Harvesting summer of second year onwards		

LEFT **A bed of seakale that will be blanched next winter. To blanch, cover the stems with an upturned bucket or special terracotta pot.**

The stems of seakale can be blanched by covering the plants in late winter or early spring with a special terracotta pot or an upturned bucket. Terracotta pots have the advantage of looking more decorative. It is important that no light enters, or the stems will turn green and taste bitter.

Harvesting

Plants and thongs can be harvested in the second year; those grown from seed in the third year. Harvest when the blanched stems are long enough and remove the covers once harvesting is complete. Discard the plants after harvesting (but remember to take root cuttings when you lift the plants in order to provide the crop for next year).

Storage

Eat seakale straight from the garden.

Pests and diseases

On the whole, seakale is trouble free. The worst pests are slugs and caterpillars, especially those belonging to the cabbage white butterfly.

Varieties
Usually listed simply as seakale, except for 'Lilywhite'.

seakale

ABOVE **Some blanched seakale after the terracotta pot or upturned bucket has been removed. The seakale is now ready for harvesting.**

LEFT **This is a blanched seakale plant that has been exposed to the light once more to grow away again.**

Florence Fennel
Foeniculum vulgare var. dulce

With a name like Florence fennel it does not take much imagination to guess that the fennel we grow today originated in Italy, during Roman times. Italy is, in fact, still the centre of cultivation because it is very widely used in Italian cooking. Although it was introduced to Britain in the 18th century it has never been widely grown until recently, because the popularity of Italian dishes has encouraged more gardeners than ever to grow it.

Fennel is a versatile plant. As a vegetable it is grown for the bulbous swelling at the base of the leaf stalks, but other parts of the plant can also be eaten. The leaves are used as a herb, for both flavouring and garnish, and the seeds are used for their aniseed flavour. Fennel also makes a superb foliage plant and is often grown just for its decorative, finely cut foliage, which has a light, airy quality

BELOW **A bed of Florence fennel, showing the bulbs and the decorative foliage.**

about it. The main vegetable forms have bright green foliage, but some perennial forms grown in the flower garden have very attractive bronze leaves. In the first year it grows to about 75cm/30in, but it gets much taller before it flowers in the following year.

It is, however, the bulbous part for which the plant is mainly grown. This consists of the overlapping swollen bases of the leaves, and it is either cooked or eaten raw in salads as a crisp, aniseed-flavoured alternative to celery.

The secret of growing fennel is to make certain that it is kept moist and grows fast. If there are any checks, especially through drought, the plants will quickly run to seed before the bulb is formed.

Cultivation

Fennel needs an open, sunny position and, because of its height, one that is sheltered from the wind. It prefers light, well-drained soil, and if your soil is heavy, a raised bed might be better. The soil should be well manured to help make sure that it does not dry out. Do not be in too much of a hurry to sow, because plants from seed sown in spring are likely to bolt. Early to midsummer is the

HARVESTING

These bulbs are nearly ready for harvesting. They can be pulled directly from the ground or cut just below the bulb so that the root produces more foliage.

best time. Sow the seed in drills 1cm/½in deep and 45cm/18in apart. Seed can also be sown in modules under glass, but the transplanting may cause the plants to check and bolt, so it is preferable as well as less time-consuming to sow in situ. Thin the resulting seedlings to intervals of 23cm/9in. Keep the bed well watered, especially during dry periods. When the bulbs begin to swell, draw some soil up round them to at least half their height. As they continue to swell, draw up more soil to blanch the bulbs, which makes them taste sweeter.

Harvesting

Florence fennel is ready to harvest when the bulb is about the size of a tennis ball, which is about two or three weeks after earthing (hilling) up. It can either be pulled from the ground and then the root and leaf stems cut off, or cut from the root while still in the ground. This has the advantage that the root will sprout again and produce new feathery foliage that can be used for flavouring or decoration. If seed is required, the plants will have to be left in the ground for a second year, during which they will flower and set seed. This can be collected on a dry day and dried thoroughly in a warm place before being stored in an airtight jar.

Storage

Fennel is best eaten when it is fresh, straight from the garden. It will then keep

for a few days if it is stored in a refrigerator but not for any longer.

Pests and diseases

Fennel is blessed as being one of the vegetables that rarely suffers from any problems with pests and diseases. Bad weather is likely to cause more of a problem.

ABOVE **This row of healthy looking Florence fennel contains a variety called 'Dover'.**

Varieties	
'Argo'	'Perfection'
'Cantino'	'Sirio'
'Dover'	'Sweet Florence'
'Fino'	('Di Firenze')
'Herald'	'Tardo'

Florence fennel

FRUITING VEGETABLES

Aubergines (Eggplants)
Solanum melongena

Surprisingly the aubergine (eggplant) is related to the potato although so different. Now popular vegetables in the shops, aubergines have never really been widely grown in the garden and the young plants especially need shelter and warmth. Things are changing, however, and more gardeners are attempting to grow these attractive fruits.

The aubergine (eggplant) is a tropical plant, coming mainly from India where it was grown over 2,000 years ago. Introduced into southern Europe, in particular Spain, in the 16th century by the Arabs, it subsequently became popular throughout the countries bordering the Mediterranean, especially Greece.

The plants grow to about 45cm/18in tall, although they will be taller under glass, and they have soft, felted leaves. Some forms retain prickly fruit stems, but this characteristic has been bred out of some of the more modern cultivars. The fruits that we usually see in shops are long and a deep, shiny purple, sometimes almost black, but those that are grown from seed can be a variety of colours. The alternative name, eggplant, derives from those forms that produce round, white, egg-shaped fruit – there is even a variety called 'Easter Egg'. Other varieties bear fruits that are striped in white and purple or white and mauve. The shapes of the fruits also vary considerably, from almost round to long and thin, and these look like a cross between a bean and a chilli pepper (to which they are, in fact, related). The variation is such that the aubergine has become something of a cult with a number of growers in much the same way that pumpkins and squashes are with others. It is easy to see why.

The aubergine (eggplant) can be cooked as a vegetable by itself or it can be combined with other ingredients in more complicated dishes. Increasing interest in Mediterranean cooking has also stimulated interest in growing these plants, and there is now good reason to grow them as a vegetable rather than just as a curiosity.

Because of its tropical origins, aubergine (eggplant) is best grown under glass unless a favoured sunny spot can be found. This is, perhaps, one reason why it has not hitherto been popular, as most greenhouses are taken up with tomatoes and cucumbers.

Cultivation
Aubergines (eggplants) need a warm, sunny position, which is usually best provided in a greenhouse. Even where they can be grown outside, they need to be started off inside. Soak the seeds in water overnight before sowing, then sow in spring in modules or individual pots. The seeds will germinate in a temperature of 21–25°C/70–77°F. If seed is sown in trays, prick out the seedlings as

ABOVE **This swelling fruit shows the glorious purple colour of the most common aubergines (egglants).**

soon as they are large enough to handle. Once they are big enough they can be planted out into growing bags (two to a bag) or into large pots in the greenhouse. If the temperature does not drop below 15°C/59°F, after hardening off they can be planted outside or moved in the pots to a sheltered position outside. The best results, however, are usually obtained by growing under glass.

Use canes or strings to support the growing plants once they get above 45–60cm/18–24in. Pinch out the tips of the plants when they reach about 38cm/15in high to encourage the formation of fruit. Keep the plants well watered, and feed once every ten days with a high-potash liquid feed once the fruit has started to develop.

Harvesting
The fruits can be picked as soon as they are large enough, which should be from mid-summer onwards in a greenhouse, but from

PLANTING IN CONTAINERS

Aubergines (eggplants) can be planted in pots or window boxes and moved outside when the weather is warmer.

autumn outside. Cut each one with a piece of stalk on it, and remember that those that have lost their shine taste bitter and are not worth eating.

Storage

Aubergines (eggplants) are best eaten fresh from the plant, straight from the garden, although they can be kept for up to two weeks before use in the kitchen.

Pests and diseases

The pests that are most likely to cause trouble are the normal greenhouse ones, such as aphids, red spider mite and whitefly. Dampen the floor of the house and spray the plants with water to maintain humid conditions to discourage red spider mite.

ABOVE **In warm areas, aubergines (eggplants) can be planted directly in the soil in the open garden.**

aubergines

Cultivation
Sowing time spring
Sowing in modules or pots
Planting time inside mid-spring
Planting time outside early summer
Planting distance 50cm/20in
Distance between sown rows 50cm/20in
Harvesting midsummer onwards

Varieties	
'Black Beauty'	'Easter Egg'
'Black Bell'	'Long Purple'
'Black Enorma'	'Moneymaker'
'Black Prince'	'Short Tom'
'Bonica'	'Slice Rite'

Peppers
Capsicum species

Increasing interest in Mediterranean cooking has been accompanied by an increase in the popularity of peppers, of which the main type are the sweet peppers or bell peppers (Capsicum annuum Grossum Group). These are the large green, red and yellow fruits we see in supermarkets – the green peppers are, in fact, the unripe versions of the red and yellow fruit. They can be used raw or cooked, usually with all the seeds removed. The plants are bushy in habit, growing up to 75cm/30in in good conditions.

Cultivation

Sowing time spring
Sowing in modules or pots
Planting time inside mid-spring
Planting time outside early summer
Planting distance 50cm/20in
Distance between sown rows 50cm/20in
Harvesting midsummer onwards

The chillies (*Capsicum annuum* Longum Group) are also a fairly recent crop for most gardeners, again stimulated by changes in eating habits, although they were probably the first types to be grown in Europe. The fruits, usually red in colour, are long and pointed. They are hot to the taste, becoming hotter as the fruit matures. It is the seed and the pith that are the main hot ingredients, and if these are removed, the fruit can be made milder. Chillies are often dried.

Finally, there are the hot or cayenne peppers or tabasco, which belong to a different species, *Capsicum frutescens*. These are smaller than chilli peppers and

are generally even hotter. The narrow fruits, which can be yellow, orange or red in colour, are often used dried. They are the most difficult and less usual of the peppers to grow.

Peppers originated in Mexico and Central America, and they were thus a relatively late introduction to Europe – sometime late in the 15th or early 16th century. They have, however, been cultivated in their native lands for at least 7,000 years and perhaps much longer. Once in Europe, they were adopted far more readily in the Mediterranean countries, where they are still used more than in northern Europe.

Peppers can be grown outside in warmer districts, but generally they do best under glass. If they are grown outside, the best method is to grow them in containers or growing bags, in a warm, sheltered position, against a south-facing wall. In warmer areas they can be grown in a border.

Cultivation
Seed should be sown in spring in a propagator, set at about 18°C/65°F. They can be sown in modules, individual pots or trays. If trays are used, prick out the resulting seedlings as soon as they are large enough to handle. As soon as they are big enough they can be transferred to growing bags (two or three to a bag) or into large pots. The advantage of pots is that they can easily be moved outside if the weather is warm enough. Pinch out the tops of the young plants when they get to 15–20cm/6–8in to make them bush out. If the bushes get above 45–50cm/18–20in they may need to be supported with canes or strings. If they are grown in an outside bed, plant them out in early summer when the temperature has warmed up and set them at 50cm/20in intervals in a fertile, but free-draining soil. Keep the peppers well watered and feed every ten days with a high-potash liquid feed once the fruits start to swell.

Harvesting
Start picking in mid- to late summer when the fruits are large enough – for peppers this is usually when they are about the size of a tennis ball. They can be harvested when they are green or have changed to

LEFT **Green peppers are the unripe fruit, yellow peppers are the first stage in the ripening process, and red peppers are the final stage.**

their final red or yellow coloration. Some cultivars are best picked green. The hot or cayenne peppers should be fully ripe and coloured before they are picked. Cut the fruit so that about 2.5cm/1in of stalk is left.

ABOVE **Not all peppers are the evenly shaped fruit that we find in our supermarkets.**

Storage

Sweet peppers are best eaten straight from the plant, but they can be kept for up to two weeks before being used. Other types of pepper can be dried.

Pests and diseases

The pests that are most likely to cause trouble are the usual greenhouse ones such as aphids, red spider mite and whitefly. Dampen the floor of the house and spray the plants with water to maintain humid conditions to discourage red spider mite. Both inside and outside the greenhouse, however, the major problem is likely to be aphids on the young shoots.

sweet peppers

chilli peppers

Varieties	
Sweet peppers	**Chilli peppers**
'Ace'	Sometime listed
'Antaro'	simply as chillies.
'Ariane'	'Apache''
'Bell Boy'	'De Fresno Chilli
'Bendigo'	Grande'
'California Wonder'	'Hot Gold Spike'
'Canape'	'Hot Mexican'
'Clio'	'Red Chilli'
'Delphin'	'Serrano Chilli'
'Gypsy'	**Cayenne**
'Hungarian Wax'	**peppers**
'Luteus'	Often listed simply as
'Marconi'	cayenne.
'New Ace'	'Cayenne Large Red'
'Redskin'	'Cayenne Long Slim'
'Sweet Spanish	'Red Cherry Small'
Mixed'	'Super Cayenne'
'Yellow Lantern'	'Tabasco'

Sweet Corn (Corn)

Zea mays

Sweet corn, maize or corn-on-the-cob (Zea mays) is a cereal. It is a rather dramatic plant, growing up to 1.5m/5ft or more. The airy spikes of male flowers decorate the top of the plant, and the cobs, with their female flowers, form where the broad strap-like leaves join the main stem. They have an ornamental quality that makes them worth growing in the decorative kitchen garden.

Although maize has a long history, going back to prehistoric times, it is a relatively recent introduction to Europe. This is because it comes from Mexico and it was only after the Spanish Conquest in the early 16th century that it was brought to the Old World. In Europe the main varieties are yellow or yellow and white, but in the Americas, where it has had such a long tradition, there are many more varieties, often with quite deeply coloured seeds, including black.

Because of its size, sweet corn (corn) takes up a lot of space in the garden, but the superior taste of fresh sweet corn, compared with corn bought in the shops,

which may be days old, makes it worth trying to find the space, even if it is only for a few plants. Sweet corn needs to be grown in a block rather than in rows, which increases the chances of pollen falling from the higher male flowers onto the female ones below. This may be inconvenient in terms of the shape of your vegetable garden, but it is worth making the effort to find room.

Sweet corn (corn) needs as long a growing season as possible, but it is, unfortunately, frost tender, so the plants have to be started off under glass and transferred to open ground only when there is no further danger of frost. Seed can be sown directly into the soil, but this may not give a long enough

ABOVE **The dying tassel of a female flower hangs from the developing cob. This is an indication that the cob is ready for harvesting. Twist the cobs so that they snap off from the stem.**

season in some regions. Seed often carries a powdery fungicide to stop it from rotting in wet soils.

Cultivation

Sweet corn (corn) needs a warm, sunny position, sheltered from strong winds. The soil should be free draining and well prepared with rotted organic material. Sow the seeds in individual pots under glass in mid-spring, and germinate under gentle heat of 13–15°C/ 55–59°F. Harden off the plants before planting out in early summer or whenever there is no likelihood of frost. Plant in a block and set 30cm/12in apart.

Seed sown outside should be sown in late spring and protected by cloches. Sow two seeds together at 30cm/12in intervals in a block rather than a row. After germination remove the weaker seedling.

Once established, growing plants should have earth drawn up around the stems for about 15cm/6in or more to support them against wind in exposed areas. Avoid deep hoeing – this can disturb the shallow roots.

LEFT **These young sweet corn (corn) plants have been grown from seed under glass and then planted out in a block.**

Cultivation

Sowing time inside mid-spring
Sowing time outside early summer
Sowing inside in modules or pots
Planting-out time early summer
Planting and sowing distance
30cm/12in
Distance between sown rows 30cm/12in
Harvesting autumn

Varieties

'Butterscotch'	'Morning Sun'
'Dawn'	'Northern Belle'
'Dynasty'	'Pilot'
'Earliking'	'Sundance'
'Fiesta'	'Sunrise'
'Honeycomb'	'Sugar Boy'
'Kelvedon Glory'	'Sweet 77'
'Miracle'	'Yukon'

LEFT **These maturing sweet corn (corn) plants clearly show the spiky male flowers which are situated higher up than the female flowers.**

mature
sweet corn (corn)

immature sweet corn
(corn)

Harvesting

Harvest sweet corn (corn) when the tassels on the cobs begin to turn brown. Twist the cobs so that they snap off from the stem.

Storage

Sweet corn (corn) is best when cooked and eaten straight from the plant, although the cobs will keep a few days after they have been harvested. Cobs can also be frozen and then kept for winter use.

Pests and diseases

The main problem with sweet corn (corn) comes from mice and birds, which steal the seed. Frit fly and corn smut are the only other likely troubles, but fortunately they are not common.

Tomatoes
Lycopersicon esculentum

Tomatoes are probably the most widely grown of all vegetables. Even people without a garden often manage to grow a plant or two on a balcony or patio. One reason for this is that tomatoes are relatively easy to grow, but another must surely be that supermarket-bought tomatoes bear little resemblance to what a gardener knows as a tomato – there is very little relationship between the two flavours. Another reason may well be the sheer range of tomatoes that you can now grow. They come in all manner of tastes, sizes and colours, and even some of the old-fashioned varieties that have the best flavours are becoming more readily available. The largest, such as the beefsteak tomatoes, can weigh up to 450g/1lb each, while the smallest are not much more than the size of grapes.

ABOVE **Cordon tomatoes should be well supported. These special spirals support the plant without the necessity of tying them**.

Tomatoes can either be grown on cordons (upright plants) or as bushes. It is well worth not only growing your own particular favourite varieties each year, but also experimenting with at least one new one. This may well result in a glut of tomatoes, but they are wonderful things to give away.

Tomatoes are a very close relation to the potato. (If you want to try your skill at grafting, graft a young tomato plant onto one of the stems of a potato plant; it is actually possible to get potatoes underground and tomatoes above.) Like the potato, the tomato comes from South America, where it had probably been grown for centuries before it was bought to Europe in the 16th century. Because they belong to the family Solanaceae, of which deadly nightshade is also a member, they were at first treated with suspicion in Europe and used as ornamental plants. However, once they were accepted, it was the Mediterranean countries that used them most often in their cuisine. They do, of course, make very decorative plants, with their red, yellow or green fruits, and they are a valuable addition to potagers and other ornamental gardens.

Tomatoes are used widely both in raw and cooked dishes. They can even be used in their unripened state, so that any that have not ripened by the time the frosts arrive can still be used.

Tomatoes are half-hardy and can be grown under glass or outside. Earlier and later crops, as well as heavier ones, are obtained under glass, but outside crops often taste better, particularly if the summer has been hot and the fruit has ripened well.

Cultivation

If you are growing under glass, sow the seed in mid-spring in a very gentle heat or an unheated greenhouse. An earlier start can be made in a heated greenhouse to obtain earlier crops. As soon as they are big enough to handle, prick out the seedlings into individual pots. When the plants are large enough, transfer them to growing bags, large pots or a greenhouse border.

LEFT **A bed of tomato plants with good exposure to the sun for ripening.**

USING GROWING BAGS

Tomatoes can be grown in bags of compost (soil mix).

PINCHING OUT SIDE SHOOTS

The side shoots on cordon varieties should be pinched or cut out.

HARVESTING

Harvest tomatoes when they are ripe, which will usually be when they turn red. Leave the stalk on.

RIPENING TOMATOES

At the end of the season, dig up any remaining plants and hang them upside down under protection to ripen.

(The soil will need changing, preferably every year, if tomatoes are planted directly into a border.) Arrange some form of support, such as strings or canes, for the tomatoes to be tied to as they grow. Remove any side shoots as they appear. Keep well watered and feed every ten days with a high-potash liquid fertilizer once the fruits begin to swell. Pinch out the top of the plant when it reaches the glass.

For cordons grown outdoors, the same procedure as above is followed, except that the plants are hardened off before being planted out, which should not be until after the last of the frosts. They should be in an open, sunny position and a fertile soil. Bush forms are treated in the same way, except

that there is no need to remove the side shoots. They will also benefit from a straw mulch to keep the fruit off the soil. The end of the season usually comes before all the fruit has ripened. Either use them in recipes that call for unripe tomatoes or dig up the whole cordon or bush and hang it upside down in a greenhouse or frost-free shed so that the last ones ripen. Alternatively, cut down the plant from its support, lay it on a bed of straw and cover with a cloche.

Harvesting
Pick the tomatoes as they ripen, which will usually be when they turn red. At this stage they should come away, bringing a short piece of stem, simply by twisting them.

Storage
Tomatoes are best eaten straight from the plants, although they will keep for a few days. They can be frozen, but then used only in cooked dishes as they lose their firmness.

Pests and diseases
Tomatoes are cursed with a number of pests and diseases. Fortunately, they are generally not troublesome enough to deter those who grow them. Pests include aphids, potato cyst eelworm, whitefly and red spider mite. Diseases include tomato blight, grey mould, potato mosaic virus, greenback, tomato leaf mould and scald. Many problems can be avoided by good ventilation. Cracked fruit is often caused by uneven watering.

Cultivation
Indoors
Sowing time early to mid-spring
Sowing inside in modules or pots
Planting time mid- to late spring
Planting and sowing distance 45cm/18in
Harvesting summer onwards
Outdoors
Sowing time inside mid-spring
Planting-out time early summer
Planting distance (cordon) 45cm/18in
Planting distance (bush) 60cm/24in
Distance between sown rows 75cm/30in
Harvesting late summer onwards

Varieties

Inside	Inside or outside (cordon)		Outside (cordon)
'Aromata'	'Ailsa Craig'	'Golden Sunrise'	'Marmande'
'Big Boy'	'Alicante'	'Harbinger'	'Outdoor Girl'
'Buffalo'	'Gardener's Delight'	'Mirabelle'	**Outside (bush)**
'Dombito'		'Moneymaker'	'Golden Sunrise'
'Eurocross'		'Sungold'	'Ida Gold'
'Grenadier'		'Tigarella'	'Incas'
'Libra'			'Marmande Super'
'Nimbus'			'Red Alert'
'Shirley'			'The Amateur'
'Super Sweet'			'Tornado'
			'Totem'
			'Tumbler'

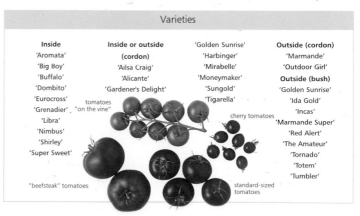

tomatoes "on the vine"

cherry tomatoes

"beefsteak" tomatoes

standard-sized tomatoes

herbs

Herbs have been an important part of gardening for generations. Indeed, some of the first gardens were herb gardens. However, our perception of herbs has changed over the centuries. Gone are the times when it was essential to grow your own headache remedies and now few people grow medicinal herbs for their own use.

On the other hand, culinary herbs are still widely grown. There are two possible approaches to growing culinary herbs: one is simply to grow those that you actually cook with and the other is to make a comprehensive collection so that you can make a feature of the herb garden. For either type of garden, there is a tremendous range of herbs from which to choose.

Herbs can be grown in a variety of ways. For many people, the traditional herb garden remains the only way to grow them and with care it can become an attractive part of the whole garden. Herbs can also be grown in the vegetable garden or mixed with flowers in the ornamental garden. Another alternative is to grow your herbs in containers which is often the ideal solution for many gardeners because they can be sited near the kitchen for convenience.

Chives

Allium schoenoprasum

Chives, a low-growing perennial with narrow, grass-like leaves, are one of the basic kitchen herbs that few gardeners will want to be without. They provide a mild onion flavouring and garnish in a wide range of dishes.

Chives also have the advantage that they are attractive, particularly when in flower, and can be grown easily in a flower border. They are excellent for a potager or decorative kitchen garden, and make a fine edging to a path or plot.

Chives are easy to grow. Initially, you will need to buy – or be given – a plant, but once you have one you can go on dividing clumps as frequently as you like. Set the plants out in spring, planting them in a sunny position at intervals of 23cm/9in. If the pot or clump is large, split it up and plant them out as separate bulbs or in small clumps. Harvest by cutting off the leaves at the base. The flower stems are tough and should be discarded. Every two years, divide the clumps to prevent them from becoming congested. Chives are best used fresh, but the leaves can be frozen, either individually or in ice cubes, or dried.

ABOVE **A white-flowered form of chive that is usually grown for decorative purposes.**

ABOVE **Use only the leaves of chives because the flower stalks are usually too tough for culinary use.**

Cultivation

Planting time spring
Planting distance 23cm/9in
Harvesting any time the plant is in growth
Storage frozen or dried

Dill

Anethum graveolens

Dill is a tall, upright herb with feathery leaves, similar to those of fennel, and yellow flowers. It is mainly used for its seeds, although the leaves can also be used. Both are used as flavourings, especially for fish dishes and salads. The seeds can also be used in pickling.

Because dill is an annual it has to be grown from seed each year. Dill grows best in an open position and rich soil. It is advisable to avoid planting dill near fennel if you are planning to use the seeds of either plant, either for cooking or for propagation, because the two herbs can cross-pollinate easily.

Sow in shallow drills, 1cm/½in deep, in spring or early summer. Thin the resulting seedlings to 23cm/9in apart. Keep watered so that the growth is not checked, or the plants will prematurely run to seed. Start picking the leaves when the plants are 10cm/4in high and continue to do so until flowers appear. Harvest the seeds when they are ripe – that is, when they turn brown. The leaves are best used fresh but can be dried. Seeds can be dried and stored.

Cultivation

Sowing time spring to early summer
Sowing depth 1cm/½in
Thinning distance 23cm/9in
Harvesting (leaves) late spring until flowering
Harvesting (seed) when ripe
Storage (leaves) dried
Storage (seed) dried

ABOVE **The feathery leaves of dill are useful for decorating dishes as well as for enhancing flavour.**

Angelica
Angelica archangelica

A tall, hardy biennial, angelica is a statuesque plant with large, white flower-heads. It can be grown in an ornamental border, and it is also an ideal decorative plant for a potager. This is a herb that nowadays is used more for its decorative qualities than anything else, but many people still use the seeds for herb teas and crystallize the young stems. The leaves are used for flavouring fish dishes and fruit desserts, especially acidic ones.

This plant needs to be regrown every two years, but if the seedheads are left on, the chances are that there will be plenty of self-sown seedlings. Angelica prefers a lightly shaded position and rich, moist soil. Station sow in late summer, in 1cm/½in drills at intervals of 90cm/3ft. Remove the weakest seedlings, leaving one at each position. Alternatively, sow in early spring in a pan or tray and prick out the seedlings into individual pots. Plant out at intervals of 90cm/3ft in autumn. They can be either grown in a herb garden or decoratively in a flower border.

Pick angelica leaves only before flowering time. They can be dried. Cut stems while they are still young for crystallizing. The seeds should be picked when ripe and then dried.

Cultivation

Sowing time late summer
Sowing depth 1cm/½in
Planting and thinning distance 90cm/3ft
Harvesting (leaves) until flowering
Harvesting (stems) while young
Harvesting (seed) when ripe
Storage (leaves) dried
Storage (stems) crystallized
Storage (seed) dried

ABOVE **Angelica seeds can flavour drinks, although the herb is mainly grown for its leaves and stems.**

Chervil
Anthriscus cerefolium

Chervil, with its delicately cut leaves and white flowers, is increasingly being used in the kitchen for the subtle flavour of its leaves, which taste like a mixture of aniseed and parsley. Its dainty appearance as well as its flavour make it a valuable addition to a decorative herb garden.

Although a biennial, chervil is primarily used in its first year. Unlike many herbs, which prefer a sunny situation, chervil can be grown in light shade, preferably in a position where it will avoid the hot midday sun, because this may cause it to run to seed prematurely.

Sow seed successively, every three to four weeks, from spring until summer in 1cm/½in drills in a sunny position and a free-draining soil. Thin the seedlings to intervals of 20cm/8in. Chervil will happily self-sow if left to go to seed. Seed can also be sown in late summer for potting up plants to keep under glass and to provide a supply of fresh chervil leaves throughout the winter.

Keep watered, especially in hot weather or they will quickly run to seed. Harvest the leaves while they are still young – that is, before flowering – and use fresh or store after drying. Combined with parsley, chives, and tarragon, it is an essential ingredient of the classic French combination, *fines herbes*.

Cultivation

Sowing time spring to summer
Sowing depth 1cm/½in
Thinning distance 20cm/8in
Harvesting late spring onwards
Storage dried

ABOVE **Chervil leaves should be harvested when they are still young.**

Horseradish
Armoracia rusticana

It is debatable whether horseradish is a herb or a vegetable. Since it is really used only in small quantities and then mainly as a flavouring, it can be classed as a herb, but it does not really matter what you call it. It is a rather coarse plant, which looks much like a dock (Rumex). It is, however, grown for its roots, which are used in the celebrated horseradish sauce (which is much better made from fresh roots than bought in a jar) or grated raw on salads. Young leaves can also be used in salads.

It is best to start growing horseradish with a bought plant or with a length of root begged from a friend. One plant may be enough for most homes, but if you need more plant them 30cm/12in apart. Horseradish likes an open position and a light, rich soil, although it will grow in most soils. Remove a root when it is required. For winter use, dig several roots and store them in trays in just-moist sand. If you dig up a whole plant take care to remove it all, or any remaining pieces will reshoot. Unless this task is performed very carefully, a forest of deep-rooted horseradish will appear throughout the garden. Do not plant horseradish near a fence if you have neighbouring farm animals as the leaves can prove fatal to them if eaten.

ABOVE **This flush of horseradish leaves shows that there is a flourishing root system below ground.**

Cultivation

Planting time spring
Planting distance 30cm/12in
Harvesting (roots) as required
Harvesting (leaves) while young
Storage (roots) in trays of sand

French Tarragon
Artemisia dracunculus

A half-hardy perennial herb, French tarragon needs winter protection or to be replaced each year. It is grown for its narrow, strap-like leaves, and although it is not a particularly decorative herb, it is very valuable in the kitchen and is one of the basic herbs that should be grown. It is especially valuable in sauces and for many French dishes, particularly those containing chicken.

You have to start by buying a specimen of French tarragon, because you cannot grow it from seed. Further increases of tarragon can be made by division or by taking cuttings in midsummer. Plant the tarragon in spring in a sunny, warm position at intervals of 30cm/12in. If necessary, cover to protect against frost in winter. The leaves can be harvested at any time. Use fresh, but they can be dried or frozen.

The seed that is sold is for Russian tarragon (*Artemisia dracunculus dracunculoides*) which is much hardier but has a more bitter taste. Russian tarragon is, in fact, often grown as a substitute for French tarragon, in spite of its inferior taste. It has the added advantage of being able to tolerate much lower temperatures than the French variety which means that it can thus be left in its position in the open garden. The taste of Russian tarragon improves the longer it is left to grow.

ABOVE **For the discerning cook, tarragon is a necessity in any herb garden.**

Cultivation

Planting time spring
Planting distance 30cm/12in
Harvesting any time
Storage dried or frozen

Borage
Borago officinalis

Borage is an annual herb with rough, greyish-green leaves, which beautifully set off the sky-blue flowers. It is not much used as a herb these days except for the flowers, which are used as decoration for drinks and dishes. The young leaves may be used in salads and drinks. It is, however, worth growing both in the herb garden and the potager for its decorative qualities.

Once you have had borage in the garden, you need not worry about being without it as it self-sows copiously. Fortunately, unwanted plants are not difficult to remove and any that are required can be easily transplanted. For a more controlled approach, sow the seed in spring to early summer in 1cm/½in drills and thin the resulting seedlings to intervals of 30cm/12in. They are not particularly fussy about the soil they grow in, but they should have a sunny position. The stems and leaves are covered in bristles, which some people may find uncomfortable, and you may like to wear gloves when touching the plant. The flowers can be harvested at any time. They can be stored by freezing in ice cubes or by crystallizing. As a contrast, white-flowered varieties are also available.

ABOVE **Borage is mainly grown for the decorative qualities of its beautiful blue flowers.**

Cultivation

Sowing time spring to early summer
Sowing depth 1cm/½in
Thinning distance 30cm/12in
Harvesting (flowers) any time
Harvesting (leaves) when young
Storage (flowers) frozen in ice cubes or crystallized

Caraway
Carum carvi

Caraway is a biennial herb with feathery leaves and flat, cow-parsley-like heads of white flowers. It is grown for its seeds, which have a distinctive flavour that was first appreciated at least as far back as the Stone Age. It has an aniseed taste and is used in a wide range of dishes as well as in breads and cakes. The leaves can also be used to impart the same flavour. It is not a particularly attractive plant but is important because of its seed.

Caraway is not the most elegant of plants. For this reason, it is best grown in a herb garden rather than in a decorative border. Although it is a biennial, it will self-sow, providing a succession of plants. If you leave the seed on one or two plants, when harvesting, it will provide enough offspring for the following year. Caraway likes a sunny position and a rich, free-draining soil. It should be given a position that it can occupy for two years because it does not flower and set seed until the second. Sow in late spring to late summer in drills 1cm/½in deep. Thin the seedlings to 20cm/8in apart. Leaves should be picked while they are still young and before flowering. Seed can be gathered when it is ripe and turns brown. Dry and store the seed.

ABOVE **The delicate flower-heads of caraway soon give way to aromatic seeds.**

Cultivation

Sowing time late spring to late summer
Sowing depth 1cm/½in
Thinning distance 20cm/8in
Harvesting (leaves) while young
Harvesting (seed) when ripe
Storage (seed) dried

Coriander (Cilantro)
Coriandrum sativum

Coriander (cilantro) is a hardy annual herb of ancient lineage. It grows to about 60cm/24in and has cut leaves and airy heads of small white flowers. It is not a particularly attractive plant but it imparts a distinctive flavour to dishes and so has an important role in the kitchen. Coriander used to be grown mainly for its seeds, but recently the lower leaves have become popular in a wide range of dishes and garnishes. Some cooks use it in the same way they do parsley and put it in nearly every dish.

This herb has seen a revival in recent years. It is now one of the most popular herbs for use in the kitchen and in restaurants. However, it has a very strong, distinctive flavour that is not to everybody's liking, so it is advisable to check that you really enjoy the taste before growing it in any quantity. Because it is an annual, it is grown from seed sown in autumn or spring. Sow it in shallow drills 1cm/½in deep in a fertile soil in full sun. Germination may be slow, but once up, thin the seedlings to about 15cm/6in apart. Cut the heads as the seed ripens and dry the seed. The lower leaves are now used more than the upper, more finely cut ones, but both can be harvested when young. Store the seed dried. The leaves can be frozen.

Cultivation

Sowing time autumn or spring
Sowing depth 1cm/½in
Thinning distance 15cm/6in
Harvesting (seed) when ripe
Harvesting (leaves) while young
Storage (seed) dried
Storage (leaves) frozen

ABOVE **The larger lower leaves of coriander (cilantro) are the most popular part of the plant.**

Fennel
Foeniculum vulgare

Fennel has already been dealt with as a vegetable, Florence fennel, but it is also used widely as a culinary herb. It is an extremely decorative plant and is certainly one to include in a potager or ornamental kitchen garden. The leaves of fennel are very finely cut and in some varieties they are bronze in colour. The tiny golden-yellow flowers are held in flat heads, from which are produced seeds that can be used in fish dishes and in sauces. The leaves can also be used in fish and other dishes. The flavour is predominantly of aniseed.

This hardy perennial needs a sunny position and a well-drained, rich soil, although it will grow in quite poor conditions. It can be grown from seed, station sown in spring in 1cm/½in drills at intervals of 45cm/18in. One or two plants should be sufficient for most uses (unless it is being used as a vegetable as well). Harvest the young leaves as you need them and collect the seed when it ripens. Remove the seeding flower-heads if seeds are not required to stop it self-sowing everywhere. It is important to bear in mind that some herbs, such as dill and coriander, will cross-breed with fennel which affects the flavour of the seeds and any plants grown from these seeds.

Cultivation

Sowing time spring
Sowing depth 1cm/½in
Thinning and planting distance 45cm/18in
Harvesting (seed) when ripe
Harvesting (leaves) while young
Storage (seed) dried
Storage (leaves) frozen

ABOVE **All parts of fennel can be used, but the foliage is the greatest attraction in the garden.**

Hyssop
Hyssopus officinalis

A shrubby perennial, hyssop has long been used in herb gardens and potagers for its decorative qualities. It is particularly useful as a low hedging plant for parterres and knot gardens, although it may not be long lived. It has small, shiny leaves and spikes of purple flowers. The leaves are used to counter fatty dishes, but they have a rather bitter taste, so should be used only in small quantities.

Although hyssop is not a long-lived plant, especially on heavier, wet soils, it is often used to create low aromatic hedges. It can be planted around the individual plots in a herb garden or potager, or even along the edge of a decorative flower border, separating the border from the lawn, for example.

Hyssop needs a sunny position and a free-draining soil. It can be grown from seed, sown in a seed bed and then transferred or sown directly where it is to grow. Sow in spring in 1cm/½in drills and thin to about 30cm/12in. Plants can be purchased and planted at the same distance.

Alternatively, take cuttings from existing plants in summer and plant these out in the following spring. Plants do not last long and may need to be replaced every three years or so. Harvest the leaves as required. The young leaves can also be dried.

Cultivation
Sowing time spring
Sowing depth 1cm/½in
Thinning and planting distance 30cm/12in
Planting and transplanting time spring
Harvesting any time
Storage dried

ABOVE **These hyssop leaves are in a perfect condition for harvesting.**

Bay
Laurus nobilis

Bay is one of the most consistently used herbs, with one or two leaves at a time being added to an enormous number of dishes, and it is one of the key ingredients of the traditional bouquet garni. Surprisingly, however, few gardeners grow it, and most cooks use old leaves from a jar, which inevitably have lost much of their vitality. They taste rather bitter when first picked but are at their best and sweetest within a few days of drying. As a decorative plant it has much to recommend it, either in the herb garden or potager or as a container plant on a patio. It is a bush that will, in time, grow into a small tree. The leaves, which are the part used in cooking, are tough and leathery.

Bay trees can be very decorative plants, especially if trained and clipped. Rather than one large bush, several smaller ones, perhaps shaped, make good structural features in a herb garden. They can be grown in containers and, in cold climates, over-wintered indoors. The simplest way of growing a bay tree is to buy a young plant. If you need further plants, then take half-ripe cuttings in the summer. Plant the tree in a warm, sunny position in well-drained, rich soil, although it will tolerate quite poor

conditions. Trim with secateurs (pruners) to keep it to the size you want – it will grow to 4.6m/15ft or more. Pick leaves as needed and keep a supply of freshly dried leaves.

Cultivation
Planting time spring
Planting distance 1.2m/4ft or more
Harvesting any time
Storage dried

ABOVE **Bay tree leaves do not look appetizing, but, once dried, they add a sweet flavour to food.**

Lovage
Levisticum officinale

Lovage is a hardy perennial with a bold appearance. In the right conditions it can grow to a height of 2.1m/7ft, which makes it a useful specimen plant for the herb garden or potager, although it is not suitable for a small garden. The celery-like leaves are still widely used in cooking, but they are not that easy to come by unless you grow lovage yourself. It has a strong flavour, which is appropriate only for more robust dishes where such flavours are required. The seed is also used by some cooks.

Whether in a pot or in the garden, lovage is a large statuesque plant and needs siting with care. Planted in the wrong position, it will overshadow its neighbours, and few herbs like shade. Lovage is large enough to act as the centrepiece of a herb bed, but it is often better situated in a decorative border. Lovage can be easily grown from seed, but because only one specimen is usually required it is often less trouble to buy it as a young plant. It can be grown from seed, sown in autumn, or from root cuttings taken in early winter. If more than one plant is required, plant them

60cm/24in apart. Harvest the leaves as you need them. Some can be stored by drying them. Harvest the seed when it is ripe.

ABOVE **Its large, bold leaves make lovage a very distinctive plant for the herb garden or border.**

Cultivation
Sowing time autumn
Sowing depth 1cm/½in
Planting time spring
Thinning and planting distance 60cm/24in
Harvesting (leaves) any time
Harvesting (seed) when ripe
Storage (leaves) dried
Storage (seed) dried

Lemon Balm
Melissa officinalis

A perennial herb, lemon balm is widely grown but seemingly not used much in the kitchen. This is a pity, because its lemon-scented, mint-like leaves have a wide variety of uses in all manner of dishes and it is not usually available other than from the garden. One of its best known uses is as an infusion to make herb tea. It is an attractive plant for the first half of the year but looks rather ragged for the remainder of the year unless it is chopped to the ground so that it reshoots with fresh growth. The other advantage of doing this is to prevent it from self-sowing, which it does with abandon.

Lemon balm, as its name suggests, has a very distinctive lemon smell. It is one of those herbs that encourages you to run your fingers through the leaves as you pass by. It is, therefore, a good plant to site near a path or on the edge of a border, so that it can be easily reached. Lemon balm will grow in any soil as long as it is not too dry, and it will grow in sun or partial shade. It shoots very readily from seed sown in 1cm/½in drills in spring. Existing plants can be divided or basal cuttings taken in

spring. Harvest the leaves while they are young. They can be dried.

ABOVE **Once lemon balm leaves begin to look tired, cut the plant to the ground to get a fresher flush.**

Cultivation
Sowing time spring
Sowing depth 1cm/½in
Thinning and planting distance 60cm/24in
Planting and transplanting time spring
Harvesting when the leaves are still fresh-looking
Storage dried

Mint
Mentha species

Perhaps one of the best known of all herbs, mint has a flavour that even someone who is not interested in cooking would recognize – even if only from toothpaste. It is a perennial herb, whose felty leaves are widely used in all aspects of cookery. There is a wide range of mints – probably more than are seriously used – and it is probably a question of finding the two or three that you like and growing those. Most cooks manage with just one.

ABOVE AND RIGHT **Many garden mints are so interbred that there are only marginal differences** between them, as these two mints show. It is best to go by flavour rather than appearance.

Grow mint from an existing plant, either by buying or otherwise acquiring one, or by dividing or taking basal cuttings from an existing plant. Plant in sun or partial shade in any garden soil, but preferably a fertile one. The questing roots have a tendency to spread far and wide, and to prevent it from taking over the entire garden, you need to contain the roots somehow – planting in a large sunken bucket with no bottom is a possible solution. Another is to plant it where it is confined between two solid structures such as a wall and a path. Pick the leaves while they are still young and fresh. They can be dried or frozen.

Cultivation

Planting time spring
Planting distance 30cm/12in
Harvesting while leaves are young
Storage dried or frozen

Bergamot
Monarda didyma

Although it is not widely used as a herb today, except in the making of herb tea, bergamot is a very attractive plant with whorled heads of bright red flowers; there are other colours, but these are best relegated to the flower borders. Simply brushing against the wonderfully aromatic leaves releases their fragrance, making it a joy to weed among them. It is also a beautifully colourful plant to grow in a herb garden or potager.

Bergamot is one of the most decorative herbs and more than holds its own as a border plant in the ordinary flower garden. It is also one of the strongest smelling herbs and should be planted near a path where it will be brushed against by passers-by, thus releasing the fragrance. It is essential to have a rich, moist soil, or bergamot will languish and die, and it is a good idea to replant it in fresh soil at least every three years. Bergamot can be grown from seed, basal cuttings or division, all carried out in spring. It looks better grown in a clump rather than in a row, and individual plants should be 45cm/18in apart. The leaves should be harvested while they are still young. Flowers can also be picked as they open. Both can be dried.

Cultivation

Sowing time spring
Sowing depth 1cm/½in
Planting time spring
Thinning and planting distance 45cm/18in
Harvesting while young
Storage dried

ABOVE **The flowers of bergamot – here *Monarda* 'Cambridge Scarlet' – are especially colourful.**

Sweet Cicely
Myrrhis odorata

Sweet cicely is one of those herbs that is not often used these days but that gardeners are reluctant to see disappear. This is mainly, one suspects, because of its spring appearance – it looks like a more wholesome version of cow parsley, with finely cut leaves and flat heads of white flowers. Later in the year it produces rather dramatic clusters of long seeds. In the kitchen it is mainly used to reduce the acidity of fruit dishes. Both the leaves and seeds are used; the seeds are usually used in an unripened state, but ripe ones can also be used.

Sweet cicely is often found growing in the wild, more often than not in hedgerows and on verges. If you are lucky enough to have a hedgerow, or even a hedge, in your garden, then growing any spare plants along it creates an attractive planting association. Sweet cicely is useful because it is one of the few herbs that will grow in shade, as long as it is not too dark. It likes a humus-rich soil. Sow seed in autumn in 1cm/½in drills, thinning the resulting plants to 60cm/24in apart. Remove the seedheads before they scatter the seeds, which self-sow prodigiously. Harvest the leaves early in the year, particularly those used for drying. Seed can be collected while still unripe and dried. Ripe seed can be collected and stored.

ABOVE **The flat heads of sweet cicely flowers stand out well against the fern-like leaves.**

Cultivation

Sowing time autumn
Sowing depth 1cm/½in
Thinning distance 60cm/24in
Harvesting (leaves) spring, early summer
Harvesting (seed) unripe and ripe
Storage (both) dried

Basil
Ocimum species

No kitchen should be without aromatic basil. It is perhaps not as versatile as many other herbs, but when it is used, it is used to great effect. It is particularly good in association with tomatoes, salads (especially mozzarella cheese and tomato salad), and in a wide range of other Mediterranean dishes.

There are several types of basil, but the basic species is *Ocimum basilicum*, often referred to as sweet basil, and there is a beautiful purple variety, *O. b.* var. *purpurascens*. The flavour of the purple-leaved form is less strong than that of the green variety. All are annuals and must be grown from seed each year. Basil can be grown in the open ground, but it is often more convenient to use containers. All basils like a warm, sunny position – although they may flag if they are exposed to a hot midday sun – and a moist, fertile soil. Sow in trays in a gentle heat in early spring and plant out after the threat of frosts is over. It can also be sown directly in the soil in late spring, but the soil must be kept moist. Plant out or thin to intervals of 23cm/9in. Pick the leaves as required. They can be dried or frozen, or puréed in a fusion of olive oil.

ABOVE **The green variety of basil is the most commonly grown.**

ABOVE **Purple-leaved basil can be used decoratively in a potager or herb garden.**

Cultivation

Sowing time spring
Sowing depth 1cm/½in
Thinning and planting distance 23cm/9in
Harvesting any time
Storage dried or frozen

Marjoram and Oregano
Origanum species

Sweet marjoram (Origanum majorana), pot marjoram (O. onites) and oregano (O. vulgare) look similar but have slightly different tastes. Sweet marjoram, as the name suggests, is the sweetest, with a delicate flavour. Pot marjoram has a strong, even bitter, taste, and tolerates lengthy cooking. Oregano has a spicy flavour and is the most widely used in a range of dishes. Pot marjoram is probably the best for the ornamental garden, especially in its golden-leaved form.

All the marjorams and oreganos grow in full sun, preferably in a rich, well-drained soil. They can be grown from seed sown in spring in shallow drills at a depth of 1cm/½in. Seed is slow to germinate. Existing plants can also be divided in the

ABOVE **Marjoram leaves give off a sweet fragrance when bruised and also have culinary uses.**

ABOVE **Marjoram in flower makes a decorative edge-of-border plant.**

spring. They should either be thinned or planted at intervals of 30cm/12in. All the species are perennial, but sweet marjoram is more tender and may have to be re-sown each year, or grown in a pot and taken indoors for the winter. Harvest the leaves while they are young. They can be dried or frozen for storage.

Cultivation

Sowing time spring
Sowing depth 1cm/½in
Dividing time spring
Thinning and planting distance 30cm/12in
Harvesting while young
Storage dried or frozen

Parsley
Petroselinum crispum

Parsley is perhaps the most used of all herbs; indeed, some overenthusiastic cooks throw a handful into nearly every dish. There are two forms – the curly leaved and the flat leaved. Curly-leaved parsley is the more attractive and is often used for decoration and garnishes, but the flat-leaved forms have a stronger taste and are increasingly recommended for adding to dishes to provide extra flavour.

In the garden, the curly-leaved forms are undoubtedly the more attractive for use in herb gardens and potagers, especially as edgings to paths or beds. Parsley does best in a sunny spot but will take light shade. Grow in a moist, fertile soil. Treat parsley as an annual, growing it from seed sown in spring to provide leaves for use during summer and autumn; a second sowing in late summer will give leaves for winter use.

ABOVE **Curly-leaved parsley is used a great deal in cooking as well as for garnishing dishes.**

ABOVE **Flat-leaved parsley has a stronger flavour than curly-leaved parsley and is becoming more popular.**

Cover the winter crop with cloches, partly to protect it and partly to prevent mud from being splashed on the leaves. Sow the seeds in 1cm/½in drills and thin to about 23cm/9in apart. Parsley is slow to germinate, especially if the soil is cold. Do not let the soil become too dry. Harvest the leaves as needed. Dry or freeze for storage.

Cultivation

Sowing time spring or late summer
Sowing depth 1cm/½in
Thinning distance 23cm/9in
Harvesting any time
Storage dried or frozen

Rosemary
Rosmarinus officinalis

What would lamb be without its traditional accompaniment? For that matter, it is difficult to imagine many other dishes without the unique flavour that rosemary contributes. This is not only a herb for the kitchen, however, for this attractive shrub, with its bright green, needle-like leaves and blue flowers, plays a key role in the ornamental herb garden or potager. It is one of those plants that you cannot resist brushing or running your hands over every time you pass.

Rosemary is one of those herbs that should be planted next to a path or patio so that you can appreciate its lovely scent as you pass by. However, rosemary can grow quite large, so do not plant it too close to the path or it will eventually cause an obstruction. If it is established in the right position, however, rosemary will grow for many years, although it may eventually get rather straggly. It is marginally tender and may succumb to a very cold winter, especially if it is wet as well. It needs a well-drained soil and a warm, sunny position. It is best to start with a bought plant or one grown from cuttings. Plant out in spring, and if you need more than one plant set them 75cm/30in apart. Pick the leaves as required, but those that are needed for drying are best picked before the flowers appear.

Cultivation

Planting time spring or late summer
Planting distance 75cm/30in
Harvesting any time
Storage dried

ABOVE **The best time for picking rosemary is before the flowers appear.**

Sage
Salvia officinalis

Sage, that almost inevitable ingredient of stuffing, is a long-lived shrub with grey, felted leaves. Its distinctive flavour is particularly appropriate with meats and dairy produce, such as cheese. It is a good, decorative shrub for the herb garden or potager, and although the normal culinary form has grey leaves, it is also available in forms with sultry purple or bright yellow and green foliage. Spikes of blue-purple flowers are borne in late spring.

All forms of sage like a well-drained soil in a sunny position. They are best grown from cuttings or purchased as young plants, although they can also be grown from seed. They should be planted out in spring and if several plants are required, they should be planted 60cm/24in apart. The leaves can be picked at any time, but those for drying are best picked before the flowers appear.

There is an attractive purple-leaved form, *Salvia officinalis* Purpurascens Group which has striking, purple, grey and green foliage. Some of its variants produce blue flower spikes. It has a strong flavour, is often used as a culinary herb and is widely cultivated for is ornamental value. Golden sage (*S. o.* 'Icterina') does not have such a good taste, but it will add colour to salads.

Cultivation

Sowing time spring
Sowing depth 1cm/½in
Cuttings taken summer
Planting distance 60cm/24in
Harvesting any time
Storage dried

ABOVE **Sage has coarse-looking leaves that feel soft and felt-like to the touch.**

Savory
Winter savory (*Satureja montana*) and summer savory (*S. hortensis*)

Although these two herbs are among the oldest of herbs, they are not widely grown or used today. Winter savory is a low-growing, spreading, shrubby perennial; summer savory is an annual with a less tidy appearance. The leaves of both species have a spicy, peppery flavour and are used in a wide range of vegetable dishes as well as in stuffings and other recipes. Summer savory is often used in bean dishes.

Both winter and summer savories are Mediterranean herbs that need a sunny position and well-drained soil. Although both herbs can be used for culinary purposes, many people find that winter savory has a less refined taste than summer savory. Savories can be grown readily from seed, which is station sown in mid-spring in shallow 1cm/½in drills at intervals of 30cm/12in. Winter savory may need pruning in spring to keep the plant neat and compact, and in cold areas it will need winter protection. Harvest the leaves at any time, but leaves for storing are best picked just as the flower-buds are opening.

Savories can be grown as alpine plants in a rockery or in a raised bed as well as in the herb garden. This is the ideal place to grow them, in many ways, because it exploits their decorative qualities while also raising them towards the light.

Cultivation

Sowing time mid-spring
Sowing depth 1cm/½in
Thinning distance 30cm/12in
Harvesting any time
Storage dried

ABOVE **The leaves of savories are best harvested just as the flowers begin to open.**

Thyme
Thymus

There are a very large number of thymes for the gardener to grow. From a culinary point of view, there is not a great deal to choose among them, because the flavour is basically the same although the intensity varies considerably, with the broad-leaved thymes having the stronger flavours. For garden display, there is a wide range of forms with coloured leaves as well as variations in flower colour, which makes thymes especially useful in ornamental herb gardens and potagers.

Thymes are good plants for growing in the cracks and crevices between paving in the herb garden. Being robust plants, they can survive being walked on. They can also be grown in the cracks between paving slabs. However, care should be taken if people are likely to walk over the thyme in bare feet, because the herbs are usually full of bees when in flower. Thymes are easy to grow, but they do need replacing from time to time as they grow rather straggly and threadbare. They like a sunny position in a well-drained soil. They can be grown from purchased plants or from cuttings taken at any time from existing plants. Set the plants about 30cm/12in apart and keep them well weeded. Trim over the more straggly forms after flowering to keep them more compact. Harvest leaves as required. They can be dried for storage.

Cultivation

Cuttings taken any time
Planting distance 30cm/12in
Harvesting any time
Storage dried

ABOVE **Thymes are colourful plants with flowers in a wide variety of pinks, purples and white.**

fruit

Fruit can be one of the most enjoyable crops that comes from the kitchen garden, and yet it is probably the most neglected area of gardening. It is difficult to know why this should be the case. In the past, it may have been that fruit was considered to take up too much space, but the modern cultivars now available even make it possible to grow apple trees in containers on a balcony.

One possible reason for people's reluctance to grow fruit is that it can take time to see results. An apple tree may take several years before it produces fruit in any quantity. However, the wait is usually worth it because fresh fruit straight from the plant is one of the great joys of life. Another reason could be that many gardeners are put off by what they see as the complicated art of pruning. But most people perform tasks that are far more complicated than this, and soon pruning becomes second nature.

One point to bear in mind if you are considering planting fruit trees or bushes is that they can be very decorative, especially trained as fans or espaliers, for example. Full-sized fruit trees also have their advantages – they are wonderful for sitting under on hot summer days.

Strawberries

Fragaria × ananassa

Strawberries are one of the best loved fruits. No matter how readily they are available in the supermarkets, there is nothing quite like wandering into the garden and picking a few to eat there and then. The taste is always better, especially if the fruit is still warm from the sun.

It is now possible to pick strawberries from early summer right through to the first frosts and even beyond, if protection is provided. Strawberries are categorized by their time of fruiting and are known as "early", "mid-season" and "late", which continue to fruit well into autumn. There are also perpetual strawberries, which produce fruit in summer, have a break and then start again in autumn. If you have space it is a good idea to plan your strawberry bed so that you have as long a productive season as possible. There are also alpine strawberries, which produce very small fruits over a long period. All strawberry plants should come from certified stock to ensure against virus diseases.

Strawberries are not very difficult to grow. If grown in beds they take up quite a bit of space, but they can also be grown in pots or in towers – a series of containers one on top of the other. They can be grown in a greenhouse, which produces earlier and later crops, but the flavour is not as good as that of crops grown outdoors.

The plants will remain productive for only about three years, and it is important to have a rolling programme to renew a third of the plants each year. Unfortunately, they really need to be planted in fresh ground, so it is not simply a question of taking out one row and replacing it with another; the new plants should ideally go elsewhere in the garden. Alternatively you can create a completely new bed in the third year, and abandon the old one immediately after the fruit has been produced.

Cultivation

Strawberries need an open, sunny site. The soil should be fertile and well drained. The plants should be set out in late summer or early autumn, at intervals of 38cm/15in, with each row 75cm/30in apart. As the plants come into fruit the following year, place clean straw under the leaves and fruiting stems to keep the fruit off the ground. Polythene (plastic) or felt mats will serve the same purpose. Deep water during dry periods.

Pruning and training

Strawberries are not pruned or trained as such, but after fruiting it is normal practice to cut off all the old leaves and burn or destroy these, together with the straw mulch, to remove any pests and diseases. Remove any runners as they are formed unless you want keep a few new plants.

Harvesting

Pick the fruit as it ripens. Pick with a short piece of stalk attached.

Storage

The fruit is best eaten straight from the plants, although it can also be frozen or

ABOVE **After fruiting, the strawberry plant sends out a series of runners that root along their length to produce new plants.**

bottled. Unfortunately, frozen strawberries go mushy when they defrost.

Pests and diseases

Birds and slugs are two of the worst problems. Birds can be kept at bay if the plants are netted while they are in fruit. Viruses and grey mould can also be problems. Burn or destroy any plant with viral disease.

CARE AFTER FRUITING

After the strawberries have produced their fruit, cut off all the leaves and burn or destroy them, along with the straw mulch. This helps prevent the spread of diseases.

RUNNERS

The strawberry runners have produced a perfect new plant through layering. The layered plants can be dug once they have rooted and used to start a new bed.

ABOVE **On this plant a succession of stages can be seen, from flowers to ripe fruit. Fruit picked straight from the plant tastes best.**

PROTECTING THE FRUIT

Place a layer of straw under the leaves of the strawberry plants in order to prevent the developing fruit from getting muddy or covered with dirt.

Varieties

Early	'Merton Dawn'	**Perpetual**
'Cambridge Early Pine'	'Montrose'	**(remontant)**
'Cambridge Prizewinner'	'Saladin'	'Calypso'
'Cambridge Vigour'	'Le Sans Rivale'	'Mara des Bois'
'Honeoye'	'Symphony'	'Rabunda'
'Maxim'	'Troubadour'	'Red Rich'
Mid-season		'St Claude'
'Cambridge Favourite'		**Alpine**
'Cambridge Sentry'		'Alexandria'
'Grandee'		'Baron Solemacher'
'Hapil'		'Delicious'
'Jamil'		'Yellow Wonder'
'Redgauntlet'		
'Tamella'		
'Tenira'		
Late		
'Cambridge Late Pine'		
'Domanil'		
'Fenland Wonder'		strawberries

Raspberries
Rubus idaeus

Raspberries are an appealing fruit, although they are often overshadowed by strawberries, which come into season at the same time. They are a good fruit for eating straight from the plant or for freezing and for making into jams and preserves. Raspberries can be used in a wide range of cakes and desserts as well as sauces for both sweet and savoury dishes.

ABOVE **Ripening and immature fruit on a raspberry cane. Ripe raspberries can be obtained over a very long period if the varieties are chosen carefully.**

It is possible to provide a good "taste" of raspberries by growing a group of just a few canes, but it is more usual to grow the canes in a row. This may take up quite a large amount of space, but it can be used as a hedge or screen, so fulfilling a double function. The canes are tied into wires that are supported on posts, which adds to the initial cost, but once the framework has been erected it will last for a long time, as will the raspberries.

As with strawberries, new varieties of raspberry have been developed so that it is possible to have a supply of fruit from early summer right through to the first frosts, which in a mild year can mean early winter. Rather than having three separate rows, which would take up a great deal of space, it is possible to divide a single row into three or even four separate sections for early, mid-season, late and autumn fruit.

Cultivation

Like most fruit, raspberries like an open situation with plenty of air circulating among them, but, unlike most other fruit, they will tolerate a little partial shade. The soil should be fertile and moisture retentive, but it should not be waterlogged. Permanent supports in the form of posts and wires should be erected. The wires should be 75cm/30in, 1.1m/3ft 6in and 1.5m/5ft from the ground. Allow 1.5m/5ft between rows. Plant the canes at intervals of 38–45cm/15–18in, spreading out their roots, during late autumn or early winter. Remove any suckers that appear out of the row, and use them as new stock if required. Mulch with garden compost or manure every spring

Pruning and training

Each autumn remove all the old fruiting canes by cutting them off at the base. Tie in the new canes to the wires. In late winter cut off the tip of each cane to a bud about 15cm/6in above the top wire. If you grow autumn-fruiting varieties, cut *all* canes to the ground in late winter.

Harvesting

Pick as the fruit becomes ripe, squeezing gently with the fingers so that the fruit slides off its "plug".

LEFT **If this crop of ripening raspberries is left uncovered in this way, there will be few to eat because the birds will strip them away.**

Storage

The fruit is best eaten straight from the plant. However, it can be stored by freezing, bottling or turning into jam or other preserves. Frozen fruit becomes mushy and loses its shape and firmness, although it is still useful as fillings and sauces. You can overcome the storage problem by selecting and growing a range of varieties. This means you will have a continuous supply of fresh fruit from early summer right through to the first frost.

Pests and diseases

Birds are a nuisance unless the raspberry canes are netted or protected in a fruit cage. Raspberry beetle – the grub is found in the fruit – is often a nuisance. Spray with derris as soon as the first fruits begin to ripen, and then make a second application two weeks later. Grey mould can cause the fruit to rot and there is also the possibility of some virus diseases. Infected canes should be removed and either burned or destroyed.

ABOVE **This double row of raspberries is supported by wires that are secured on a well-constructed wooden framework.**

ABOVE LEFT **These raspberry canes are tied into wire supports by twisting a continuous piece of string around the wire in order to trap the canes.**

Varieties	
Early	'Malling Orion'
'Delight'	**Late**
'Glen Clova'	'Augusta'
'Glen Coe'	'Leo'
'Glen Moy'	'Malling
'Malling Exploit'	Admiral'
'Malling Promise'	'Malling Joy'
'Sumner'	**Autumn**
Mid-season	'Autumn Bliss'
'Glen Lyon'	'Fallgold'
'Glen Prosen'	'Heritage'
'Julia'	'Norfolk Giant'
'Malling Jewel'	'September'

raspberries

Growing raspberries on posts and wires It is essential that raspberries have a strong supporting system of posts and wires. The plants are set at 38–45cm/15–18in intervals. Each year, new raspberry canes are thrown up. When fruiting has finished on the old canes, these are cut out and the new canes are tied to the wires in their place. This sequence is followed every year. Raspberry plants put out suckers which can become established in the gangways between the rows. These should be dug up as soon as they appear.

Blackberries and Hybrid Berries
Rubus fruticosus

Although blackberries that are picked in the wild have a great deal to offer, there are advantages to be gained from growing cultivated forms. The first is that they are conveniently at hand. Second, the fruit is usually much larger and often sweeter. Then there is the fact that you can get thornless varieties, which makes picking much easier. A disadvantage, however, is that you do need quite a bit of space to grow them successfully, although they do not need to be a free-standing crop. They can, for example, be grown along a boundary fence, which may well be a good use of space as well as acting as a deterrent to intruders.

Cultivated blackberries are derived from their wild relatives; the hybrid berries are crosses between various *Rubus* species, often involving blackberries and raspberries in their parentage. Each of these berries, including loganberries, boysenberries and tayberries, has a distinctive flavour and is grown in the same manner as blackberries.

They come into fruit from late summer onwards and are, therefore, available later than most other soft fruit, which is another advantage. Like most fruit, blackberries and hybrid berries are best eaten straight from the garden, but they can also be used in a wide range of dessert dishes and sauces.

Blackberries are usually grown on post and wire supports, the wires being placed at 38cm/15in intervals up to about 1.8m/6ft. The thornless varieties are not as vigorous and take up less space. In a really large garden, blackberries could be left to grow free, like their wild cousins, but this is not recommended because cultivated varieties are often much more vigorous than wild forms.

Cultivation
Blackberries prefer a sunny spot, but will grow in a modicum of partial shade. The soil should be well prepared, with plenty of added humus. Plant the canes in late winter or early spring, placing them 3.5–4.5m/12–15ft apart (thornless varieties can be closer together), and immediately shorten them to a bud about 23–30cm/9–12in above ground. Do not plant deeply; the soil should only just cover the roots, which should be spread out in the planting hole. Mulch with manure in the spring and water in dry weather. They can be increased by bending down a vigorous shoot and planting its tip to form a layer. A new plant will quickly form and can be severed from the parent.

Pruning and training
In autumn cut out all the old fruiting stems and tie in the new growth. There are several methods of training blackberries and hybrid berries. One is to tie in all of one year's growth to one side, several canes to each wire, and

ABOVE **Blackberries fruit over a long season, as is shown by a sprig of ripe and immature blackberries.**

RIGHT **This vigorous stand of blackberries shows the prodigious nature of many of these plants.**

the new growth to the other side. Another is to tie the fruiting growth along the wires, allowing the new growth to grow up the middle. A more formal and higher yielding method is to create a fan, with the shoots tied in a radiating pattern from the base, again leaving the centre free for new growth.

Harvesting
Pick as fruit becomes ripe, without any stalks.

Storage
Fresh blackberries last a day or so but can be frozen, bottled or used in preserves.

Pests and diseases
Blackberries are prone to the same problems as raspberries.

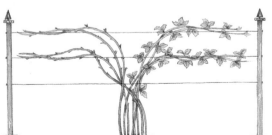

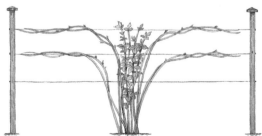

Alternate bay One way to train blackberries is to tie all the new growth to one side of the wirework. After fruiting, remove the previous year's growth from the other side and then use this for the next year's new growth. Repeat each year.

Rope training A second way to train blackberries is to temporarily tie in all new growth vertically to the wirework and along the top wire. The current fruiting canes are tied in groups horizontally. These are removed after fruiting and the new growth tied into their place.

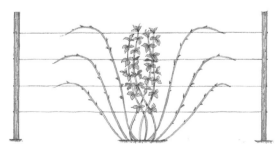

Fan training The new canes are temporarily tied vertically and along the top wire, while the fruiting canes are tied in singly along the wires. Any excess canes are removed. After fruiting, these canes are taken out and the new growth tied into their place.

Varieties

Blackberries	'Merton Thornless'	Marionberry
'Ashton Cross'	'Oregon Thornless'	Sunberry
'Bedford Giant' – early	'Smoothstem'	Tayberry
'Himalayan Giant'	'Thornfree'	Tummelberry
'John Innes'	**Hybrid berries**	Vietchberry
'Loch Ness'	Boysenberry	Worcesterberry
'Merton Early'	Loganberry	

tayberries

blackberries

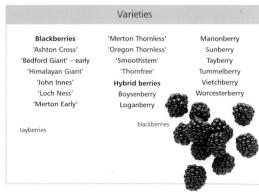

Red and White Currants
Ribes rubrum

The only difference between red and white currants is the colour of the fruit. Both types of currant have a very distinctive, slightly tart flavour, but, unlike many other types of fruit, they have a comparatively short season, around midsummer. Red currants in particular are very attractive, and the bushes can be trained into standards, cordons or fans and used as a decorative feature.

As well as being used as fruit in their own right, both are widely used as decoration on cakes and in a wide range of desserts and savoury dishes.

Cultivation

Both red and white currants prefer a sunny site and a rich, moisture-retentive soil. Plant between autumn and early spring at intervals of 1.2–1.5m/4–5ft. Cordons can be 30cm/12in apart and fans can be 1.8m/6ft apart. Mulch in spring with well-rotted organic material. Propagate from hardwood cuttings taken in early autumn.

Pruning and training

Initially, prune back all main stems to four buds. After that, prune in spring and summer, reducing the growth on the new leader by about half and that on laterals to about 8cm/3in in spring and to four or five leaves in summer. Once the bushes are established, cut back all side shoots to one bud and take the tip out of the main stems. Let new shoots from the base replace older wood. If you are growing them as cordons, in early spring remove a third of the new growth on the leader and cut back laterals to three buds. In summer cut back all laterals to five leaves.

Harvesting and storage

Pick when the currants are ripe, taking the whole cluster of fruit. They can be frozen or turned into preserves – but remove the stalks first.

Pests and diseases

Birds, which will attack both buds and fruit, are likely to be the biggest problem. Aphids and black currant gall mites may also be troublesome. Grey mould may be a problem and coral spot can affect the branches.

BELOW **These cordons of red and white currants have been tied to vertical canes which are, in turn, tied to horizontal wires.**

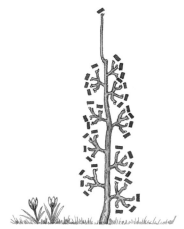

Pruning a red or white currant cordon On planting, cut back the leader by half of its new growth and cut back the side shoots to one bud. Thereafter, cut back the side shoots every summer to five leaves and, in winter, further reduce these to one bud.

Pruning a red or white currant bush After planting, cut back each shoot by about half. Subsequent pruning involves ensuring that the plant becomes an open bush. Cut back all new growth on the main shoots and reduce the new growth on all side shoots to one bud.

Varieties

Red currants	White currants
'Jonkheer van Tets'	'Versailles Blanche'
'Junifer'	'White Dutch'
'Laxton's Number 1'	'White Grape'
'Red Lake'	'White Pearl'
'Redstart'	
'Rondom'	
'Rovada'	

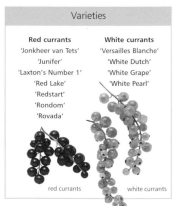

red currants   white currants

Blackcurrants

Ribes nigrum

Varieties	
'Baldwin'	'Malling Jet'
'Ben Connan'	'Mendip Cross'
'Ben Lomond'	'Wellington XXX'
'Ben More'	
'Ben Sarek'	
'Boskoop Giant'	

blackcurrants

Not only do blackcurrants have a unique flavour, but they are much valued for their high vitamin C content. They are used widely in desserts as well as jams and drinks. Blackcurrants, like red and white currants, tend to have a relatively short season compared with other soft fruit, but although related to red currants it is important to realize that they are pruned in a different way. Because the fruit is produced on the previous season's growth, it is important that this is not removed. Unlike red currants, blackcurrants can only be grown on bushes.

They are long-lived plants, lasting up to 15 years or more. Joostberries, a cross between blackcurrants and gooseberries, are grown in the same way.

Cultivation

Blackcurrants prefer a sunny site, although they will tolerate a little light shade. The soil should be well prepared and have plenty of well-rotted humus added to it. Plant between autumn and early spring, setting the plants at intervals of 1.5m/5ft. Mulch in spring with a layer of organic material. Water during dry spells but not when the fruit starts to ripen or it may split. Propagate from hardwood cuttings taken in autumn.

Pruning and training

After planting, reduce all shoots to one bud above the ground. The following winter remove any weak wood. After that remove any weak wood and up to a third of the older wood so that new growth is produced. Never reduce the lengths of the shoots.

Harvesting and storage

Pick the fruit as it ripens, retaining the stalks. Store by freezing or preserving, removing all stalks first.

Pests and diseases

Birds are likely to be the biggest problem. Aphids, big bud mite and gall mites may also be troublesome. Leaf spot and powdery mildew can also be a problem.

RIGHT **Blackcurrants and red currants are usually picked in bunches, complete with their stalks. They can be collected in a trug for convenience.**

Pruning a blackcurrant bush After planting, cut blackcurrant bushes back to a single bud above the ground. The following winter, remove any weak or misplaced growth. Subsequent pruning should take place after fruiting and consists of cutting out up to a third of two-year-old or older wood in order to stimulate new growth. Also remove any weak or misplaced stems.

Gooseberries
Ribes uva-crispa

Because most people think that gooseberries need cooking and so do not fit into the world of convenience foods, they are not, perhaps, as popular as they were in the past. This is a pity, partly because gooseberries have a very distinctive flavour, suitable for a range of dishes and sauces, but also because gooseberries can be eaten raw – there are some delicious dessert varieties. Unfortunately, these rarely find their way into shops, and so it is only gardeners who are likely to appreciate them – an excellent reason for growing your own.

Gooseberries are easy plants to grow, the only drawback being the thorns, which can be very sharp, but well-trained bushes and the use of cordons make it easier to get at the fruit without being torn to pieces. Typical gooseberries are green, but there are also red and yellow varieties.

Cultivation
Gooseberries require an open, sunny position, although they will take some light shade. The soil should contain plenty of well-rotted organic material. Plant the bushes at any time between autumn and early spring when the weather and soil are favourable. They should be set 1.5m/5ft apart. Mulch in spring with a good layer of manure. Avoid hoeing because the roots are only just below the surface and can be damaged. New plants can be propagated by hardwood cuttings taken in autumn.

Pruning and training
Gooseberries can be grown as bushes, cordons or standards. They are treated in the same way as red currants. Keep the centre of the bush open so that plenty of air can circulate as well as making it easier to get at the fruit.

Harvesting and storage
Start harvesting before the fruit is quite ripe. Such fruit can be cooked or frozen. Wait until fruit is fully ripe if it is for eating raw. Continue picking as the fruit ripens. Pick with a stalk, although this must be removed before storing. Store by freezing, bottling or by making jam or other preserves.

Pruning a gooseberry The basic aim when pruning gooseberries is to create an open framework. Establish a framework, first of all, by removing the basal shoots and cutting back the main shoots by about half in their first and second years. After this, cut back the new growth on the leaders in winter by about half and reduce the side shoots from these to two buds. Remove any damaged wood and any branches that cross or rub. Remove suckers and basal growth. In summer, prune the side shoots back to five leaves, but leave the main stems uncut.

Pests and diseases
One the whole, gooseberries are not prone to a great many pests and diseases. The main problem is powdery mildew, and one way to prevent this is to ensure that plenty of air can circulate around and through the bushes. Birds can also be a nuisance in spring when they strip off buds.

Varieties

'Broom Girl'	'Lancashire Lad'
'Careless'	'Leveller'
'Early Sulphur'	'Whinham's Industry'
'Greenfinch'	'White Lion'
'Invicta'	'Whitesmith'
'Jubilee'	'Yellow Champagne'

gooseberries

LEFT **Gooseberries can be grown as single cordons. This is achieved by tying them into canes which are supported by horizontal wires.**

Blueberries
Vaccinium corymbosum

The high-bush blueberry is becoming more popular in the garden. The rich, fruity flavour that is a characteristic of the berries has made it popular as a fruit to be eaten straight from the bush and for inclusion in an ever-increasing number of desserts and other dishes. Its disadvantage as a garden fruit, at least for some people, is that it must have acid conditions. In chalky or limestone (alkaline) regions bushes could be grown in large containers away from the normal garden soil, but this could become quite a chore, no matter how tasty the resulting berries.

The bushes and berries are decorative and are a useful addition in the potager or ornamental border.

Cultivation
Choose a sunny site, although a little light, partial shade will be tolerated. The soil must be acidic. Add ericaceous compost (soil mix) if your garden soil is just on the borderline. Set out the plants at any time the weather and soil conditions allow between autumn and early spring. Plant them as free-standing bushes, 1.5m/5ft apart. Mulch with manure, but only if it has not been "sweetened" with chalk or limestone. An ericaceous compost can be used or marginally acid soil. Do not allow the soil to become dry, watering regularly as necessary. Propagate from softwood cuttings taken in midsummer.

Pruning and training
Because the fruit appears on the second- or third-year wood, do not prune until cropping starts. After that, cut out any dead or weak wood and then remove up to a third of the oldest wood to promote new growth. Prune in winter or early spring.

Harvesting and storage
Pick as the fruit ripens and store, if necessary, by freezing or bottling.

Pests and diseases
Blueberries are remarkably trouble free. The worst problem will be birds, which will steal the fruit, but netting will solve this.

ABOVE **This healthy looking cluster of ripening blueberries clearly shows the distinctive powdery bloom of the fruit which most gardeners try to retain when picking.**

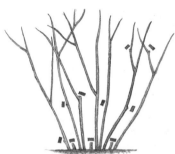

Pruning an established blueberry bush Blueberries fruit on older wood, so no pruning is needed for several years. Thereafter, cut out any weak or misplaced shoots as well as the old wood that has ceased fruiting in order to stimulate new growth.

BELOW **A vigorous blueberry bush, such as this, with plenty of ripening fruit, must be protected to stop birds from stripping away the fruit before it ripens.**

Varieties

'Berkeley'	'Goldtraube'
'Bluecrop'	'Herbert'
'Bluejay'	'Patriot'
'Bluetta'	'Spartan'
'Duke'	

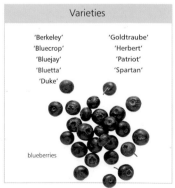

blueberries

Apples
Malus domestica

Apples are a staple fruit, grown in many countries around the world, but although there are, literally, thousands of varieties, the number available in shops can be limited. Unlike many other fruits, in which the taste is only marginally different from one variety to another, apples exhibit a great range of flavours and textures. Some are suitable for cooking, others are dessert (eating) apples, and others combine these qualities.

To help you choose among the vast range of apple varieties, visit one of the open days held by specialist apple nurseries and collectors. It is usually possible to taste several different varieties of ripe fruit and see the trees themselves, which you can often buy or order.

One aspect of apple growing that may restrict your choice is pollination. Most apples need another variety to pollinate them, and because the flowering time varies from variety to variety it is essential to choose two that flower during the same period.

Another question that will have to be addressed is what type of plant do you want. The old standard trees look best and produce a heavy crop, but they are usually too large for today's smaller garden, and ladders are needed for pruning and harvesting. Cordons take up the least space, but the crop is small. On the other hand, cordons allow you to have several different varieties in a small space. There are, however, all kinds of shapes and sizes between the two extremes, some of them very decorative. Always check the rootstock of the plants you buy to see how vigorous and large the tree will be ultimately.

Cultivation

Apple trees will be in position for years, so prepare the soil well, adding plenty of organic material. An open, sunny position is best. Plant young trees at any time of year between late autumn and early spring, as long as weather and soil conditions are favourable. The planting distances vary considerably depending on the type and size of tree. Cordons, for example, may be only 75cm/30in apart, whereas the full standards can be 10m/ 30ft or more apart, so check first with your supplier. Stake young trees, especially in a windy position. Newly planted trees should not be allowed to dry out. Mulch around the tree every spring with organic material. If necessary protect the blossom from late frosts with fleece.

Rootstocks
The rootstock on an apple tree affects the size and rate of growth of the tree.
M27 an extreme dwarfing stock (bush, dwarf pyramid, cordon)
M9 dwarfing stock (bush, dwarf pyramid, cordon)
M26 semi-dwarfing stock (bush, dwarf pyramid, cordon)
MM106 semi-dwarfing stock (bush, spindle bush, cordon, fan espalier)
M7 semi-dwarfing stock (bush, spindle bush, cordon, fan espalier)
M4 semi-vigorous stock (bush, spindle bush)
MM4 vigorous stock (standard)
M2 vigorous stock
MM111 vigorous stock (half-standard, standard, large bush, large fans, large espaliers)
M25 vigorous stock (standard)
MM109 vigorous stock
M1 vigorous stock

Thin the apples in early and midsummer if there are too many of them – a good guide is to ensure that individual fruits should not touch each other. If branches begin to sag under the weight of fruit, the fruit may need thinning or the branches may need to be supported.

BELOW **These pole apples have been grown as vertical cordons. The bottoms of the trunks have been protected against attacks by rabbits.**

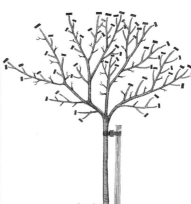

Spur pruning an apple bush tree After planting, cut back the leader to about 75cm/30in above the ground. Leave any side shoots that appear just below this cut and remove any others lower down. The following year, reduce all new growth by about half. This will form the basic framework. Subsequent pruning is restricted to reducing the length of new growth by about a third and removing overcrowded growth.

ABOVE **Apples are not only delicious when they are picked straight from the tree, but they also retain their qualities when stored. This crop of ripening apples will make for a successful harvest.**

LEFT **Training cordon apples against a fence in this way is a suitable method of growing fruit if you only have a small garden.**

Pruning and training

Pruning is not difficult once you have done it the first time. Apple trees fall into two groups, depending on where the fruit is borne. On tip bearers the fruit develops near the tip of the shoots, so it is, obviously, important that you cut back shoots in spring. Trees in the other group produce fruit on spurs, which are found on older wood. Most training and pruning involves cutting out dead or weak wood and maintaining the shape and open nature of the tree. Larger trees are pruned in winter only, but those with a more controlled shape need to be pruned in both winter and summer.

Harvesting and storing

Apples should be picked when ripe, which is usually when the fruit comes away easily with a quick twist of the wrist. Some apples store better than others; in general, early apples do not store as well as later ones. If possible, store in a dark, dry, cool place, and ensure the fruits do not touch. Only store sound fruit. Freezing is appropriate for apples that have already been cooked and puréed.

Pests and diseases

A wide range of pests and diseases can affect the trees and fruit. Birds, wasps and codling moths are three of the most important pests. Canker is one of the worst diseases.

Varieties	
Dessert (eating)	'Millers Seedling'
'Blenheim Orange'	'Ribston Pippin'
'Cox's Orange Pippin'	'Starking'
'Discovery'	'Sturmer Pippin'
'Egremont Russet'	'Worcester Pearmain'
'George Cave'	**Cooking**
'Idared'	'Bramley's Seedling'
'James Grieve'	'Grenadier'
'Jonathan'	'Howgate Wonder'
'Laxton's Fortune'	'Lord Darby'
'Laxton's Superb'	'Newton Wonder'
'Lord Lambourne'	

apples

Planting and pruning an apple cordon Cordons are planted as feather maidens at 45° to the wirework. All side shoots are cut back to three buds on planting. Subsequent summer pruning (above right) consists of cutting back any new side shoots to three leaves and new growth on existing side shoots to one leaf. Winter pruning consists of thinning out any of the older spurs if they have become congested.

Pears
Pyrus communis

In the past, pears were, like apples, widely grown, partly for eating and cooking, and partly for turning into perry, a drink akin to cider. Pears for cooking and perry did not have to be the luscious juicy ones that are wanted for eating, and so many people have inherited trees in their gardens that bear pears that are as hard as bullets. This, unfortunately, has put them off growing pears altogether, which is a shame, because ripe eating pears, picked straight from tree can be mouth-watering.

Pears can be grown as standard or dwarf trees as well as in the form of cordons, espaliers and fans. For the smaller garden, cordons are ideal as they make it possible to have several different varieties in a relatively small area. This means that you do not have a glut of one variety but can spread the harvest over a longer period. Pears need warmth to grow well, which is one reason that they are frequently grown against a wall. The warmth is needed not only during the spring at blossom time – they flower early and are particularly susceptible to frosts – but also during summer and autumn so that the fruit can ripen properly. In cold years, when the pears remain hard, they can still be cooked, often by poaching, to make them soft and edible.

Pear trees are vigorous and are, therefore, often unsuitable for small gardens and for some of the smaller forms in which the trees are grown. It is more usual to grow a

pear tree that has been grafted onto a quince rootstock to curb its vigour. This means that any suckers appearing below the graft should be removed.

As with apples, pears must be grown near a different variety so that the blossom can be pollinated. Unless there happens to be a compatible tree in a neighbouring garden, you will have to plant at least two trees. Unfortunately, you cannot use any variety – the trees must be compatible. Consult your supplier about suitable pairs.

Cultivation

Pear trees must have a sheltered, warm site and fertile, free-draining, but moisture-retentive, soil. Add plenty of organic material while preparing the ground. Set out new plants at any time between late autumn and spring with favourable weather and soil conditions. Planting distances vary according to the type of plant. Bush trees can be up to 4.5m/15ft apart, dwarf pyramids 1.5m/5ft apart, cordons 75cm/30in apart, and espaliers and fans 4.5m/15ft apart. Stake free-standing trees to prevent wind-rock. Mulch with manure in the spring. Thoroughly water during dry spells. If the crop is heavy, thin out young fruit in early to midsummer so that they do not touch.

Pruning and training

Most varieties of pears are spur-bearers, which means that they produce fruit on spurs that grow on two-year-old or older wood. The leader's new growth can, therefore, be safely cut back in winter by about a third of its length, and laterals can be pruned to three or four buds. Spurs are readily produced and

LEFT **These pears have been grown in a cordon against trellis, a method suitable for small gardens.**

ABOVE **Conference pears have a distinctive elongated shape. These healthy specimens are ripe for picking and enjoying.**

should be thinned once the tree is established. Before starting to prune and shape a tree, always remove any dead, dying or weak growth and then work with what is left.

Harvesting and storage

The picking time for pears is crucial. The fruit should be just ripe; any that is left on the tree beyond this stage will soon become overripe. Pick as soon as the fruit comes away readily to a twisting motion of the hand. Early varieties can be picked just before they ripen, but mid-season and late varieties should be left until they are ripe. Pears can be stored in slatted trays in a cool room. Only store sound fruit and position them so that they do not touch each other.

Rootstocks

As with apples, the rootstock on which a pear tree grows affects the size and rate of growth of the tree.
Quince C moderately dwarfing stock (bush, cordon, dwarf pyramid, espalier, fan)
Quince A semi-vigorous stock (bush, cordon, dwarf pyramid, espalier, fan)
Pear vigorous stock (standards, half-standards)

RIGHT **A pear tree trained in the shape of a cone.**

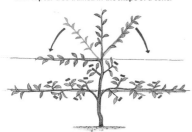

Pruning an espaliered pear After planting, cut back to two buds above the bottom wire. In the first summer, tie the central growth to a vertical cane and the next two shoots to canes at 45°. Cut back all other shoots to two leaves. In autumn, lower the two side shoots to the horizontal and tie the cane to the bottom wire. In winter, cut back the leader to two buds above the second wire and repeat the above until the espalier covers all the wires. When established, cut back all new shoots to three leaves each summer.

Pruning a dwarf pyramid pear After planting, cut back the leader by about a third. Cut side shoots back to about 15cm/6in. In the first summer, cut back the new growth on the main side shoots to about five leaves and on the secondary shoots to three leaves. Thereafter, cut back new growth on the main stems to five leaves and reduce other new growth to one leaf. During the winter, thin out any congested spurs.

Pests and diseases

Pears are prone to a number of problems, including aphids, codling moth and pear midge. Diseases include fireblight, canker, scab and brown rot. Fireblight will probably mean the removal of the entire tree; it must then be burned or destroyed. For other pests and diseases, check on the latest controls with your local nursery or garden centre.

Varieties		
'Beth'	'Glou Morceau'	
'Beurré Hardy'	'Jargonelle'	
'Black Worcester'	'Joséphine de Malines'	
'Concorde'	'Louise Bonne of Jersey'	
'Conference'	'Merton Pride'	
'Doyenné du Comice'	'Onward'	
'Durondeau'	'Williams' Bon Chrétien'	

pears

Cherries
Prunus species

Although cherries are a really delicious fruit, they are not widely grown in gardens. One reason for this is that until relatively recently cherries could be grown only on large trees. This was a problem in small gardens as well as creating a problem in trying to prevent birds from stealing the whole crop since it is virtually impossible to net a large tree. Now that dwarfing stock are available, much smaller trees can be grown and it is worth finding the space to grow them.

There are two types of cherry: sweet cherries (*Prunus avium*) and sour or acid cherries (*P. cerasus*). Sweet cherries are perfect for eating, while the sour varieties, typified by "Morello" cherries, are cooked or bottled. Most people prefer sweet cherries, but the sour forms are easier to grow in a small garden. This is because they are less vigorous, and when they are on "Colt" dwarfing stock they do not make very large trees. They are also self-fertile, so one tree is sufficient.

If you do not have room for a big tree, sweet cherries are best trained as fans on a warm wall, where their size can be controlled and they can be easily covered against marauding birds. Improvements are being made in the development of dwarfing stock for cherries, and it may soon be possible to grow them as small trees, smaller than the current 4m/13ft. Sweet cherries generally need two varieties in order for pollination to be effective, except for 'Stella', Sunburst' and a few other self-fertile varieties.

Cultivation

Cherries need a warm, sunny position – a south-facing wall is ideal. The soil should be well-drained so that it is not waterlogged but it must be sufficiently moist to provide the precise conditions that cherries like. Plant full-sized trees 9m/30ft apart. Smaller trees and fan-trained cherries can be 4.5–5.5m/15–18ft apart. Stake young trees firmly so that the lower part of the trunk and the rootball are not rocked by the wind. If possible, mulch with manure or other organic material to help retain moisture. Water cherries in dry spells but keep the level of moisture even, because a sudden glut of water during a dry spell is likely to crack the fruit, which ruins it. There is no need to thin cherries.

ABOVE **The delicate blossom that appears in early spring is an attractive feature of cherry trees and a welcome bonus.**

Pruning and training

Sweet cherry trees need little pruning, apart from removing dead or damaged growth, unless they are trained as fans, when new growth is cut back to five leaves every summer. In early spring remove all new side growth. Sour cherries grow

Sour cherry fan Once established, there are two purposes to pruning a cherry fan: to keep the fan shape and to ensure that there is a constant supply of new wood. To keep the shape completely, remove any shoots that are pointing in the wrong direction. For renewal, cut back in summer all shoots that have fruited, preferably as far back as the next new shoot. Tie these new shoots to the cane and wire framework.

Sour cherry bush or tree Once established, bush and full-sized sour cherry trees need little pruning other than to remove a third of the old fruiting wood, cutting back to a new growth. Also remove any crossing branches.

on year-old wood, and so some of the older wood is removed each year so that new growth is produced. After picking the fruit in summer, cut back existing, one-year-old shoots on which the fruit was borne to the first new growth. In early summer reduce the number of new side shoots to about one every 8cm/3in. Remove all shoots that face towards or away from the wall. Remove any "water" shoots that appear from the bottom of the tree. Bush and full-size trees need little pruning.

Harvesting and storage

Pick sweet cherries as they become ripe. If you have a lot of cherries to pick, early in the morning is the best time because the leaves are crisp and stand up, revealing the fruit. Later in the day, especially if it is hot, the leaves tend to be limp and hang over the fruit, hiding it. Pick the fruit with the stalks on. The stalks of sour cherries should be cut rather than pulled to avoid tearing,

which would allow disease to enter. Cherries can be frozen or bottled. They should be stoned (pitted) first.

Pests and diseases

Birds are the worst problem – given the chance, they will eat every cherry long before the gardener can get to them. Aphids can also be a problem. Canker, silver leaf and brown rot are the most likely diseases.

Varieties	
Sweet	'Stella'
'Colney'	'Sunburst'
'Early Rivers'	'Waterloo'
'Governor Wood'	**Sour or acid**
'Greenstem Black'	'Kentish Red'
'Kent Biggarreau'	'May Duke'
'Merton Bigarreau'	'Montmorency'
'Merton Favourite'	'Morello'
'Merton Glory'	'Nabella'
'Napoleon Bigarreau'	'Reine Hortense'
'Noir de Guben'	'The Flemish'

ABOVE **This fan-trained cherry has been netted to protect it against marauding birds. Here, it is trained against wires, but it could also be trained against a wall or fence.**

sweet cherries

Plums
Prunus domestica

Plums are one of the great unexplored parts of the fruit world. In the past there were many different varieties, all with different flavours and textures, but now all knowledge of such fruit seems to have been lost. At most, one or two varieties surface occasionally in shops, but few people seem to know of the treasury of delights that could be available. Fortunately, many of the old varieties are available from specialist nurseries, and anyone who takes the trouble to search them out is really in for a treat.

The name "plum" actually encompasses a great diversity of fruit, including damsons, bullaces and the gages. Plums come in all shapes and sizes as well as a range of colours, from red to black and from yellow to green. The flesh, too, varies from red to yellow. As with the other main tree fruits, distinctive cultivars have been developed for dessert (eating uncooked) purposes and for cooking. The former are succulent and mouthwatering; the latter are firmer and less sweet.

In general, plums like a sunny situation, but there are plums for all sorts of climates and you may well find that some are better suited to local conditions than others.

ABOVE **A cluster of plums that would have benefited from thinning out – they are growing too close together and could have filled out more.**

Check to see what varieties are still grown in your neighbourhood area and what may have been grown in the past when they were more widely grown.

Plums are mainly grown as trees, varying from full-sized standards to spindle bushes and pyramids. They can also be trained as fans. Unfortunately, they cannot be grown as cordons. Plums trees are not usually large and can be accommodated, even in small gardens.

Damsons were traditionally grown as hedgerow trees and can be planted in a hedge, saving a lot of space and yet producing a good crop of fruit. Plums vary in fertility, some being self-fertile, but they all do better for having a pollinator in the area.

Cultivation

Plums must have a sunny position; in cooler areas, a position against a wall will be ideal. They flower early and so should not be planted in frost pockets, where the blossom will be lost. The soil should be

Pruning a plum fan in spring and summer The main aim when pruning a plum fan is to maintain the fan shape. In spring, cut out any new side shoots that are pointing to or away from the wall. If necessary, reduce the number of new shoots to about one every 15cm/6in. In summer, cut back all new shoots to about six leaves, leaving any that are needed to fill in gaps in the main framework. In autumn, after cropping, further cut back the shoots to three leaves.

Rootstocks

The rootstock on which a plum tree grows affects the size and rate of growth.
Pixy dwarfing stock (bush, pyramid)
Damas C moderately vigorous stock
St Julien A semi-vigorous stock
(bush, fan, pyramid)
Brompton A vigorous stock
(half-standards, standards)
Myrobalan B vigorous stock
(half-standards, standards)

Varieties

Dessert	'Merton Gem'
'Ariel'	'Oullin's Gage'
'Cambridge Gage'	'Victoria'
'Coe's Golden Drop'	**Cooking**
'Early Laxton'	'Belle de Louvain'
'Greengage'	'Czar'
'Jefferson'	'Early Rivers'
'Kirke's Blue'	'Laxton's Cropper'
'Marjorie's Seedling'	'Pershore Yellow'

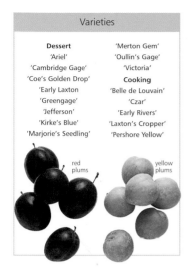

red plums   yellow plums

fertile and moisture retentive, although they will tolerate drier soil than many other tree fruits. Plant the trees at any time between autumn and early spring, as long as weather and soil conditions allow. Planting distance will vary from 3m/10ft to 7.5m/25ft, depending on the size of tree. Fan-trained trees will need to be 3–4.5m/10–15ft apart. Smaller trees and fan-trained varieties should be covered if frost threatens while they are in blossom. Mulch in early spring with a good layer of organic material. If the crop is heavy, thin the fruit as soon as the stones begin to form. Thin so that they are 5–8cm/ 2 3in apart.

Pruning and training

Any pruning should be carried out in summer to reduce the chances of the tree being infected with silver leaf. Once the initial shape has been determined, larger trees do not need any pruning apart from the removal of dead or damaged wood. On fans, remove all new shoots that face towards or away from the wall. Shorten any retained new growth to six leaves.

Harvesting and storage

Pick the plums as they ripen. For cooking and preserving pick a little earlier, just before the fruit is ripe. Keep the stalk on the fruit as you pick them. They can be

frozen or bottled for storage, but it is best to remove the stones first.

Pests and diseases

Wasps and birds can cause problems as can larger animals such as rabbits and hares. Other insect pests include aphids and

ABOVE **Ripening damsons are suitable for cooking once they have coloured. Eat fresh when fully ripe.**

winter moths. The main diseases are silver leaf, canker and brown rot. Trees that are affected with silver leaf and canker should be burnt or destroyed at once.

Peaches and Nectarines
Prunus persica and P. p. var. nectarina

Peaches and nectarines are closely related, the main difference between the two is that peaches have a downy skin, while nectarines are smooth skinned. They are treated similarly in the garden, although nectarines do better in warmer conditions and are less hardy.

B oth fruits can be grown as free-standing trees, but in cooler climates both are better grown as fans against a warm, south-facing wall or even a solid fence.

Cultivation
Peaches and nectarines need a warm, sunny site. The soil should be free draining, but it is also important that it is moisture retentive, so plenty of organic material should be added to the soil. Plant the trees or fans in autumn or early winter, with both at a distance of 4.5m/15ft. Trees should be staked to avoid wind-rock. Mulch in the spring with a good layer of manure or garden compost. If frosts are forecast when they are in blossom, cover the plants with fleece or polythene (plastic) frames. Water during dry periods.

It may be necessary to assist pollination by hand pollinating. Use a soft brush to transfer pollen from the anthers of one flower to the stigmas of another. The flowers should be fully open and the weather dry and warm. With a good fruit set it will be necessary to thin them, removing the excess fruits so that they are 15cm/6in apart.

Pruning and training
Mature trees do not require much pruning apart from the removal of dead or damaged wood and the cutting out of some of the older wood to promote new, vigorous growth. Remove all the shoots that face towards or away from the wall. Initially, thin other shoots to intervals of about 15cm/6in, tying them to the wires and removing the tips if they are longer than about 45cm/18in. Once the plant is established, allow a new bud to form at the base of each lateral in spring, but remove all other buds.

After fruiting, remove the fruiting wood and tie in the new lateral to replace it. Remove the tip if it is too long.

Harvesting and storing
Pick the fruit as it ripens. They are best eaten straight from the tree but can be kept for a few days in a cool place. They can be stored for longer periods by freezing or bottling.

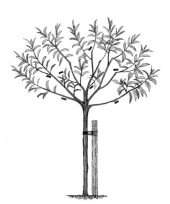

Varieties

Peaches	'Rochester'
'Amsden June'	'Red Haven'
'Bellegarde'	'Royal George'
'Duke of York'	**Nectarines**
'Dymond'	'Independence'
'Peregrine'	'John Rivers'
	'Lord Napier'
peaches	'Pineapple'

nectarines

Pests and diseases
Birds and aphids can be a common problem with peaches and nectarines as can earwigs and red spider mites. Diseases include peach leaf curl, powdery mildew and canker.

Peach bush tree Not a great deal of pruning is required for a peach bush tree. In spring, cut back some of the older barren wood as far as a replacement new shoot. Also remove any awkwardly placed branches and keep the bush open and airy. Avoid making large cuts, as this is likely to allow canker to infect the tree.

LEFT **Fan-trained peaches such as this healthy specimen provide a decorative feature for a wall.**

Rootstocks

The rootstock will affect the size and rate of growth of the tree.
St Julien A semi-vigorous stock (bush, fan)
Brompton A vigorous stock (bush)

Apricots

Prunus armeniaca

Apricots are not grown as frequently as most other fruit, partly because they are not very easy to grow and partly because, with limited space, most gardeners prefer to grow the more luscious peaches. Home-grown apricots may well be a revelation, however, because they taste much better than shop-bought fruit ever does.

One of the problems with apricots is that they flower very early and are susceptible to frosts. They are, therefore, suitable only for warm areas. Their need for warmth means that they are best grown as fans against a south-facing wall, which will help to protect them from the cold. They are self-fertile, so there is no need for different varieties and only one tree need be grown if space is limited.

Cultivation

A warm, sunny, frost-free site is required to grow apricots successfully. The soil should be free draining but moisture retentive. You will have to incorporate plenty of organic material before planting. Plant in autumn or early winter, placing fans about 4.5m/15ft apart. The blossom will need to be protected if there is the possibility of frost. Mulch the ground with a good layer of

manure and keep the ground watered during dry spells. If there is a potentially heavy crop, thin out the fruits to about 8cm/3in apart.

Pruning and training

On mature fans pinch out the laterals in summer to about 8cm/3in. Remove any laterals that face towards or away from the wall. Later, in summer, remove any more laterals that have developed. Apart from that, little pruning is required because most apricot fruit is borne on old wood. Every few years, remove some of the older wood and allow new laterals to develop in order to replace it.

Harvesting and storage

Pick the fruit once it has fully ripened and can be removed easily from the stalk. Apricots do not store well, although they can be frozen or dried.

Pests and diseases

Protect fruit from birds by netting. Aphids may also be a problem. The most likely diseases are silver leaf, canker, brown rot and die back.

Apricot fan Once the fan has been established, the object of most subsequent pruning is to maintain the shape. Cut out any shoots that are pointing in the wrong direction, especially those that point towards or away from the wall. Thin new shoots, leaving one every 15cm/6in. Prune the remaining shoots to five leaves in the spring and then again, after fruiting, back to three leaves.

LEFT **An elegant fan-trained apricot spread out across a large wall. The canes, supported by wires, help to maintain the fan shape.**

Rootstocks

The rootstock will affect the size and rate of growth of the tree.
St Julien A semi-vigorous stock (bush, fan)
Brompton A vigorous stock (bush)

Grapes
Vitis vinifera

Grapes have long been appreciated, not only as fresh fruit, but also for making wine. Varieties of white or black grapes are specially selected for their purpose, and growing grapes for wine-making in particular is a very specialized business. Soil and weather conditions as well as choice of variety or varieties can make all the difference. If there ever was a case for checking what other gardeners in your area are doing, this is it.

G rapes need a great deal of sun, and in cooler areas it is easier to grow them under glass, especially if they are for eating. Outside they can be grown in the open if they are trained onto wires, but they may well do better if they are grown against a warm, south-facing wall. From a decorative point of view they make excellent climbers to cover a pergola or arbour, when they provide a dappled shade that is perfect for sitting under. However, with vines climbing over such large structures it is not easy to protect the ripening fruit from the birds.

Patience is required because it will be at least three years before grapes in any quantity are produced, but once they are established the vines may live up to 50 years, so investment in thorough initial work will be well repaid.

There are several methods of training grapevines. They can be grown against a wall as single, double or multiple cordons; in the open on wirework the double guyot is a good method. Although pruning and training are not complicated, the formative work takes place over several seasons and it is worth consulting specialist publications to check on the best methods and techniques.

Cultivation

Grapes must have a warm, sunny situation. The soil must be very free draining, and if your soil is heavy it will need a lot of work before it can be used. South-facing hillsides, with a gravelly, lightish soil are perfect. Plant the new vines in spring at intervals of 1.5m/5ft. Apply a mulch of manure in spring. Water during dry spells.

Dessert grapes need to be thinned to produce large grapes. Bunches should be thinned to 30cm/12in intervals and then the grapes themselves thinned to allow

them to swell and the air to circulate. Use long-pointed scissors for the thinning. Net to prevent fruit loss to birds.

Pruning and training

Whether they are grown under glass or outside, against a wall or as free-standing plants, vines need wire supports. Immediately after planting reduce the leader to 45cm/18in. From this the various basic shapes will be grown. Specialist books should be consulted for formative and established training and pruning methods for vines grown under glass. The guyot system of training and pruning may be used for outdoor vines, the double guyot system is illustrated opposite.

Harvesting and storing

Pick the grapes when they are ripe by cutting the entire bunch from the vine. It is usual practice to cut a little of the

Varieties
Outdoor
'Brant' black, wine
'Chardonnay' white, wine
'Chasselas' ('Royal Muscadine') white, dessert
'Léon Millot' black, wine
'Madeleine Angevine' pale green, dual-purpose
'Madeleine Silvaner' white, wine
'Müller-Thurgau' white, wine
'Noir Hatif de Marseilles' black, wine
'Perlette' black, dual-purpose
'Pirovano 14' red-black, wine
'Précoce de Malingre' white, wine
'Riesling' white, wine
'Siegerrebe' golden, dual-purpose
'Triomphe d'Alsace' black, wine
Greenhouse
'Alicante' black, dessert
'Buckland Sweetwater' white, dessert
'Foster's Seedling' white, dessert
'Gros Maroc' black, dessert
'Reine Olga' red-black, dessert
'Schiava Grossa' ('Black Hamburgh') black, dessert
'Seyval Blanc' white, wine

white grapes

black grapes

LEFT **These bunches of wine grapes are growing on vines that are supported on wirework.**

RIGHT **Small quantities of grapes can be grown over trellis and archways as long as they have a warm, sunny situation. Grown in this way, they provide a highly decorative feature which is ideal for a small garden.**

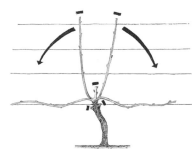

Established double guyot, winter pruning Each year remove the horizontal branches that carry fruiting stems, leaving three vertical central shoots. Pull two of these down on each side of the central shoot, so they are horizontal, and tie in place on the wire. The third shoot should be cut back to leave three strong buds which will form the three verticals for the following year.

Established double guyot, summer pruning In the summer, train the new shoots from these buds vertically, removing any side shoots that develop on them to one leaf. Allow the vertical fruiting shoots to grow on the horizontal branches, removing any side shoots that appear. Cut back above the top wire to three leaves. After fruiting, completely remove the horizontal branches and train the remaining three central shoots as described above.

woody vine stems on each side of the bunch in order to form a useful "handle". A mature vine should provide about 7kg/15lb of grapes. It is advisable to store the grapes in a container with a soft lining so that the delicate fruits are not bruised or damaged. Grapes are best eaten straight away, but they can be kept for a couple of weeks if a longer handle is cut and placed in a tall container of water so that the fruit hangs down outside the container.

Pests and diseases

Wasps and birds are two common nuisances, but scale insects, mealy bugs and red spider mite can also be a problem. Grey mould and powdery mildew are among the diseases.

Melons
Cucumis melo

It is debatable whether melons should be regarded as a fruit, which they strictly are, or as a vegetable together with marrows (zucchini) and cucumbers, to which they are closely related. However, since they are grown to be eaten as fruit, they have been treated separately from their relatives.

Melons are tropical fruit and therefore need plenty of warmth, both during germination and for their subsequent growth. In temperate climates, therefore, they are really suited only to greenhouse culture, unless they can be grown in a particularly warm position. It is possible to grow them in cold frames in the same way as in a greenhouse, except that they are grown horizontally over framework (or even on the ground) rather than vertically up canes and wires.

There are several types of melon. The cantaloupes are often considered the sweetest and best flavoured, but the honeydew, or winter, melons are popular with some growers because they can be kept for up to a month after harvesting.

Cultivation

Seed is sown in individual pots in a propagator at about 18°C/64°F. When the plants are large enough to handle, plant them in the greenhouse border or into containers, such as growing bags. Grow them as single cordons, when they should be 38cm/15in apart, or as double cordons, when they should be 60cm/24in apart. The temperature in the greenhouse should be 30°C/86°F during the day, dropping to 24°C/75°F at night. A framework of canes and wires or plastic netting should be erected to provide support. Pinch out the top of single cordons when the plant reaches 1.8m/6ft. Pinch out the leader for a double cordon low down and allow two shoots to develop. As the fruit develops support each in a net.

Harvesting and storage

Harvest melons when the fruit is ripe. A good indication of this is that the stems will start to crack and the fruit has a sweet smell. All types of melon can be stored for a few days, but honeydew melons can be kept for up to a month.

ABOVE **These melons have been grown vertically under glass. The plants are supported on a wire frame and the ripening fruit is held in a net.**

Pests and diseases

Aphids, whitefly, red spider mite and powdery mildew are likely to be the worst problems.

Varieties	
'Alaska'	'No Name'
'Amber Nectar'	'Ogen'
'Blenheim Orange'	'Ring Leader'
'Charentais'	'Romeo'
'Classic'	'Superlative'
'Galia'	'Sweet Dream'
'Hero of	'Sweetheart'
Lockinge'	'Sweet 'n' Early'
'Honeydew'	'Venus'

melons

LEFT **Melons can be grown horizontally in a cold frame. The fruit can be kept clear of the soil by resting it on straw or saucers.**

Cobnuts and Filberts

Corylus avellana and *C. maxima*

Cobnuts or hazelnuts are not very large nuts, but they are sweet, tasty and easy to crack. The trees are easy to grow and have the advantage of producing catkins or tassels of male flowers from midwinter to early spring. The female flowers are inconspicuous red tufts. Fortunately, both types are wind pollinated, which compensates for the lack of pollinating insects so early in the year. There are several self-fertile varieties, so it is not necessary to grow more than one if you are short on space. They are perfect for providing shade in which to sit plants as well as to grow shade-loving plants. They are really a large bush, rather than a tree, growing to no more than about 4m/13ft high, which makes them suitable for a small garden, unlike many of the other nut trees.

ABOVE **The bracts and shells will eventually go brown as the nuts ripen on this typical cluster of cobnuts.**

The main visual difference between cobnuts and filberts is that the husk surrounding the shell does not completely cover the cobnut – you can still see the tip of the nut – whereas on the filbert the husk completely encloses it. The trees produce better crops if they are pruned and maintained, but they can be planted in a wilder part of the garden and left to their own devices if you prefer.

Cultivation

Unlike most fruit, cobnuts like a partially shaded spot that is sheltered from strong winds. The soil should be free draining but moisture retentive, and it should not be too rich. Plant the young bushes in autumn or early winter at distances of about 4.5m/15ft. Mulch with manure to help retain moisture around the roots.

Pruning and training

Both can be grown in two main ways. They are either grown as a tree with a short "trunk" about 45cm/18in high with up to a dozen branches or as a stool, in which all the main stems come directly from the ground, more in the manner of a bush. Whichever way you choose, train the plants to be open centred. Heavier crops can be obtained by "brutting" which opens up the bush so more female flowers can form. This involves the curious practice of part-breaking some of the outer side shoots and letting them hang down to

Harvesting and storage

Pick the fruit as the husks are beginning to turn yellow. The nuts are borne after three

to four years. They can be eaten fresh or dried and then stored until you need them.

Pests and diseases

These plants have few problems with the exception of squirrels that steal the nuts.

BELOW **A hazel bush can be used for decorative as well as nut-producing purposes. For larger crops, the bushes should be trained.**

Varieties	
Cobnuts	**Filberts**
'Cosford Cob'	'Butler'
'Fuscorubra'	'Ennis'
'Pearson's Prolific'	'Gunslehert'
	'Kentish Cob'
'Webb's Prize Cob'	'Red Filbert'
	'White Filbert'

cobnuts

GARDENING CALENDAR

Winter

AW *all winter* EW *early winter* MW *midwinter*
LW *late winter*

General
Clean and maintain tools and equipment AW
Plan next year's crops AW
Order seed and plants AW
Order sowing and potting composts (soil mixes) AW
Order manure AW
Continue digging soil when conditions allow AW
Avoid treading or working on waterlogged soil AW
Clean and prepare pots and propagators AW
Compost any organic waste AW

Vegetables
Sow early vegetables under glass for planting
under protection MW–LW
Sow early vegetables for planting out LW
Check stored vegetables AW
Plant rhubarb MW–LW
Sow broad (fava) beans MW–LW
Sow parsnips if conditions allow LW
Plant early potatoes if conditions allow LW
Protect overwintering crops such as peas and broad
(fava) beans with cloches AW
Protect brassicas from birds AW
Force rhubarb LW

Herbs
Continue to remove dead stems from
herbaceous material AW
Continue to prepare ground when
conditions allow AW
Use cloches for protection or to promote
winter growth AW

Fruit
Prune fruit bushes AW
Prune apple and pear trees AW
Heel in bare-rooted trees and bushes when
they arrive AW
Plant bushes and trees when conditions allow AW
Prevent birds stripping buds from fruit bushes AW–LW
Check stored fruit AW
Check supports and ties on supported
trees and bushes AW
Take hardwood cuttings EW

Spring

AS *all spring* ES *early spring* MS *mid-spring*
LS *late spring*

General
Prepare seed beds AS
Finish winter digging and ground preparation ES
Keep weeds under control AS
Water in dry weather LS

Vegetables
Mulch permanent beds with manure ES–MS
Begin main sowing and planting of hardy vegetables AS
Continue successional sowings MS–LS
Sow tender vegetables like runner beans under glass LS
Plant tomatoes, aubergines (eggplants), cucumbers and
peppers in heated greenhouses ES–MS
Plant tomatoes, aubergines (eggplants), cucumbers and
peppers in unheated greenhouses MS–LS
Plant Jerusalem artichokes, potatoes and onions ES–MS
Plant permanent crops such as globe artichokes
and asparagus ES
Plant out tender vegetables after last frosts LS
Protect vulnerable new growth from frosts AS
Erect supports for peas and beans MS–LS
Force rhubarb ES
Mulch vegetables LS

Herbs
Finish removing last year's dead growth ES
Sow seed for annuals and perennials ES
Sow tender herbs ready for planting out
after frosts MS–LS
Plant out hardy herbs AS
Prune shrubby herbs ES
Plant out tender herbs after last frosts LS
Take basal cuttings ES–MS
Divide herbaceous herbs ES–MS

Fruit
Mulch bushes and trees with manure ES–MS
Finish winter pruning ES
Remove any winter-damaged branches ES
Finish planting bushes and trees ES
Hand-pollinate early fruit trees ES
Protect blossom from frosts AS
Prune plum trees LS
Thin gooseberries LS
Mulch strawberries with straw LS

Summer

AS *all summer* ES *early summer* MS *midsummer*
LS *late summer*

General
Keep weeds under control AS
Water when necessary AS
Keep an eye out for pests and diseases AS
Take soft and semi-ripe cuttings MS–LS

Vegetables
Plant out greenhouse-sown tender vegetables ES
Sow tender vegetables ES
Sow winter crops MS–LS
Continue successional sowings ES–MS
Harvest early vegetables as required AS
Shade and ventilate greenhouse vegetables AS
Dampen greenhouse floor to maintain humidity AS
Pick greenhouse vegetables as they ripen AS
Pinch out side shoots from tomatoes AS
Earth up vegetables that require it AS
Lift and dry onions, shallots and garlic LS

Herbs
Harvest herbs as required AS
Harvest herbs for storing before they flower ES–MS
Plant out tender herbs ES
Deadhead as necessary unless seed is required AS
Cut back herbaceous plant to stimulate
new growth AS

Fruit
Pick early soft fruit ES–MS
Continue to pick soft fruit MS–LS
Pick cherries and early tree fruits MS
Net soft fruit against birds AS
Tie in new growth on cane fruit AS
Summer prune tree fruit AS
Thin tree fruit if necessary ES–MS
Remove spent raspberry canes and tie in
new growth LS
Remove foliage and mulch from spent strawberries LS
Pot up or transplant strawberry runners LS
Tip-layer briar fruit LS

Autumn

AA *all autumn* **EA** *early autumn* **MA** *mid-autumn*
LA *late autumn*

General

Continue weeding **AA**
Compost all waste vegetation **AA**
Water if necessary **EA**
Start autumn digging on heavy soils **MA–LA**
Clean and oil tools before putting away for winter **LA**

Vegetables

Lift and store potatoes **EA–MA**
Lift and store root crops in cold areas **LA**
Remove and compost finished crops **AA**
Plant garlic **LA**
Plant spring cabbage **EA**
Sow broad (fava) beans **LA**
Sow salad crops under glass **EA**
Protect globe artichokes, celeriac (celery root) and
celery with straw in cold areas **LA**
Protect brassicas from birds **AA**
Check stored vegetables **LA**

Herbs

Harvest seed as it ripens **AA**
Tidy away dead material as necessary **AA**
Protect tender herbs **MA–LA**
Plant perennial and shrubby herbs **AA**
Move container herbs under protection **MA–LA**
Divide herbaceous herbs **EA**

Fruit

Pick tree fruit as it ripens **AA**
Store apples and pears **AA**
Pick late crops of strawberries and raspberries **AA**
Plant new strawberry beds **EA, MA**
Remove old fruiting canes from briar fruit and
tie in the new **MA**
Finish removing old raspberry canes and tying
in the new **EA**
Take hardwood cuttings **LA**
Plant new fruit trees and bushes **MA–LA**
Check stored fruit **LA**
Check all supports and ties **EA–MA**

WINTER **It is advisable to protect
permanent plants, such as globe
artichokes, from winter cold and
frost. A straw-filled box is a good
source of insulation.**

SPRING **Leeks can be harvested
between early autumn and late
spring by simply digging them
out with a fork. Autumn varieties
are not as hardy and should be
harvested before midwinter.**

SUMMER **Harvest globe artichokes,
in summer, from the second year
onwards. Take off the flower-
heads before they open and
while they are still green, cutting
2.5cm/1in below the head with a
sharp knife or secateurs
(pruners).**

AUTUMN **Potatoes can be
harvested from early summer to
autumn, depending on whether
they are first earlies, second
earlies or maincrop potatoes.**

INDEX

ACKNOWLEDGEMENTS

The publishers would like to thank the following for their kind permission to photograph their plants and gardens for this book:

Hilary and Richard Bird; the RHS Garden, Wisley; The Priest House, West Hoathly, Sussex

The publishers would also like to thank the following picture agencies for allowing their pictures to be reproduced for the purposes of this book:

KEY
l = left r= right t = top
b = bottom c = centre

The Garden Picture Library: 2 (Gil Hanly); 4 (Mayer/Le Scanff); 6 (John Glover); 10b (Juliette Wade); 11 (JS Sira); 24t (Mayer/Le Scanff); 24b (Brian Carter); 25 (Ron Sutherland); 38 (Stephen Robson); 39t (Jacqui Hurst); 54t (Mayer/Le Scanff); 54b (Marijke Heuff); 55 (Jacqui Hurst); 56t (Mayer/Le Scanff); 56b (Juliette Wade); 58 (Clay Perry); 61t (Mayer/Le Scanff); 62t (Michael Howes); 67b (Steven Wooster); 70 (Brigitte Thomas); 73 (Eric Crichton); 74b (Christii Carter); 79t (Brigitte Thomas); 97t (Lamontagne); 102t (Mayer/Le Scanff); 103b (Mayer/Le Scanff); 115 (Lamontagne); 119t (Alec Scaresbrook); 120t (Michael Howes); 121t (Michael Howes); 123t (Lamontagne); 140t (John Glover); 140b (Jerry Pavia); 144t (John Glover); 144b (Brian Carter); 145t (Mayer/Le Scanff); 145b (Howard Rice); 146b (John Glover); 147t (John Glover); 148b (John Glover); 149t (Sunniva Harte); 155t (Gil Hanly); 157r (David Askham); 158l (Chris Burrows); 158r (Chris Burrows); 161t (Christii Carter); 161b (Christii Carter); 162t (Philippe Bonduel); 163l (Brian Carter); 163r (Jacqui Hurst); 164br (Christopher Fairweather); 165t (Mayer/Le Scanff); 165b (Howard Rice); 166l (Mayer/Le Scanff); 168b (Mayer/Le Scanff); 170t (David Askham); 171t (Mayer/Le Scanff); 179 (Ron Sutherland); 186b (Michel Viard); 199t (Jacqui Hurst); 203t (Lamontagne); 204 (Brian Carter); 205t (Lamontagne); 228b (Michael Howes); 231t (Lamontagne); 235t (Howard Rice); 235b (Lamontagne); 240 (John Glover); 241 (John Glover); 249t (John Miller); 249c (Didier Willery); 256 (Steven Wooster).

The Harry Smith Collection: 6t; 34bl; 90t; 122t; 148t; 156; 157l; 164t; 168t; 169r; 187l; 187r; 191t; 229l.

Jonathan Buckley: for the soil samples featured on page 56.

NOTES

NOTES

NOTES

NOTES

NOTES

NOTES

NOTES

NOTES